Another Day

More Stories from the Early Colonial Records of Virginia's Eastern Shore

JENEAN HALL

KWE PUBLISHING

Hall, Jenean. *Another Day: More Stories from the Colonial English Records of Virginia's Eastern Shore*

Copyright © 2023 by Jenean Hall.

ISBNs: 978-0-9832660-3-7 (paperback), 978-0-9832660-4-4 (e-book)

Library of Congress Catalog Number: 2023918044

First Edition. All rights reserved. No portion of this book may be reproduced, stored in a retrieval system, or transmitted in any form or by any means - including by not limited to electronic, mechanical, digital, photocopy, recording, scanning, blogging or other - except for brief quotations in critical reviews, blogs, or articles, without the prior written permission of the publisher, KWE Publishing.

Front cover: Sunrise, Long Branch, New Jersey, 1850, by Sanford Robinson Gifford, Courtesy Wikimedia Commons, Public Domain.

Background photograph, a Northampton County court record page, by the author.

Cover design by Michelle Fairbanks | Fresh Design

Independently published, IngramSpark, and KWE Publishing, LLC, 2023. KWE Publishing: www.kwepub.com

Dedicated to Douglas B. Quelch, my cousin and friend, who has the patience of his Uncle Whitfield B. Hall, who was my father.

A Bill Nelson map.

TABLE OF CONTENTS

Acknowledgments	*vii*
Introduction	*ix*
Glossary	*xi*
Chapter 1 - Abandoning Yeardley's Commission	1
Chapter 2 - Dales Gift	23
Chapter 3 - Yeardley and Epps	35
Chapter 4 - The Last Years of Thomas Savage	43
Chapter 5 - First Known African Inhabitants of the Eastern Shore	47
Chapter 6 - First Minister	55
Chapter 7 - First Church, First Glebe, First Parsonage	63
Chapter 8 - The Second Burial Ground	71
Chapter 9 - The Chapel of Ease	83
Chapter 10 - Burdett's Prenuptial Promise and Frances's Last Will and Testament	89
Chapter 11 - Shameful Politics	95
Chapter 12 - Argoll Yardley	101
Chapter 13 - The Laughing Kings	115
Chapter 14 - The Horns	129
Chapter 15 - A Petticoat War	133

Chapter 16 - A Curious Sequence of Events: the "False Raid"   137

Chapter 17 - Scarburgh's Brother   153

Chapter 18 - The Event in Hack's Old Fields   155

Chapter 19 - The Northampton Protest   175

Chapter 20 - Elizabeth Charlton, Or Edmund Scarburgh's Finest Speech   183

Chapter 21 - Bridget Charlton Foxcroft's Victory   211

Chapter 22 - The Nuswattocks Community of 1656   223

Chapter 23 - Edmund Scarborough, the Father of Edmund Scarburgh   229

Chapter 24 - The First Chesapeake Bay Retriever?   235

Chapter 25 - Joane Windley, the Eastern Shore's First Attorney   239

Chapter 26 - An English Trick   243

Chapter 27 - Dunking Was Not Always About Doughnuts   249

Chapter 28 - Northampton   259

Chapter 29 - Merchant   265

Appendices   *273*

Bibliography   *287*

Index   *299*

About the Author   *325*

Acknowledgments

Many people and resources contributed to the development of this project. My long-standing gratitude to the exceptional staffs in the offices of Accomack County Clerk of the Circuit Court, Northampton County Clerk of the Circuit Court, and Eastern Shore Public Library.

Also, no work such as this could be completed without the help of the resources housed by the Virginia Museum of History and Culture and the Library of Virginia. The Historical Map and Chart Collection (National Oceanic and Atmospheric Administration, U. S. Department of Commerce) is invaluable for mining historic information found in old maps.

The works of Susie May Ames, William Waller Hening, Susan Myra Kingsbury, Howard Mackey, Henry Read McIlwaine, and Frank V. Walczyk are requisite to any attempt for bringing clarity to seventeenth-century events on Virginia's Eastern Shore. Other works are, of course, beneficial; many of them are listed in the bibliography.

Special thanks to friends and family (Aunt Bev, Brice, Carla, Carolyn, David, Dawn, Dean, Diane, Eliza, FC Nancy, Kathy, Nancy Megan, Pam, Rick, Tony, Uncle Bob, and Woody) who encourage my writing and inspire my enthusiasm for telling these stories. My cousin and friend Doug Quelch spent countless hours reading these pages and talking via the phone from his home in Florida, discussing—sometimes debating—fine points of grammar. His counsel has been invaluable.

An especial thank you to Kim Eley of KWE Publishing, and her staff, Taylor Mills, Michelle Fairbanks, and Emily Deaton. Thank you for your talents, competence, and patience. Working with you is a joyful experience.

My abiding gratitude and love to my sister, Janice, and my brother-in-law, Ken Thompson, who have always been my home away from home, and also to Beno, Tina, and Ryder, who never complain when I commandeer an end of their island for writing.

And thank you, reader; you are ever the inspiration for telling the story and telling it as accurately as possible.

Introduction

In *An "Uncertaine Rumor" of Land*, several stories were relegated to be told another day. Here, in *Another Day: More Stories from the Early Colonial Records of Virginia's Eastern Shore*, you will find those promised stories, plus others.

The first essay picks up the story of Sir George Yeardley's commission to create a new, large settlement on Virginia's Eastern Shore after the devastating attack on the colony in March of 1622. This commission outlined a plan to send 300 to 400 colonists across the bay to the Eastern Shore. We can only imagine the preparations for such an event, yet it is seldom noted in the writings of historians. Perhaps historians seldom mention it because the plan became a nonevent when the Virginia Company got wind of it. The colony was struggling to survive, but it was the Virginia Company that never recovered.

For the most part, the chapters do not follow chronological time. Each chapter will pick up a new topic; however, many of the topics are related to the chapters preceding, so it will be best to start from the beginning. The most extreme example of this involves Chapters 18 and 19. These chapters tell the story of two consecutive years when incendiary papers were written to be considered by the Grand Assembly. The stories of these papers are presented out of sequence for the purpose of underscoring the fact that they were two very separate papers. Previous writers have melded the two papers into one, thus missing the more noteworthy consequences of the "lost" paper.

This book has many hidden gems that could be the subject of dissertations. While writing the stories, it has felt as if I am opening windows, letting in fresh air on old, musty stories. It is my hope that some readers will find subjects to pursue further, recognizing that I have but skimmed the surface of some momentous events in Eastern Shore and Virginia history.

As in *An "Uncertaine Rumor" of Land*, this book begins with a glossary. Many of the terms are repeated from the previous book, but not all. I have placed the glossary at the front of the book, as several people told me that was a helpful feature in the previous book. May that be true here also.

Glossary

Accomack/Northampton Records: The English settlement on the Eastern Shore was named Accomack (with several spellings). The name Accomack was used when the settlement was designated as a county in 1634. In 1642, the county was renamed "Northampton." In 1663, Northampton was divided into two counties; the southern county retained the name "Northampton" and the northern county was named "Accomack." Today, Northampton County maintains the original earliest records whereas Accomack County has a copy of these records.

Accomack/Acchawmacke Creeke or River: Cherrystone Inlet today. In early records, this body of water and the land adjacent were called Cherrystones/Cherry Stones.

Adventurer: Within this book, the word "Adventurer" most often refers to a stockholder in the Virginia Company. Some people adventured with money and others adventured with their persons in going to the colony as Company employees. Some people adventured with both purse and person. The phrase, "by personal adventure," meant that a person had paid their own way.

Accompt: Account (archaic).

Against: As used in early geography descriptions, "against" (agaynst) usually meant "opposite" or "across from."

Ancient Planter: A planter who had been in the colony since before the time of Sir Thomas Dale and had stayed at least three years. The definition of an ancient adventurer and planter was given in the Virginia Company's 1618 instructions to George Yeardley. These instructions have come to be known as "the Great Charter."

Apostrophes: In 1890, the U. S. Board of Geographic Names was created to maintain uniform geographic name usage throughout the federal government. At that time, most creeks, rivers, and places that had possessive names lost their apostrophes. For example, King's Creek became Kings Creek. In this book, the apostrophes for creeks and other place names are usually omitted so that the current names can be recognized. However, it is also true that the early court writers very rarely used apostrophes.

APVA: The Association for the Preservation of Virginia Antiquities was founded in 1889. Today, the organization is known as Preservation Virginia.

Arrest: In the early years, arrests often were notifications of custody rather than actual, physical custody. Jails were scarce, perhaps because they were not necessary in most cases of arrest.

Attachment: The court could "attach" one's property in order to pay a debt. For example, if you didn't have enough money or tobacco to pay what was owed, the court could "attach" your property to pay the debt. Efforts were made to do this fairly, by having disinterested people appraise the value of whatever was being "attached."

Attorney: A person representing someone else in court. In the early records, men (and women) who acted as attorneys rarely had training in the law.

Beating the mortar; making the mortar ring: Early terms for grinding corn in a mortar and pestle. Early mortars and pestles were often made of metal and could be very heavy.

Bodkin: A straight, flat needle with a hole at one end, used to thread. Also used to tie corsets. www.bu.edu/today/2008/a-stitch-in-time/.

Buff coats: Thick leather overwear worn by some seventeenth century soldiers.

Burgess: An elected representative to the General Assembly (later Grand Assembly) of colonial Virginia.

Calendar: In these early years, England still used the Julian or Old Style (OS) calendar in which the legal year began on March 25. England did not change to the Gregorian or New Style (NS) calendar until 1752; at that time, January 1 became New Year's Day. Today, we use the New Style (NS) calendar. To synchronize with the New Style, England dropped eleven days from its calendar in 1751.

In this book, when you see a date written with two years between January 1 and March 24, the first year is OS and the second year is NS. (For example, March 24, 1632/33, would be followed by March 25, 1633, because March 25 was the first day of the new year.

Remember: the use of two years is necessary only for events that happened between January 1 and March 24 in any year before 1752. When only one year is written, that year coincides with today's calendar.

Cherrystone: See Accomack/Acchawmacke Creek.

Chirurgeon: An early word for surgeon. This profession did not have the high level of training required for a physician, but it did have a level of training, probably including an apprenticeship. It seems that chirurgeons attended to wounds and illness, something a physician also did, but physicians additionally dealt with theories of treatment and epidemiology.

Coif: A woman's close-fitting cap. (See Quoife.)

Commodities: Products that could be sold or purchased.

Commonwealth Government: In England, the period from 1649 to 1660 when the country was ruled as a republic, first by Parliament, then by Oliver Cromwell as the Lord Protector, and then by Parliament again until the monarchy was restored in 1660.

Cooper: A barrel and cask maker.

Council of State: Also called the council or the governor's council. The council was composed of men appointed by the king to assist the governor. Members of the council along with the governor formed the Quarter Court and the General Court. Men appointed to the council were usually wealthy and from prominent families. The council, along with the governor and burgesses, made up the General (Grand) Assembly.

Court Commissioner: The men of the local courts were commissioned by the governor for their positions, thus they were called "commissioners." Only a very few times in the early years were they called "justices;" this was a title that came later.

Cozen: To cheat or trick. This word also shows as a spelling for "cousin."

Crop: "At this crop" meant the current crop. "At the next crop," meant the future crop. These terms were used in reference to tobacco payments.

Cupping: Cupping was a medical procedure in which a heated glass was placed on the skin to form a partial vacuum which drew blood to the surface of the skin. In dry cupping, the suction created a bruise. In wet cupping, the suction was strong enough to draw blood through the skin.

Dales Gift: In 1614, Deputy Governor Thomas Dale sent Captain Samuel Argall and Thomas Savage, the interpreter, to the Eastern Shore Indians to negotiate for land and corn. The land they procured was at the lower end of the peninsula. It was named "Dales Gift." (See "Apostrophe" for an explanation of why the possessive case apostrophe is not used.)

Demand: In early colonial days, this word seems to have had a different meaning than today. Its meaning seems to have been "to ask, expecting an answer."

Divident: An early term for dividend, or a person's designated portion of land. This word was used frequently in the early records but seems to have disappeared from use today.

Dress cloth: An apron.

Execution: Putting an order into effect, sometimes by forceable means. For example: "...shall performe the said Order according to the true intent and meaneing of the Court and pay Court Charges or else execution etc."

Fire dogs: Andirons. Mulling fire dogs were made with elevated, small receptacles used for warming cups or bowls. (Imagine a metal, footed stick, topped with a small metal basket).

Folio: (abbreviation: fol.) The leaves of the old court records were often numbered with the first page (always on the right) as folio 1. After turning the page, the page on the right (recto) was called "folio 2," whereas its opposing page on the left (verso) was called merely "page 2." Theoretically, this pattern would follow throughout the book: page 3, folio 3; page 4, folio 4, etc.

Form: Bench.

Freedom dues: What was due to a servant upon completion of the contract, or indenture. These "dues" usually consisted of one or two suits of clothes and some amount of corn or tobacco. The dues could be unique to a contract, but they often were the same from contract to contract.

General (Grand) Assembly: In the Virginia Company's 1618 instructions, George Yeardley was told to form "a laudable form of Government by Magistracy and just laws for Happy guiding and governing of the people there inhabiting like as we have already done for the well ordering of our own courts here and of our officers and actions for the behoof of that Plantation..." Yeardley called together elected representatives from each plantation. Together with the governor and the council of state, these representatives formed the "General Assembly." (In February 1631/32, this legislative body changed its name to "Grand Assembly." Years later, it would change back again to General Assembly.)

General Court: By 1661, this was the name given to Virginia's highest court. Earlier it was termed merely "Court" and "Quarter Court." It was composed of the governor and the Council of State. In the colony's early years, this court most often met in James City and sometimes in Elizabeth City.

Gentleman: In the early records, this appears to be a title of respect. A gentleman's name was preceded by the prefix "Mister." The Virginia criteria for a man receiving this title is not entirely clear; however, all court commissioners and sheriffs received this designation unless they already were known as "Captain."

Glebe: Land set aside by the parish for the minister's house and fields. The intent was for the land to supplement the minister's income.

Goodman: An early prefix meaning Mister, or the male head of household, as in: "Goodman Jones." Most often the prefix seemed to reflect a social standing below that of someone who was called "Mister."

Goodwife: An early prefix meaning the female head of household, as in: "Goodwife Jones." Most often the prefix seemed to reflect a social standing below that of someone who was called "Mistress." This term was sometimes abbreviated as "Goody."

Grand Assembly: See "General Assembly."

Headright: In 1619, the Virginia Company, through its instructions to Governor Sir George Yeardley, introduced the headright system. In this plan, a certificate for fifty acres somewhere in Virginia was granted to each person who came to the colony. That person was counted as one headright. Each headright equaled fifty acres. The land didn't necessarily go to the person who arrived, it went to the person who paid the transportation costs. Ownership of a headright could be transferred or assigned to another person.

Hogshead: Tobacco was shipped in barrels of a standard size. The hogshead is made to hold 64 gallons, liquid, whereas a barrel holds half that amount.

Hundred: The term "hundred" comes from the English practice of locating ten towns, or tithings (groups of ten families), at a settlement. (See Encyclopedia Virginia). In Virginia, the term was used for the investment plantations which were usually larger than an average, single-owner plantation.

In-law, father-in-law, mother-in-law: In the early records, an in-law was what today we call a "step___." In the early records, what we call a stepfather was often just called a father. The term "step___" had not yet been created. A spouse's brother was your brother; your mother's new husband was your father-in-law; your father-in-law's son was your brother.

James City: Jamestown. The Eastern Shore records refer to Jamestown as James City. In the early Virginia records, this is the name used most often.

Kequohtan, Kicotan, Kecoughtan: The name of the Indian village that the early settlers found at the site of today's independent city, Hampton, Virginia, on Hampton River. In the early days, the English called that river Southampton River.

Lingaskin: In 1786, the Indians who were living at Indiantown on Virginia's Eastern Shore wrote a petition to the Virginia legislature. They referred to themselves as The Tribe of the Lingaskin.

Magatty Bay: Originally, this was an area just south of today's Old Plantation Creek. It may be that Magatty Bay originally was what today may be thought of as the mouth of Old Plantation Creek, and Magatty Bay Pond was just south of that, at what today is Costin Pond. Magatty Bay became all of the area hugging the bayside, from what today is the mouth of Old Plantation Creek down to today's Wise Point. Today, maps will show Magothy Bay (or a similar spelling) on the east side (seaside) of the Eastern Shore, but originally, it was a bayside area.

Mainland: Virginia's Eastern Shore is separated from the main body of Virginia by the Chesapeake Bay. The mainland is the main portion of Virginia.

Mattawoman Creek: The body of water to the south of today's Wilsonia Neck. It separates Wilsonia Neck and the neck to the south of it, called Old Town Neck.

Mattawombes town: Believed to have been the name of the town on Mattawoman Creek where Indians lived when Argoll Yardley came to claim the land. These Indians were moved to what became known as Gingascount town, on the seaside. One theory holds that Mattawombes was the name of the town where the Laughing King lived and where he may have died.

Mortar: see "Beating the mortar."

Moveables: Personal property that can be moved.

Neck: An isthmus. On the Eastern Shore (a seventy-five-mile-long peninsula) the necks jut out from the sides, especially the bayside. Most of the necks are named, as in Savages, Old Town, Old Plantation, Wilsonia, Church, etc.

Neck and Heels: This term may have different meanings in the records, but as a phrase, it seems to mean "wholly" or "completely." For example, to say, "He was tied neck and heels," may have meant that the man was immobilized, or tied in such a way that he could not move.

New Style (NS): see "Calendar."

New Year's Day: March 25: see "Calendar."

Old Style (OS): see "Calendar."

Ordinary: An ordinary was the same as what we might call an "inn" or "tavern." This use of the word has an interesting history. Early courts, a collection of ordinaries (judges), met in private homes until someone of the community found the means to build a house where food and drink could be sold with a room large enough for a court meeting. When court wasn't in session, the house still was often called "the ordinary." Over time, the word "ordinary" was used less in relation to the court and more often in relation to its provision of drink, food, and lodging. Throughout the seventeenth century, Virginia's laws pertained to ordinaries as the word "tavern" was not yet in use.

Paper: This is the term often used for an official document, such as contracts, receipts, bills, treatises, etc.

Passing speeches: An early term for "gossiping."

Patent: Land that was acquired by certification of headrights. It was the king's grant.

Personal Adventure: A term used when a person paid his or her own passage to Virginia.

Pestle, mortar and pestle: Tools used for crushing. The colonists used a mortar and pestle for crushing corn before the handmill was invented or affordable. See "Beating the mortar."

Phisick, Physick: Medicine.

Pillory: A punishment device consisting of a stand with a hole for the head and holes for the hands. This is different from stocks which has holes for the feet.

Pillow-bere, pillowbeere, pillow bier: Pillowcase.

Pinnace: A light boat, powered by oars or sails. In colonial days, it was often used as a tender to carry passengers and goods from larger boats to the shore.

Plantation: In colonial Virginia, the earliest use of this term seems to have been in reference to the large corporations formed for growing tobacco. The term then could be used interchangeably with "settlement" and with "hundred." Later, the term seems to have been used for what today is called "a farm" and size was not a defining factor. (Later still, outside the scope of this book, the term came to mean a very large farming operation.)

Pounds, shillings, and pence: In colonial days, 1 pound = 20 shillings; 12 pence = 1 shilling. The amount 4 pounds, 2 shillings, 3 pence would be written as £4.2.3.

Powhatan: Powhatan was a paramount Indian leader who presided over an empire of Indians known as the Powhatan. Their language was Algonquin. This empire covered most of today's eastern Virginia, from the Potomac River to the Dismal Swamp. The chief was also known as Wahunsenacawh, but the English called him Powhatan.

Pretend: In the early records, this term's meaning was to state or to affirm. It did not have the connotation of deception as it does today.

Quarter Court: The Virginia governor and Council of State met as a colony court to try cases that were of greater value than the local courts were allowed to handle. This court also heard appeals from the local courts. When the court began a quarterly schedule, it was called the Quarter Court. Quarter Courts became General Courts in 1661.

Quoife: A woman's close-fitting cap.

Roanoke, ronoke roanoake: Indian currency. It was made from shells rubbed smooth and joined together as in beads or ropes. Peake is another word meaning Indian money.

Rug, rugg: An early word for "coverlet" or "blanket."

Sabbath: The English church held divine services on Sunday, so Sabbath translates to Sunday in these early writings.

Salvage: A word often seen in the records to refer to an Indian. It is an early spelling of the word "savage."

Scanning the business: In early Virginia court records, this phrase was used to mean that the court was reading or viewing the clerk's copy of the matter under discussion.

Security: Surety, bond, bail. Putting up money to guarantee a pledge. A person would lose the money if the pledge were not kept.

Servant: A servant was a person who was working off a debt, usually of transportation to the colony. The contract for transportation was usually seven years, but it could vary by contract. At the end of the obligation, the servant received "freedom dues;" this usually was two sets of clothes and a quantity of corn. (See "Settlers/Colonists/Tenants/Planters.")

Settlers/Colonists/Tenants/Planters: Early English men and women were referred to in the records by several descriptors. A planter was usually the owner or head of what today might be termed a farm. If you had not paid your own passage (and you were not a family member) you usually were a servant under contract (indentured servant); however, most of the early Company contracts were tenant contracts that allowed a sharing of profits. Servants worked to pay an obligation but did not share profits. EVERYONE was a colonist, having come to the Colony of Virginia. Everyone was also a settler, but that term often referred to the specific plantation (farm) where you lived. For example, you were a colonist in Virginia, helping to settle the Elizabeth City Plantation; therefore, you were an Elizabeth City settler. Colonist and settler are usually interchangeable words.

Shallop: A small, heavy workboat used for sailing and rowing in shallow waters. John Smith used a shallop to explore the Chesapeake.

Stocks: A punishment device in which a person sat with his legs outstretched and his ankles secured.

Summer Sickness: In the early years of the colony, the mortality rate increased in the summer months. This seems to have been due primarily to a lack of fresh drinking water and the increased exposure to contaminated waters due to changes in tidal flows. New colonists were particularly prone to sickness because of their weakened condition upon arrival, but even seasoned colonists were at risk in the presence of poor water and unsanitary conditions.

Tenant: A person who leased land. During Company times, the term was used in reference to people brought in to work for the Company for a share of the profits. Later, after the Company was dissolved, contracts for workers would be set up on an individual basis. (See "Settlers" above.)

Tithes, tithable: Tithes were taxes. A tithable was a person who met the criterion to be taxed. The criterion changed over time. Most males who were of age (sixteen years) to work were tithable. African and Indian servants, male and female, sixteen years of age and older, were considered tithable. Some planters would hire English women to work in the fields to avoid the tax. The lawmakers got wise to that and changed the law in 1662 to include all women who worked in the fields as tithable.

Truck: Any product used for small trade, such as vegetables, nuts, fruits, handmade items, etc.

Undersheriff: The sheriff's second in command, what today is called "deputy." (The sheriff was the "high" sheriff; thus his deputy was the "under" sheriff.)

Vestry: A local, court-appointed committee of parishioners who conducted the business of the local church.

Virginia Company of London: In 1606, King James approved the charter of this joint-stock company for which shares were sold at £12 10s. The plan was to outfit ships, go to America, come back with riches, and pay dividends to the investors. Over its eighteen years, the company was headed by two men: Treasurer Sir Thomas Smith and Treasurer Sir Edwin Sandys. By the time King James I dissolved the Company in 1624, it was into its fourth charter and was in debt for no less than £9000. (It is sometimes called the London Company.)

Virginia Peninsula: Today's name for the peninsula surrounded by the York River, the James River, Hampton Roads, and the Chesapeake Bay. It is on mainland Virginia.

Watchet: A pale shade of blue.

Werowance, werowans: The English often adopted Indian terms. This term became interchangeable with the word "king" in reference to Indian leaders. A werowance was the person of highest authority in a tribe.

Whissoponson Creek: Today this creek is known as The Gulf. It is the creek that separated Thomas Savage's divident from Sir George Yeardley's divident, as defined by the Laughing King. For a time, the creek was known as Savages Creek.

Ye: The early English abbreviation for "th" was a symbol that looked very much like the letter "y." It evolved to a Y and a superscript e. Today this is often written as Ye. In early English, it was probably pronounced as "the," not as "ye." Yt (superscript t) was an early abbreviation meaning "that." Yn (superscript n) was an early abbreviation meaning "than." Yrfore was an early abbreviation meaning "therefore."

Chapter 1

Abandoning Yeardley's Commission

One of the most underreported and misunderstood events of Virginia history took place in the summer following the Powhatan Confederation's 1622 attack on the English colony.[1] At that time, Virginia was still a privately chartered colony governed by the Virginia Company of London. The Company-appointed governor was Sir Frances Wyatt. He had been in office just four months at the time of the attack.

At noon on March 22nd, across the entire mainland colony, Native people ambushed the settlers. At the end of the day, 357 English men, women, and children lay dead. That number represented a fourth of the English population in Virginia. The aftermath of the colony's terror, panic, and chaos can only be imagined these 400 years later.

Sir George Yeardley had been the colony's governor for three years prior to Sir Frances Wyatt's arrival. Upon Wyatt's installation into office in November 1621, Yeardley became his right-hand man. In the weeks and months after the attack, every available and able man was called upon to help. People streamed into Jamestown, seeking safety. Food and shelter were scarce. A sickness spread throughout the colony, and by summer's end, it would kill as many as had died in the attack.

On June 20, 1622, Governor Wyatt announced a commission, assigning Sir George Yeardley to find a place to settle 300 to 400 settlers on the Eastern Shore. (This commission can be found in Appendix I.) Such an assignment did not happen in a vacuum. Conversations, debate, and events shaped its content. Yeardley likely suggested the commission following his recent success in settling three small plantations on the Eastern Shore while he was governor. These three were: John and Frances Blower at "old plantation" (c. late 1620), John Wilcocks at Accomack (c. mid 1621), and ten tenants on the Secretary's Land (c. late summer 1621). In addition, preliminary steps had been taken to reset the salt works on Smith Island, a barrier island on the southern end of the Eastern Shore peninsula. Only the site had been chosen; no men or equipment had yet been assigned when the March 22nd attack thwarted all plans. No able men could yet be spared.

Yeardley's commission permitted him to use as many ships, pinnaces, and shallops as he needed to take as many people as he felt were necessary. It directed him to find a place to leave these settlers, allowing them four acres each. The plan called for the first group to build and clear in preparation for the next shipment of people who would come after the crop. The total number of people to be sent was estimated at three to four hundred. Such a plan, it was hoped, would relieve the suffering and disease brought about as a result of the mainland people abandoning remote plantations and crowding to safety in protected areas. In places such as James City and Elizabeth City, this overcrowding was compounded by the arrival of hundreds of new settlers who had known nothing of the recent devastation in the colony. Imagine the collective dismay of these new people when they heard the news of the colony's disarray. They had been promised safe, adequate shelter, but none was to be found. That the governor and council would try whatever they could to relieve the people and attempt to regain the colony's footing is what one would expect of moral leadership. Yeardley's commission was their most valiant effort.

Yeardley did as he was commissioned; he went to the Eastern Shore and worked to create a new, large settlement. However, after only twelve weeks, he was called back by a new commission written on September 10, 1622.[2] Those twelve weeks undoubtedly saw an extraordinary number of decisions and a remarkable amount of work. During the time he was on the shore, Yeardley would have designated Company Land for a fort and the distribution of four acres per person for the expected 400 people. At the most, this would have been about 1,600 acres.

The English had an agreement for land on the Eastern Shore under the work of Sir Thomas Dale in 1614. At that time, the local Indian werowance had allowed the English to inhabit a tract of land. This tract was dubbed "Dales Gift," but it belonged to the Company, not to Dale personally.[3] Its parameters are unknown, but I suggest that the agreement may have allowed the English to use land south of today's Cherrystone Inlet. That agreement would have been for fishing, salting and encampments to support those operations, certainly not for a major settlement of hundreds of people.

Under the intent of his June 10th commission, Yeardley would have found it necessary to negotiate with the Eastern Shore werowance. This man was a known friend to the English. He had warned them about the mainland Indians' plan to attack, but most telling, he had befriended the trader and interpreter, Thomas Savage. The werowance referred to Savage as "Newport, my son."[4]

Yeardley enlisted Savage as his interpreter to negotiate with the werowance. Savage had interpreted for Yeardley before this time, so Yeardley was keenly aware of Savage's skills and of the fondness Savage shared with the Eastern Shore werowance. The day they met with the werowance to clear the way for a major settlement was one of the most extraordinary days in Eastern Shore history, yet no one knows when or where the meeting took place.

By the end of that meeting, the werowance (a man who has come to be known as the Laughing King) not only gave his approval, but he also gave each man—Savage and Yeardley—great tracts of land. Savage's tract was bordered to the south by today's Cherrystone Inlet, and Yeardley's was bordered to the north by today's Mattawoman Creek. The tracts were separated by Whissoponson Creek, later called Savages Creek, and now called The Gulf. The tracts began at the bay and spanned across the peninsula to the ocean. After the time of the negotiations between Yeardley and the Laughing King, the Indians appear to have migrated northward, leaving the southern Eastern Shore to the English, the boundary being generally at Mattawoman Creek.[5]

It has been said these gifts were the Laughing King's attempt to contain the English. In other words, the gifts were meant to create an English reservation.[6] Indeed, it may be true that the great man harbored a hope that this land he allowed for English habitation would provide enough space to contain the English, and that this would satisfy their appetite for land.

The people who accompanied Yeardley in his ships, pinnaces, and shallops would have been put to work building shelter as well as planting a summer crop. In one or more of those vessels, Lady Dale's people and cattle were brought across the bay and put ashore on the southeast side of what came to be known as Old Plantation Creek. For the next twenty years, Lady Dale's cattle would thrive on the inland grasses of the land allotted to the English.[7]

Yeardley's work on the Eastern Shore—clearing the way to move a large portion of the Virginia colony—was impressive, yet the story has never been fully explored. It seems that the Company's harsh response offset the plan and extinguished the zeal. The venture was underreported and subsequently misunderstood.

The Company in London received word of the March attack in July and formulated a response by August 1, 1622. By this time, the colony had suffered through four months, clawing its way to recovery, with any progress hampered by sickness and starvation. In the meantime, in Virginia, Governor Wyatt had sent Captain Isack Maddison to defend the Patomack Indians and their corn. He had sent Yeardley to the Eastern Shore, and he had given Captain William Tucker command of Elizabeth City and Newport News, east and west of Southampton River. On June 21st, Governor Wyatt had issued stern proclamations to the colonists against drunkenness, swearing, and stealing oars; these edicts illustrate the leadership's desperation for bringing order into the swelling chaos.

The Company's response from London blamed the colonists for the attack. As the Company saw it, "excesses in apparell and drinkeing" and "neglect of the Devine worshipp" had brought this calamity on them. After this stern castigation, the Company then turned its attention to what most concerned them: profits. It reported that the king had now given Virginia and the islands of Bermuda sole authority to import tobacco, and that this would improve private profits as well as Company profits. The Company said it was gathering arms and people to send to Virginia. The settling of private people was probably the only way that the colony would prosper, the Company said, and it left the matter to the "wisdomes and judgements" of the governor and council to see that new people were settled. The Company recommended against straggling settlements, but encouraged houses to be built together into what would make handsome towns. That Charles City, Henrico, the iron works, the college, and Martins Hundred had been abandoned caused the Company not merely discontent but "evil fame." The Company was afraid that the shutting down of these formerly prosperous places would cause investors to turn away. Company tenants needed to be employed upon the Company land, it said. If necessary, give them ten acres above and beyond what would be due to them. Any men remaining for the iron works were to be employed under Maurice Berkeley in any way that best profited them until the work could be continued. The Company's letter concluded with advice about vanquishing the Indians who had attacked the colony, suggesting that the colonists pay the Indians' enemies to join the fight. Young

Native people were to be spared for labor and service, the Company said, and thus, would be turned "to civilitie, and afterwards to Christianitie."

These were hard, bitter words from the Company, but harsher words apparently came to the governor and council at some point in these summer months. Someone rebuked them for their plans to send a large number of people to the Eastern Shore. The thought of such a plan had invoked panic in the London leadership, a panic so great that it resulted in warnings of treason.

The first inkling that something was afoot may be reflected in a letter written by Sir Edwin Sandys to John Ferrar, both highly placed Company officials. Sandys explained to Ferrar what letters he had written and to whom copies were sent. It's merely a shadow, but the idea of conspiracy seeps through. "But the Companies letters I only saw," Sir Edwin wrote.[8] Was he reassuring Ferrar that he had made no copies, perhaps particularly of that letter of first response in which the Company gave the Virginians permission to use their own "wisdomes and judgments" to settle people? Those words could come back to haunt them.

By late fall into early winter, Governor Wyatt and the council had abandoned the grand plans for the Eastern Shore. They granted many petitions, allowing men to return to their James River plantations. The Company had ordered them to do so.

George Yeardley's June 10th commission was essentially voided. It became a nonevent to the Company. However—make no mistake—this commission was monumental to Eastern Shore history, yet scarcely anyone ever talked about what happened.

On January 20, 1622/23, Governor Wyatt and the council wrote to the Company, updating it on the progress of recovery since the attack. Essentially, this letter was a response to the Company's first reaction and to other sentiments that had been expressed to the Virginia leadership through missives that apparently have not survived (or yet been discovered). The Virginians thanked the king for the arms and munitions that were sent over, and they thanked the Company that it was still committed to the success of the colony. They reported progress toward vanquishing the enemy and securing prizes of corn. The Company had wounded them, they said, by passing "soe heavie a Censure uppon us as if we alone were guiltie." They reminded the London leadership that it had encouraged them to take the Indians into their own houses. As for the Company thinking that they had ignored a warning, the governor and council told the story of "the Kinge of the Easterne shore" having given notice to Sir George Yeardley that Opechancanough was plotting to kill the colonists. This warning had not been ignored; Yeardley had personally visited all the plantations to assess their arms and warn them.

"Wee were in good hope that you woulde not have added sorrow to afflictione, woundinge our reputationes with such disgrasfull reprooffes, unworthie of our sufferinge if not of our industrie." With bold acerbity, they agreed that their sins must be great as they had lost more men "by the Imediate hand of God" than they had lost "by the Trecherie" of the Indians. Who, they asked, had sent them excessive quantities of wine, "in qualletie base and infectious"? In regard to apparel, the Virginians reminded the Company that it was responsible for the tax on gold and silver in clothing. (In other words, it was a luxury tax, permission for such excess as long as you shared your wealth with the Company.) Regardless of that permission, the Virginians said, the majority of the colony was poor and practically naked.

Finally, the governor and council came around to the subject of the Eastern Shore. "The Removeall to the Easterne shore which you calle an abandoninge of this River (beinge a place indeede that Comands not only this but all the Rivers in the Baye, was a thinge only in dispute & speculations: But uppon the Consideratione, that it might be at first sight a taint to our reputations, & noe way lawfull to forsake our stations withowt leave, that preceded noe farther, as all our Accons [actions] may Sufficyently prove."[9]

In this way, the Virginians cleared themselves of accusations that they were unlawfully abandoning the James River enterprises to go to the Eastern Shore. If they had wanted to press the issue, they could have reminded the Company of its permission to use their own "wisdomes and judgement." Yet they did not. In fact, they seemed to step lightly; perhaps that was because treason had been put on the table.

The idea that the Virginians' actions were treasonous came to light through George Sandys's correspondence. George Sandys was the colony's treasurer in Virginia and a brother of Sir Edwin Sandys who was a Company leader in London. In a letter written to a Company investor on March 28, 1623, George Sandys promised that he would be more careful about what he wrote. Reading between the lines, it appears that Sandys had written to someone about the "proposition of removeinge to the Easterne Shore," intimating that he had been the source of the brouhaha that led to expressions of treason. Sandys was more than a bit defensive in his explanation. See for yourself:

> *How am I touched in particuler about that ignominious proposition of removeinge to the Easterne Shore, when I onelie* [only] *related the Arguments, and nomynated the Author, And although the Governour and my selfe gave way that the place might be survaid for the planting of a Partie there as better furnished with all sorts of provisions and fit thereafter for fortification: yet never was it so much in our Thoughts (though manie* [many] *ranne violentlie that waye) to quit the places which wee held and I for my part would first have beene torne in peeces. But I wilbe more warie hereafter what I write.*[10]

Sandys seemed tormented that his reputation was being sullied by this talk about the Eastern Shore, yet he had been but a messenger. He and Governor Wyatt had agreed merely to a survey there, he said, and maybe to the planting of a small party. Two days after writing that letter, he was still burning. The more he thought about it, the angrier he became. In a letter to his brother Samuel, he wrote:

> *Yet are we taxed with indiscretion and Cowardize for draweinge theis miserable people to places of securitie; Who had neither victuall nor munition) nor Could wee helpe them with either) nor of strength to defend themselves: so that of necessitie they must have perished either by the Enimye, or famyne* [famine]. *But men that are ambitious to bee Counted wise will rather Justifie then acknowledge their Errors and impute the fault to the execution, when it is indeed in the project.*

His disgust with the Company is unmistakable. A few sentences later he addressed the Eastern Shore, confessing that he had been the one to tell brother Sir Edwin of the proposal.

> *Sir Edwin writes that strucke with a Panicke feare wee proposed a Removeall of the Collonie to the Easterne shore. Indeed I writt home of such a proposition and named the Proposor with his Arguments which were hotlie mantayned by others, (and no question but that place had beene better, at the first, to have seated on, in regard of fertilitie, Convenience, all sorts of provision and strength both against the Native and Forreiner) yet theis were refuted by us in points of Reputation, being besids, as wee alledged, an intollerable presumption for us to attempt such a Change without your Consents: however wee thought it fitt that the place should bee further survaied, and a Partie there seated, and this is that treason against God and man, for which wee deserved to bee hanged.*[11]

His sarcasm reveals the depth of his wounds. The word *treason* had shaken him, especially from someone who was not only his brother, but a man who held the authority to act on a charge of treason. George Sandys walked the line, backing himself and Governor Wyatt away from any serious considerations of moving the colony to the Eastern Shore.

It ended there. The Virginians pressed it no further. The Company pressed it no further. The James River plantations were reopened. There would be no transfer of commerce to the Eastern Shore. The word "treason" had done its job.

Still, Governor Wyatt's commission to Yeardley is on record, and it was much more than a survey and the planting of a small party. Who was "the Proposor," the "Author" of the plan, the man whose reasoning for such a move was "hotlie mantayned by others"? Little doubt exists that Sir George Yeardley was that man.

George Sandys's letter leaves no doubt that the Eastern Shore had been unanimously praised as the better place for the seat of the colony. It was more fertile; it was filled with provisions; and it was a better place for defense against attacks from any source. That position had been hotly debated before Yeardley received his commission to go.

What did Yeardley accomplish on the Eastern Shore in those twelve weeks? In March 1622/23—one year after the attack and a half year after Yeardley left the Eastern Shore—George Sandys told John Ferrar that Yeardley had lost two thirds of his estate that year. Sandys was impressed with Yeardley. "To give him his dew," Sandys said, "he hath behaved himselfe very nobly in the service of the Country to his great expenses."[12] Yet, is this the story that has come down to us through the centuries? The story that is most often repeated about Yeardley's execution of his commission and his work on the Eastern Shore comes to us from Captain John Smith. Again, see for yourself:

> *About the latter end of June, Sir George Yearley accompanied with the Councell, and a number of the greatest Gallants in the Land, stayed three or foure daies with Captaine Nuse, he making his moane to a chiefe man amongst them for want of provision for his Company, the great Commander replied hee should turn them to his green Corne, which would make them plumpe and fat: these fields being so neere the Fort, were better regarded and preserved then the rest, but the great mans command, as we call them, was quickly obeied, for though it was scarce halfe growne either to the greatnesse or goodnesse, they devoured it greene though it did them small good. Sir George with his company*

went to Accomack to his new Plantation, where he staied neere six weekes; some Corne he brought home, but as he adventured for himselfe, he accordingly enjoyed the benefit...."[13]

John Smith's contempt for Yeardley and his companions is apparent, yet Smith had been nowhere near Virginia since he left thirteen years before. Perhaps Smith's source was a man such as William Capps of Elizabeth City. Capps had complained of being thrown off his land at Elizabeth City because the Company had claimed it in the instructions of the Great Charter. In 1623, a still-bitter Capps wrote in a letter that Governor Wyatt had been blinded by Yeardley, "that Sir George had throwne a mist before his [Wyatt's] eyes."

Sir George surely had many detractors, but why would we believe John Smith instead of the Virginia Company Records? Perhaps Smith thought he was telling the truth as told to him by others, not realizing his sources were soured, as George Sandys said, by "men that are ambitious to bee Counted wise." Such men would "rather Justifie then acknowledge their Errors and impute the fault to the execution, when it is indeed in the project."

Smith wove a tale about which he knew nothing. The issues of Yeardley's commission were so quickly suppressed, that very few people spoke of them. And the majority of those who did know—those who went with Yeardley to the Eastern Shore—were not interested in the politics; they were simply, desperately trying to survive.

For twelve weeks in the summer of 1622, an unknown number of men (and perhaps women also) worked on the Eastern Shore to prepare at least 1,600 acres of land for habitation by 300 to 400 colonists. By September, the project was called off, and most of the able-bodied men who had accompanied Yeardley probably left with him to march against the Indians under his new commission. Over a year later, in February 1623/24, seventy-six colonists lived on the Eastern Shore. In the two years since Secretary John Pory placed tenants on the Secretary's Land, the Eastern Shore's English population had more than doubled; in all probability, it had tripled.

THE FURNACE

Those are the facts that can be pulled from the records. However, one more story awaits the telling, but this one is a mystery. It has yet to be proven—or disproven. It may or may not involve Sir George Yeardley's twelve-week commission on Virginia's Eastern Shore.

This story is a theory, but it has roots in some amateur archaeology conducted in 1963. In that year, Dr. R. K. Brown, an Eastern Shore physician, discovered the remains of a pig-iron furnace on Indiantown Creek. According to architect and historian H. Chandlee Forman, this furnace was made of brick and was at least twenty-two feet wide. Forman, working from Brown's sketch, said the furnace dated from the early eighteenth century, but he did not explain further. In fact, no record has yet surfaced to explain this large structure.[14] Its presence poses a puzzle that can be solved only by archaeological research. However, all solutions begin with imagination.

The creek known today as Indiantown Creek branches off a deep-water channel that ran directly from Smith Island, north through today's Magothy Bay, and joined up to Sand Shoal Inlet between Cobbs and Wreck Islands. In early colonial days, a barge out of Indiantown could easily have carried goods to the ocean and vice versa.

Imagine if you will that Sir George Yeardley had this furnace built in the first quarter of the seventeenth century. His purposes would have been several: putting specialized survivors and newcomers to work; fulfilling the Company's order for iron; and, eventually, increasing the value of his own property.

Sir George Yeardley had become an Eastern Shore enthusiast. His love of the land on the other side of the bay probably began during exploratory voyages in the time of Sir Thomas Dale's deputy governorship. It was further enhanced during his own governorship when Blower, Wilcocks, and Pory each pursued land for their own purposes. In the chaos of April and May in 1622 (following the attack of March 22), Yeardley championed a major settlement on the Eastern Shore to relieve the crush and suffering on the mainland. At what point he fashioned the idea to dovetail his own interests with those of the Company is unknown. A reasonable guess is that it came about as he argued for the plan, promising to use his own resources to develop a self-sustaining plantation on the Eastern Shore; he could be compensated in land and eventual profits. It was not the greed that John Smith portrayed; it was more what George Sandys described: "he hath behaved himselfe very nobly in the service of the Country to his great expenses." Sir George Yeardley saw what we today might call "a win-win situation:" a win for the Company and a win for himself and the colony.

The furnace remnants are on land that Yeardley probably viewed as his side of the divide between Savage's great tract of land and his own. In those early years before surveyors could do their work, Yeardley may have drawn a line from the more prominent middle branch of Whissaponson (the creek dividing those two tracts). His line may have intersected the Eastern Shore's north-south ridge at a right angle rather than the true north-south line.[15] To the north of his west–east line would have been Yeardley's gift and would have included all of the creek now called Indiantown and a portion of land to the south of that creek.[16] (See Figures 1A and 1B.)

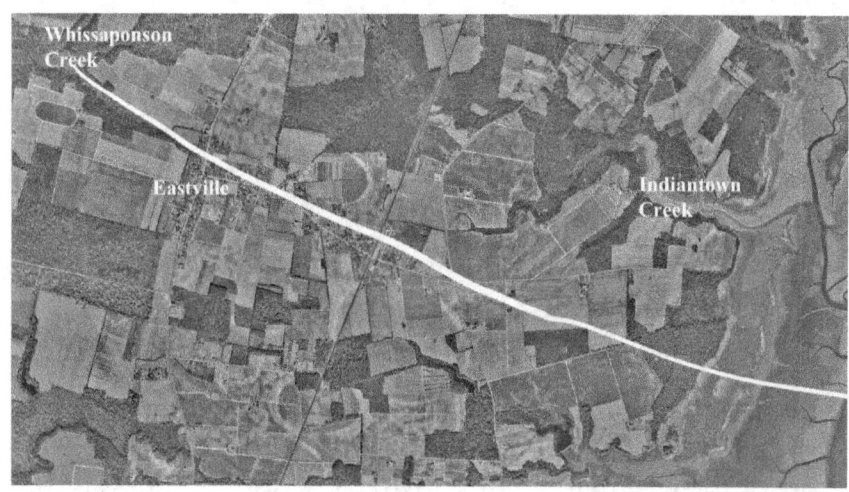

Figure 1A: 1952 (Historic Aerials, NETRonline), author's collection.

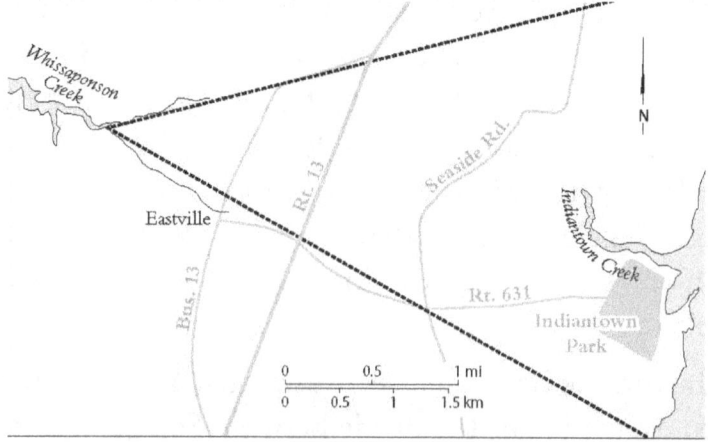

Figure 1B: (a Bill Nelson map)

Yeardley had the authority to make such decisions, and Thomas Savage was not in a position to challenge him, even if he were inclined to do so. Sir George Yeardley, knight of the realm, late governor, and senior councilor, would have faced no such challenge in his lifetime. If he said, "This is the line," that was the line. It was not a nefarious act; given the Eastern Shore's land features, such a line makes perfect sense.

The Eastern Shore held several advantages as a possible location for settlers, safety being primary among them. Also, land was available and bay and seaports provided avenues for trade. What a boon to all if iron were found on this healthful peninsula, especially in the wake of that daunting attack and the fatalities of the summer sickness. The Company's pleas for iron had been dogged. Surviving ironworkers needed work. Other men needed work. Why would someone not look to the Eastern Shore? Not to think of it at this unique time in the colony's history would have been poor leadership.

If this furnace was built under Yeardley's patronage, it certainly reflected ambitious hope. With no time to waste, production would have begun immediately. Yeardley would have envisioned the Company's gratitude for his initiative, and he would have expected reimbursement, at least in part.

Maurice Berkeley probably accompanied Yeardley to the Eastern Shore. Maurice's father had been killed at Falling Creek Ironworks and Maurice would be named by the Company to pick up where his father had left off. Maurice may have known a little something about iron. Yeardley may have charged Maurice—along with any ironworkers who had come into the colony since the attack—to find a promising site for an ironworks on his land. It would have been a hasty survey, but it would have been the best they could do under the circumstances. Once the site was chosen, they would have begun work on building shelters, making bricks, clearing land, putting in a crop of corn, building a dam and running a flume (a wooden channel) to bring water to the furnace. The number of men put to work on such a project would have been perhaps a hundred or more.

Was the work halted when word came that the Company wanted no part of "removeall" to the Eastern Shore? Did Yeardley take the workers away with him on his new commission to fight the Indians? Did the iron resources prove insufficient to support continuation? Is it an unfinished structure that is dissolving into detritus on that marshy, tidal creek bank?

George Sandys had said that Yeardley lost two-thirds of his wealth in that year. If this were indeed a viable iron furnace, Yeardley surely would have had every intention to go back, despite the Company's threats of treason. The manufacture of iron would eclipse treason, if not immediately, at least once the colony had survived its deep wounds.

If the furnace was built in the days of Yeardley, either its viability was too weak to risk further resources, or a calculated decision was made to abandon it until a later time. If anyone was waiting for the right moment to request Company money to further the work, that moment never arrived. In less than two years, the Company's finances failed, and its charter was ended. If Yeardley had dreams to go back, time was not on his side. After the Company's demise, he spent a year working with the governor and council to keep the colony afloat. He then spent a year in England, petitioning the king on behalf of the Virginians.

He returned to the colony in the summer of 1626 as the newly appointed governor. Just over a year later, he died at the age of forty.

At the time of Yeardley's death, the Accomack settlement had not expanded the six miles or so northeastward to where that furnace rests. That land would remain dormant until Yeardley's heir, Argoll, returned years later.

Until trained archaeologists can tackle it, the site should remain untouched. When it can be excavated, the results may prove to be as exciting as this theory, or it may prove to be an iron endeavor of a later generation. Either way, its colonial origins are undisputed, and thus promise to be an interesting, future tale for Eastern Shore storytellers.

NOTES, Chapter 1:

1. The Powhatan Confederation consisted of the Algonquin-speaking Indian tribes who lived in the Tidewater area of colonial Virginia. Their leader in 1622 was Opechancanough, as Chief Powhatan had died several years before. The attack took place on March 22, 1621/22. (For an explanation of the use of double years in a date, please refer to "Calendar" in the Glossary.)

2. Susan Myra Kingsbury, ed., *The Records of The Virginia Company of London. Vol. I-IV* (Washington, D.C.: Government Printing Office, 1906-1933), Vol. III, 678-679 (hereinafter: Kingsbury, *VCL-1*, *VCL-2*, *VCL-3* or *VCL-4*).

3. A question may arise about whether or not an apostrophe should be added to Dales Gift to make it "Dale's Gift." Occasionally, early writers would use the possessive case apostrophe; however, they most often did not. Please refer to "Apostrophes" in the Glossary for a discussion of the use (or nonuse) of apostrophes in this book.

4. "Newport" was a name that apparently lingered from 1608 when Captain Christopher Newport presented Savage as his son when Newport left Thomas to live with Chief Powhatan, the paramount leader of the Powhatan Indians. Some writers have questioned that Thomas's name was Savage, being that this was a term often used in relation to the Indians; however, Savage is a common surname in England. It was first recorded

in the Domesday Book in 1086. The name (and the word) had various spellings, including *salvage* and *sauvage*. Thomas's name was listed as Salvage on the ship manifest of the First Supply. Accompanying him on that voyage was another of that name, Richard Salvage.

5   The documentation of these gifts from the Laughing King is found in the patent of Thomas Savage and in the testimony of William Jones who was questioned about the land in 1668 (Virginia Land Office Patents, Vol. 1, 275; Howard Mackey and Marlene Groves, *Northampton County, Virginia Record Book: Deeds, Wills &c, Volume 6 and 7-8, 1655-57* (Rockport, ME: Picton Press, 2002), 263–264 (hereinafter: Mackey, *Vol. 6, 7 & 8*)). "Gift" is a word that has been applied to this transaction these many years later. Jones reported that the Laughing King said, "I gave that neck of land…" In the patents, the land is spoken of as having been "granted" to Savage "as by deed." The old orders contain sundry instances of land transfers between Indians and Englishmen. In most of those cases, some type of compensation was given to the Indians. This may have been true, too, for Savage and for Yeardley; however, as noted, the records reflect only the words "gave" and "granted."

6   Hinman, Michael "Fierce Arrow," historian of the Accohannock Tribe, lecture, Eastern Shore Public Library, summer, 2014.

7   A 1990s study revealed a slot trench on the south shore of Old Plantation Creek. This trench cut through a post-in-the-ground building that is thought to date to the mid-1600s. Such trenches are said to have been used for building fortification palisades during the 17th century (Nicholas M. Lucketti, "Archaeology at Arlington: Excavations at the Ancestral Custis Plantation, Northampton County, Virginia," (The Association for the Preservation of Virginia Antiquities, Williamsburg, 1999), 14). I suggest that this trench may have been built when Lady Dale's cattle and cattlemen were placed here in 1622. Two years later, the General Assembly required all dwellings to be surrounded by a palisade (William Waller Hening, ed., *Statutes at Large, Being a Collection of all the Laws of Virginia, Vol. I-[XIII]* (Richmond: George Cochran, 1819-1823), 127; hereinafter: Hening, *Statutes*). The post-in-the-ground building may have belonged to William Burdett, who had worked for Lady Dale.

8   Kingsbury, *VCL-3*, 691.

9   Kingsbury, *VCL-4*, 9-17.

10 Kingsbury, *VCL-4*, 67.

11 Kingsbury, *VCL-4*, 73–75.

12 Kingsbury, *VCL-4*, 23.

13 John Smith, *The Generall Historie of Virginia, New England, & The Summer Isles* (London, 1624, Reprint, Bedford, MA, Applewood Books, 2006), 302 (hereinafter: Smith, *Generall Historie*).

14 H. Chandlee Forman, *The Virginia Eastern Shore and its British Origins: History, Gardens & Antiquities* (Easton, MD: Eastern Shore Publishers' Associates, 1973), 56. Dr. Brown consulted an archaeologist who worked with the National Park Service, but nothing has yet been found referencing the Indiantown site in the archaeologist's records at Swem Library, College of William and Mary, Williamsburg, Virginia.

15 The Eastern Shore's railway ran from north to south following this ridge at a northeast–southwest slant. The rail line can be seen in the center of Figure 1A.

16 Whissaponson was the early name for Savages Creek. Today, the body of water is called The Gulf. In early years, today's Indiantown Creek was called by several names: Angoods and Governor Hawleys are two known names. This same theory of a west–east line drawn against the ridge could help to explain later in this history why Yeardley's son moved Indians off his land at Old Town Neck to land that is now considered a part of Savage's gift; perhaps at the time (in pre-survey days), Argoll Yardley thought that portion of land belonged to him. Early records show that the tract of land defined by the two middle branches of Whissaponson was in dispute throughout the mid-seventeenth century; Yardley dealt with that dispute by disclaiming the tract (Howard Mackey and Marlene A. Groves, *Northampton County, Virginia, Record Book: Court Cases, Vol. 9, 1664–1674* (Rockport, ME: Picton Press, 2003), 128 (hereinafter: Mackey, *Vol. 9*).

Constant Troyon (French, 1810–1865), *Cows and Sheep under Trees*, c. 1850, courtesy of The National Gallery of Art, Washington, D. C., public domain.

Chapter 2

Dales Gift

In 1614, Virginia's deputy governor, Sir Thomas Dale, authorized the establishment of a saltworks and fishing operation on an ocean island at the southern end of Virginia's Eastern Shore. Earlier explorations to these lands at the convergence of the Atlantic Ocean and the Chesapeake Bay had revealed an abundance of naturally forming salt as well as dense schools of fish. Dale's emissaries negotiated a purchase of land from the local Native people. They named the land "Dales Gift." Within a decade, people lost sight of the exact history and the ownership became "an uncertaine rumor of a great quantity of land." In this chapter, we will follow the records to see how that uncertain rumor developed into a persistent misunderstanding of ownership. In short, the misunderstanding about Dales Gift seems to have come about because Lady Dale's cattle and cattlemen were brought to the Eastern Shore, and after Lady Dale's death, a great quantity of land was claimed in her husband's name.

Sir Thomas Dale had served as a naval commander for which King James knighted him in 1606. He married Elizabeth Throckmorton in 1611, and then went to Virginia to serve as the colony's marshal under Deputy Governor Sir Thomas Gates. Dale's wife did not go with him to the colony. From 1614–1616, Dale served as acting deputy governor of Virginia. He left the colony in 1616.

In 1617, John Rolfe wrote about all of the English-inhabited places in Virginia. "Dales-Gift" was one of those places. Rolfe said it consisted of seventeen men under the command of Lieutenant Cradock, and that it was a seasonal fish and salt operation at Cape Charles.[1]

During the time of Sir Thomas Dale, according to the Virginia Company records, "sundry Saltworks" were "sett upp to the great good and benefitt of the Plantation" (the "Plantation" being the whole of Virginia). By March 2, 1619/20, the Company noted that the sundry saltworks had "wholly gone to wrack and lett fall in so much that by defect therof the inhabitants are exceedingly distempred by eatinge porke and other meats fresh & unseasoned."[2]

Lieutenant Cradock's saltworks were no doubt abandoned by October of 1617 when he was recommended for appointment as a provost marshal on the mainland plantation called Bermuda Hundred. The next month, Deputy Governor Samuel Argall asked the Bermuda Hundred citizens to allow the colony servants to stay at their plantation that year. On February 20, 1617/18, Deputy Governor Argall officially appointed William Cradock to be "provost Marshall of the Bermuda City and of all the Hundred thereto belonging."[3]

The time of quitting the saltworks at Cape Charles can be estimated from Cradock's appointment to Bermuda

Hundred; however, it is merely a guess that the colony servants who hoped to be housed at Bermuda Hundred that year were Cradock's men from the salt and fishing operation. The evidence is compelling, but circumstantial.

Bermuda City and Hundred was a private enterprise and therefore not specifically under the rule of the Virginia Company. Argall was an investor in that enterprise, but he did not have the authority to impose his will on the citizens who lived there; thus, he asked permission. The site of Bermuda Hundred is now occupied by the large industrial plant that can be seen to the northwest from the James River's Benjamin Harrison Bridge that connects Charles City and Prince George counties.

The next reference to Dales Gift was uttered by Secretary John Pory. In the summer of 1620, Pory wrote about a conversation with several men who had served at Smith Island. Though Pory did not mention the land by name, he noted that Sir Thomas Dale had bought the land from the Indians "for the Company."[4] That is the last mention of Dales Gift in the records.

Sir Thomas Dale died in India in 1619, and his will was probated in January 1619/20. He left his estate to his wife. After Dale's death, George Yeardley sent Lady Dale's tobacco home to her, after arranging prepayment of the freight for her convenience. In his report of this transaction, Yeardley noted the "love and service" he owed to Sir Thomas Dale.[5]

At the time of Dale's residency in Virginia, personal land patents had not yet been devised, although investors could have shares in land. As early as August of 1619 (seven months after the probate of Dale's will), the Virginia General Assembly noted that Lady Dale's venture (as well as those of some others) was not united into a "settled Colony" (such as a Hundred). If she (and others) were to unite, the same privileges could be afforded her as were afforded Hundreds.[6] The following June, goats were sent to Virginia for Lady Dale.[7] A year later, in June of 1621, Lady Dale desired and was granted a patent for "a particular Plantation."[8] In September of 1621, Lady Dale authorized the gift of a cow to her cousin, George Thorpe. Henry Watkins was then managing Lady Dale's cattle.[9] Eight months later, in May of 1622, Lady Dale requested the Company to write a letter of commendation to the governor for a man she was sending to Virginia to oversee her people. She felt that her people were cheating her of profits and this man, with the governor's assistance, would help to correct this situation.[10] Eight months later, Charles Harmoun [sic] petitioned the governor to require payment for a cow that one of Captain Nathaniel Butler's men killed when Butler sailed to Chickahominy in the winter of 1622.[11] A few days later, the Virginia governor and council used Lady Dale's cattle and cattlemen as an example to explain to the Company why plantations had to be "quit" in order to protect the people after the Indian attack of the previous March.

> *A muster taken of my Lady dales family, which consisted of two and twentie wherof eight were boys, most of the men were new and untrayned with very little munitione, and but six peeces and one Armour amongst them, and 54 headd of Cattle, which all those men were nott Sufficyent to guarde, except eyther the place or Industry of inclosure had given advantage.*[12]

The implication is that Lady Dale's plantation was one of the places abandoned after the March 22nd attack. The

Indians were still striking where they could, and Lady Dale's cattlemen were not able to protect the cattle, much less themselves. It is a reasonable theory that Sir George Yeardley took at least some of Lady Dale's cattle and cattlemen to the Eastern Shore during his three-month's commission, but no documentation has yet been found that tells us exactly that.[13]

Snippets in the records that do support the idea include the muster of February, 1623/24, showing that Lady Dale's overseer, Henry Watkins, lived on the Eastern Shore by the end of 1623. It's known that Charles Harmar had arrived about a year before to take up the court causes for Lady Dale, but his name does not show in that early muster. In the next year's muster, 1624/25, Charles Harmar had taken up residence on the Eastern Shore, but Henry Watkins was not in the muster. In 1627, Harmar delivered Lady Dale's account to the next manager, William Hamby. Harmar noted that this account included all that had remained in his custody since he received the same from Henry Watkins.[14]

It was in the next year, 1628, when Charles Harmar sought to lease a parcel of land south of the mouth of Old Plantation Creek. In response to Harmar's request, the James City court noted that "there hath beene an uncertain Rumor of a great quantity of land there or neere unto the same belonging unto the Lady Dale." The court noted that "no certain knowledge" about this land remained upon record or otherwise. Also, the court deemed it "unreasonable and unlikely that so great a tract of land as from Cape Charles thither should belong to any Particular divident." (Divident is an obsolete word meaning "dividend." Please see the glossary.) Consequently, the court allowed Harmar 100 acres with the condition that if anyone proved it belonged to

Lady Dale, Harmar would be forced off the land.[15] No one ever came forward to attempt such a claim.

The point of all this is to say that no one knows exactly when Lady Dale's cattle and cattlemen were brought to the Eastern Shore. It stands to reason that Sir George Yeardley had a hand in the move. The reasons being that he was somewhat solicitous toward Lady Dale, he was heavily engaged in moving settlers after the attack, and he had a vested interest in the Eastern Shore becoming a successful settlement of the Virginia colony. The addition of Lady Dale's enterprise to the mix would lend credibility and confidence to the endeavor. He would have placed Lady Dale's people and cattle on the lower shore, on land that he personally knew was Company land acquired during the two years of Sir Thomas Dale's deputy governorship (1614-1616).[16] It is not known whether Yeardley had a plan to address a patent for Lady Dale on the Eastern Shore, but that would have been the least of his concerns during the time of his Eastern Shore commission. As it played out, such a patent never concerned anyone during Lady Dale's lifetime.

When the king revoked the Virginia Company's charter in 1624 and Virginia became a royal colony, all the old Company land became the king's land. On the Eastern Shore, after Harmar took his 100 acres to the south of Old Plantation Creek, other men stayed within the old bounds and did not move southward until six years later. By the time Lady Dale died in 1640, her cattle had been grazing for almost eighteen years on that "uncertaine rumor" of land.

Lady Elizabeth Dale's will was probated in England, but a copy of the will was recorded in the local Virginia county record on March 29, 1641. Her lands in Virginia were noted to be at Charles Hundred and Sherlie Hundred. Five hundred acres, unspecified, were left to a niece.

In January 1641/42, the Eastern Shore received official notice that Samuel Chandler was authorized to represent Lady Dale's executors, Richard Hanby and William Shrimpton. Mr. Chandler was to take possession of any land, tenements, and property in Virginia that had belonged to the Dales.

In April of 1642, Chandler began selling cows, bulls, and oxen belonging to Lady Dale's estate. The buyers were prominent Eastern Shore men, including Argoll Yardley, Nathaniel Littleton, William Stone, John Holloway, John Stringer, Obedience Robins, and Phillip Taylor. By October of 1643, Hanby died, leaving Shrimpton as the sole executor.

After Hanby's death, William Shrimpton appears to have begun a quest for documentation to support land claims in the name of Sir Thomas and Lady Elizabeth Dale. In October of 1643, a notary public in England verified copies of two documents. The first was from the Virginia Company's Council of Virginia thirty-three years before. This 1610 document showed that Sir Thomas Dale's contributions as an Adventurer (Company investor) and in other assignments entitled him to be rated at a sum of £700 which would merit him "such Lands Tenements and hereditaments as shall from tyme to tyme bee there Recorded Planted and Inhabited."[17] The second document was apparently written one day later on February 27, 1610/11, also under the seal of the Virginia Company.[18]

Whereas Sire Thomas Dale Knight Marshall of Virginia hath pay'd in ready mony to Sir Thomas

> *Smyth Knight Treasurer of Virginia The Summe of Three hundred seaventye and Five pounds For his Adventures towards the said voyage. It is agreed that For the same hee the said Sir Thomas Dale his heyres Executors Administrators or Assignes shall have ratably according to his Adventures his full part of all such Lands Tenements and hereditaments as shall from tyme to tyme bee there Recorded Platted and Inhabited, And of such Mynes and Mineralls of gold Silver and ther mettalls or Threasure Pearles Presious stones or any Kinde of Wares or Marchandizes Comodityes Proffitts whatsoever which shalbe obtayned or gotten in the said voyage according to the Portion of Money by him imployed to that use in as Ample matter as any other Adventurer therein shall Receave for the like Summe.[19]*

In the meantime, after Lady Dale's death, William Burdett took on the management of Lady Dale's Eastern Shore cattle and laborers. By the summer of 1643, Burdett was terminally ill and unable to carry on. He assigned management to his second, Edward Douglas.[20] In London, Shrimpton was not aware of Burdett's illness and subsequent death, and he wrote Burdett, giving him power of attorney to pursue payment from Argoll Yardley, Edward Littleton, Richard Holwell, Samuel Lucas, William Stone, and Obedience Robins.[21] These men had apparently not paid for the cattle they had procured from Lady Dale's estate. A full year passed before Shrimpton corrected the power of attorney and placed it with the current manager, Edward Douglas.[22]

A month after he appointed Douglas as his attorney to manage affairs in Northampton County, Shrimpton wrote a lengthier document. In this document, he reiterated that Edward Douglas was authorized to collect debts and any beasts belonging to him as Lady Dale's executor. He refreshed the list of men who were in debt to him: Argoll Yardley, Nathaniel Littleton, John Holloway's executors, William Stone, Obedience Robins, John Parramore, James Perreen, John Stringer, Phillip Taylor, William Whitby, Goodman Wyatt, and William Burdett's executors. Also in this document, Shrimpton appointed Edward Douglas "to procure and obtain all such lawful grant and grants of moiety of such proportion and proportions of lands in Accomack aforesaid which are not planted and granted as in respect of the Adventures of the said Sir Thomas and Dame Elizabeth or either or them with the Virginia Company and for servants transported thither doth or shall appertain or may by any lawful ways and means be had or taken up there to my use."[23] In other words, Shrimpton instructed Douglas to determine what Eastern Shore land might be available to claim in right of Sir Thomas and Lady Dale (now both deceased) for Shrimpton's own use. This passage reveals that no land had yet been claimed in the name of Dale.

Shrimpton appointed William Stone as Edward Douglas's second, in case Douglas were to die. However, Douglas continued to manage the business in Northampton for some years more.

In October 1645, Shrimpton was awarded a 1,000-acre patent in Northampton County as the surviving and sole Executor of Dame Elizabeth Dale "and due unto her as being the sole Executrix of Sir Thomas Dale and due unto him by bill of Adventure as appeareth by said bill of Adventure into this Colony recorded under this Patent...."

(The 1610 document from the Virginia Council in London was recorded under the patent.) Four years later, Shrimpton renewed the patent, but claimed 2,000 acres this time. The bounds for both patents were the same: the bay to the west, the ocean to the east, the woods to the north, and Edward Douglas to the south.[24] At an unknown date, Douglas purchased the 2,000 acres from Shrimpton.[25]

Nothing about Dales Gift appears in any of the documents relating to Shrimpton's land acquisitions on the Eastern Shore for which he used Sir Thomas Dale's rights as an Adventurer and contributor to the Virginia Company. It appears that the acquisition of the 2,000 acres was the result of a brilliant bit of estate administration. An opportunity presented itself and Shrimpton pursued it. Letters or other documents may one day surface to show whether or not Edward Douglas (or any other Eastern Shore person) had a hand in the planning of this successful endeavor.

In summary, Dales Gift was Company property that transferred to the king upon the Company's demise in 1624. Lady Dale's cattle wound up on the Eastern Shore, apparently as a result of the 1622 Indian attack and Yeardley's knowledge of and fondness for the Eastern Shore. Over the years, the Virginia leadership lost sight of any particulars about Lady Dale's people and cattle being on the Eastern Shore. When given the opportunity, no one came forward to dispute the patenting of land in the Eastern Shore's southern reaches. Lady Dale's cattle continued to graze to the southeast and east of Old Plantation Creek under the watchful eye of her managers, who took up patents in that same area. After Lady Dale's death, her surviving executor devised a brilliant plan to claim a large portion of land on the Eastern Shore in Sir

Thomas Dale's name. This land eventually came into the possession of Lady Dale's last manager, Edward Douglas.

NOTES, Chapter 2:

1 John Rolf[e], "A True Relation of the State of Virginia left by Sir Thomas Dale Knight in May last 1616." https://encyclopediavirginia.org/entries/a-true-relation-of-the-state-of-virginia-lefte-by-sir-thomas-dale-knight-in-may-last-1616-1617/
2 Kingsbury, *VCL-1*, 318.
3 Kingsbury, *VCL-1*, 76, 91. Bermuda Hundred was located at the confluence of the Appomattox and James rivers.
4 Kingsbury, *VCL-3*, 304.
5 Kingsbury, *VCL-3*, 126. The exact date of this letter is unknown.
6 Kingsbury, *VCL-3*, 168.
7 Kingsbury, *VCL-3*, 293.
8 Kingsbury, *VCL-1*, 483. The word "particular" in relation to plantations, seems to have meant "special;" in other words, Lady Dale was asking for some very good, preferably exceptional land.
9 H. R. McIlwaine, ed., *Minutes of the Counsel and General Court, 1622–1630, 1670–1676* (Richmond, VA: Virginia State Library, 1924), 48 (hereinafter: McIlwaine, *Minutes*).
10 Kingsbury, *VCL-2*, 14.
11 Kingsbury, *VCL-4*, 8. "Harmar" would later show as the correct spelling of Charles's last name. In the winter of 1622, either Lady Dale's cows had not yet been placed on the Eastern Shore, or she had cows on both sides of the water.
12 Kingsbury, *VCL-4*, 12.
13 Eastern Shore historian Nora Miller Turman also concluded from her reading of the Records of the Virginia Company that *George Yeardley* took Lady Dale's tenants to land on the Eastern Shore (Nora Miller Turman, George Yeardley, (Richmond, Virginia: Garrett and Massie, Incorporated, 1959) 144). Historian Dr. Susie Ames said that Lady Dale's tenants were placed on the Eastern Shore in 1622. Dr. Ames concluded that Lady Dale's land was not surveyed and recorded, but that it was generally recognized as her land (Susie M. Ames, *Studies of the*

Eastern Shore in the Seventeenth Century (Richmond, VA: Dietz Press, 1940), 40). I agree with Mrs. Turman and Dr. Ames, except that the land in question became that "uncertaine Rumor," and when the time came to claim it, Lady Dale's executor had to start from scratch, so to speak.

14 McIlwaine, *Minutes*, 146.

15 McIlwaine, *Minutes*, 179.

16 Dale had expressed good faith in Yeardley when he left Yeardley in charge of the colony in 1617, awaiting the new deputy governor's arrival. As such a close associate to Sir Thomas Dale, Yeardley was probably well aware of Dale's investments. John Pory was secretary during Yeardley's governorship. Yeardley is probably the person who told John Pory that Dales Gift belonged to the Company. Still, that Dale's name was applied to the tract may mean that Dale had expressed an appreciation for the lower shore. If so, Yeardley would have known this and perhaps thought it a good place to put Lady Dale's cattle, intending to deal with the paperwork later. When Yeardley died and his contemporaries were also gone, the nuances of land ownership were lost, leaving only an uncertain rumor.

17 Susie M. Ames, ed., *County Court Records of Accomack-Northampton, Virginia 1640-1645* (Charlottesville, VA: The University Press of Virginia, 1973), 346–347 (hereinafter: Ames, *1640*).

18 Ames, *1640*, 343. In Ames's transcription the year is given as 1620/21; however, this appears to be a mistake as Dale was deceased by that date and Smyth was no longer Treasurer of the Company.

19 Ames, *1640*, 343.

20 Ames, *1640*, 344.

21 Ames, *1640*, 347.

22 Ames, *1640*, 404.

23 Ames, *1640*, 408–410. (spelling modernized)

24 Nell Marion Nugent, Virginia Genealogical Society, and Virginia State Library, *Cavaliers And Pioneers: Abstracts of Virginia Land Patents And Grants, 1623-1800, Vol. 1* (Richmond, VA: Press of the Dietz Print Co., 1934), 163, 181 (hereinafter: Nugent, *I*); Library of Virginia, *Virginia Land Office Patents and Grants, Patent Book No. 2 (1643-1651)*, 68, 167.

25 Nugent, *I*, 414; Library of Virginia, *Virginia Land Office Patents and Grants, Patent Book No. 4 (1655-1664)*, 504–505. The 1661 patent for Edward Douglas's heir states that Edward Douglas purchased the 2,000 acres from Shrimpton.

Chapter 3

Yeardley and Epps

Sometime in the last century, a writer spun the tale that Sir George Yeardley and Captain William Epps colluded against Thomas Savage, the interpreter and trader. It has become an oft-repeated story, told as truth.

As the story goes, Epps drummed up a charge of slander against Savage, and Yeardley orchestrated the trial and conviction, all for the purpose of wresting the corn trade from Savage to give to Epps. It is an intriguing story, but the part about Yeardley's involvement is not supported by the records. Most likely, that was someone's theory that went awry and gained a life of its own. In this essay, we will explore the facts that are the basis of this persistent myth.

The story began about June 22, 1623, when Captain William Epps, commander of the Accomack settlement, went to Thomas Savage's home, accompanied by Charles Harmar. Epps's purpose that day was to accuse Savage of slander. Epps said that Savage had said he was afraid Epps would kill him. Epps confronted Savage and restrained him "neck and heels," but Savage "used no ill language."

Nine months later, on March 5, 1623/24, the Grand Assembly concluded that unrestricted access of trade with the Indians increased the colonists' vulnerability to attack. It decreed "that all trade for corn with the salvages as well publick as private after June next shall be prohibited."[1] The intention was to reduce the colonists' contact with Indians by ending the unsanctioned corn trade. It was hoped that this measure would result in increased safety across the colony.

Thomas Savage had been trading with the Eastern Shore Indians for several years. These Indians considered Savage their friend; in fact, the werowance referred to him as "my son." If the law were to be obeyed, Savage would have to discontinue his trading, no matter how special the relationship.

In the colony's Quarter Court, two days after the Assembly, someone questioned whether or not Savage had been honest in accounting for corn obtained from the Laughing King. The werowance, with Savage as his interpreter, confirmed Savage's account.[2]

Three months later, on June 21, 1624, Charles Harmar told the Quarter Court about Epps's visit to Savage's home when Epps accused Savage of slander. The court did not record any action on this information.

Eight months later, on March 7, 1624/25, the Quarter Court (consisting of Governor Francis Wyatt and the Virginia Council) commanded that Thomas Savage interpret "for the good of ye Plantation of Acomack," and he was to do so at the direction of Captain Epps. If Savage did not comply, the court said, he was to put up a bond of £200 with sureties to

Epps, guaranteeing that he would have no "conference at all or familiarity with the Indians of those parts."[3]

Within the hour after that decree, the Quarter Court returned to the issue and clarified that no one could trade with the Eastern Shore Indians for corn without a special license from the governor and council. Further, they authorized Epps to seize the corn of any offender and to send the offender to James City for censure. And then the court said something that reveals the probable crux of the matter: "That if it shall appear there shall be any extreme need of corn in that plantation, the court resolves to proceed by employing Captain Epps, as they have done with Captain Ralph Hamer."[4]

The very next week, Epps was back, standing before the governor and council to say that the Eastern Shore had an extreme need for corn. He said that Accomack, "by receaving many planters into them, was likely to be in great want of Corne."

The colony had just taken a muster of the population, so an appeal to numbers was credible. Accomack had compiled its count on February 7, just five weeks before, and indeed, about fifteen new freemen were in the mix. Corn had been counted in that muster, so Epps, as the plantation commander, would have been privy to that information. However, note how he used the information. He cried "extreme need," then he noted "many new planters," and then he said that it was "likely" they would need more corn.

Given this spin, the Quarter Court ordered Epps to inspect every man's store of corn. Depending on what he found, he had the court's permission to trade with the Eastern Shore Indians for however much corn the settlers needed. He could do this, the court said, as long as he went with enough men and arms for protection. Also, he was to trade with the "trucking stuff" brought to him by the settlers. Those who brought items to trade were to be given one third of everything he bought with that truck. The rest could be distributed as needed. This plan, the court said, would prevent "the enhancing of prizes and disorderly trading."[5] The Quarter Court then granted Epps the commission.

Those are the facts.

Indeed, someone seems to have harassed Savage in the two years leading up to Epps's commission. First, Epps showed up at Savage's home to accuse him of slander, yet Savage said nothing offensive and apparently did not resist when Epps restrained him. Nine months later, someone implied that Savage had not delivered all the corn sent from the Laughing King, yet the Laughing King was present to refute that claim. In June 1624, when the new trade law was to take effect, the Quarter Court heard about Epps's visit to Savage's home. Eight months later, the Quarter Court ordered Savage to interpret for the good of the plantation at the direction of Epps or else to put up the princely bond to Epps, promising that he would have no interaction with the Eastern Shore Indians. Epps came back to the court a week later, essentially describing impending disaster if he did not have the corn trade. He got the corn trade.

To create a theory that plants Sir George Yeardley as the mastermind behind this harassment takes a leap that is not impossible, but is improbable and ill-suited. Yeardley had championed Epps years before when he appointed Epps to command Smyths Hundred, and later, to Accomack's command. In both of those instances, Yeardley had been in desperate need of commanders. Not enough evidence exists to say that Epps was Yeardley's puppet. The author of that theory surely overlooked the substantial likelihood that Yeardley had a healthy respect for Thomas Savage. No doubt exists that Savage was a primary factor in Yeardley's acquisition of 3,700 Eastern Shore acres.[6]

Epps appears to have been the sole author of Savage's broken alliance with the Eastern Shore Indians. His display of hubris upon accusing Savage of slander should be evidence enough, but then that was topped by his cry of impending disaster for want of corn on the Eastern Shore. However, even though he wrangled the commission, it was not a commission equal to that of men such as Ralph Hamor, who had been able to profit from his trade. The court's order tied Epps's hands; if he followed instructions, he would not make a personal profit.

Two years later, George Yeardley took the corn commission from Epps and gave it to Captain John Stone. This was one of Yeardley's first actions in his second term as governor.[7]

Before leaving this story, two items bear scrutiny. First, some people say that Savage was exploited, forced to work for Epps. A thorough reading of the records gives credence to the conclusion that Savage did not work for Epps and that he did not violate the Quarter Court's order. Most likely, he walked away. Thomas Savage was his own man.

In support of the idea that Savage walked away, note the Quarter Court's directive to Captain Epps to take enough men and arms for protection when he went to trade with the Eastern Shore Indians. If Savage had accompanied Epps, no such protection would have been needed; and if anyone had thought Savage might sabotage Epps, the court would have known that not enough men and arms existed to protect him.

The second item that bears scrutiny is the possibility that Savage found this event so contemptible that he resolved to leave his original homestead near the old Accomack Company land in order to develop his divident on the other side of Accomack River, as far away from Epps's reach as possible. Many writers have assumed that Savage took up residence on his divident immediately after the Laughing King granted the land to him. However, his primary residence was probably closer to other men and women, particularly after he married and had a baby. Hannah Savage's 1627 patent gives us our most reliable indicator that the couple's residence was just next to old Company land on the south side of Accomack River (today's Cherrystone Inlet). The patent describes Hannah's fifty acres as a small neck of land "whereon they are now seated."[8] Eight years later, before Hannah remarried, she allowed her future husband, Daniel Cugley, to patent 400 acres on Savages Creek (now The Gulf), next to her land known as Savages Choice.[9] From these patent records, it can be inferred that the Savages moved from Accomack plantation to Thomas's divident between 1628 and 1633 (the estimated year of Thomas's death).

That Savage ever again interpreted "for the good of ye Plantation" is highly unlikely. Savage's troubles illustrate the interpreter's importance within the colony, but they also show how having such a rare skill could be utterly oppressive.

NOTES, Chapter 3:

1   Hening, *Statutes I*, 126.
2   McIlwaine, *Minutes*, 11
3   McIlwaine, *Minutes*, 48.
4   Modern spelling was used in this quotation.

5   McIlwaine, *Minutes*, 50. (Modern spelling used.) The court was trying to quash profiteering.

6   John Camden Hotten, ed., *The Original Lists of Persons of Quality: Emigrants, Religious Exiles, Political Rebels, Serving Men Sold for a Term of Years, Apprentices, Children Stolen, Maidens Pressed, And Others, Who Went From Great Britain to the American Plantations, 1600–1700* (London: Empire State Book Co, 1874), 274 (hereinafter: Hotten, *Lists*). These were the acres granted by the Laughing King and recognized as Yeardley's divident.

7   McIlwaine, *Minutes*, 104.

8   Library of Virginia, *Virginia Land Office Patents and Grants, Patent Book No. 1 (1623-1643 Vol. 1&2)*, 57–58.

9   Library of Virginia, *Virginia Land Office Patents and Grants, Patent Book No. 1 (1623-1643 Vol. 1&2)*, 189.

Founding of Jamestown, 2-cents stamp, issue of 1907, U.S. Bureau of Engraving and Printing, U. S. Post Office, Smithsonian National Postal Museum, courtesy Wikimedia Commons, public domain.

In 1624, Thomas Savage was one of five men who owned a boat on Virginia's Eastern Shore. (Five men represented a quarter of the heads of households and ten percent of the entire Shore population at that time.) It is not known what kind of boat he owned, but it was likely similar to one depicted in the image above. Savage's special relationship with the local Native people probably meant that he explored the local waters far beyond where his contemporaries held back for fear of their safety. It is believed that Thomas Savage made his final home on the south shore of what today is known as The Gulf, not far west of today's Eastville.

Chapter 4

The Last Years of Thomas Savage

As shown in the last chapter, it had been a strained time for Thomas Savage. That year, 1624, ended in what must have felt like betrayal and defeat. After this, Savage essentially disappeared from the records, but he would live nine years more.[1] The last known references about Savage's activities were in 1631 when William Claiborne employed him as an interpreter on the first visit to Kent Island, and in May 1634 when Savage was listed in an account pertaining to several voyages made by the *Virgine*, probably in 1633.[2] In 1633, Hannah Savage was noted to be a widow; that is the earliest indication of Thomas's death.

Savage had married by 1624 and was settling into a good situation on the Eastern Shore. He and his wife, Hannah, had a newborn baby, a son named John. Savage's ability to communicate with Native people and his close relationship with the Laughing King had earned him a land grant and, one would think, the right to flourish as a freeman. Then, in 1624, that ugly business with Epps profoundly affected Savage's career for the rest of his life.

Three years later, in December of 1627, Hannah Savage was granted a patent for fifty acres in her own name, having used her own headright. In that same year, the patent for the large quantity of land given to Thomas Savage by the Laughing King was issued, but that record has not been found. Eight years later, in August of 1635, the widow Hannah reapplied for and was granted the patent for that now famous gift, and the patent was then renewed in the name of her son, John Savage.[3]

Whitelaw suggested that Thomas Savage was a quiet, unassuming man who left "little direct information about himself."[4] This is certainly understandable when we remember that Savage was not a man of English literacy, nor of habits that were entirely English. He had spent enough formative and working years among a people altogether foreign to the English.[5] In addition to the possible influence of the Native people's culture on Savage's personality, the marks of disappointment and betrayal most certainly affected his psyche. It is no wonder that Savage seems to have spurned official society. When it came time to apply for legal leases and patents, it seems entirely reasonable that Hannah was the one who faced the men and labyrinth of English law.

Hannah had been called Ann (a short form of Hannah) in the 1624 muster. She was not listed with Thomas in the first count of 1623, so it stands to reason that she and Thomas married between those two counts.[6] Some genealogists have suggested that Hannah's maiden name was Elkington, based primarily on a grandson's name.

To add a further bit of intrigue to the matter, note that Hannah arrived in 1621 on the *Sea Flower* with Captain Ralph Hamor; therefore, Hannah (or Ann) should have been listed in the first muster. No Hannah (or Ann) Elkington was listed in that muster, so we then look for another Hannah (or Ann) under another name. Starting at the most logical place, Captain Hamor's household in James City, we find an Ann Addams, but that name appears again in the Hamor household in the next muster. Given the assumption of the genealogists, another name in the Hamor household jumps from the page: Elkington Ratclife (also Ratliffe). This man, a servant placed at Hogs Island (James River), also came to the colony on the *Sea Flower*, perhaps on the same voyage with Hannah.[7]

It may be more useful to pursue Hannah's maiden name through Ann Addams than through the naming of a grandson many years after her death. The 1624/25 muster could have counted one young woman twice, especially if the muster in James City preceded the muster on the Eastern Shore by any length of time. She could have been a maiden in James City and married by the time the muster was taken in Accomack.

Imagine further that young Ann (later to be known as Hannah) had befriended Elkington Ratclife on the voyage to Virginia. He may have protected her, or she may have protected him. Hannah may have recounted the voyage in stories to her son. In the Savage home, Elkington may have been a beloved name in rainy-day and bedtime stories. Hannah may have said to John, "If I'd had another son, I would have named him Elkington." This is a theory; it is as good as any, better than others.

Hannah's true origins may never be known; however, it is notable that she came to Virginia by personal adventure. That means she paid her own way.[8]

NOTES, Chapter 4:

1. Nugent, *I*, 9. Susie M. Ames, *County Court Records of Accomack-Northampton, Virginia, 1632–1640* (Washington, D.C.: American Historical Association, 1954), 5 (hereinafter: Ames, *1632*).

2. Raphael Semmes (editor), "*Claiborne vs. Clobery* in the High Court of Admiralty," *Maryland Historical Magazine*, 28 (1933): 32. In 1631, Thomas Savage traveled to Kent Island with Claiborne on the *Affryca*; Ames, *1632*, 16–17. The voyage of the *Virgine* took place before 1634; it was probably in 1633.

3. Nugent, *I*, 23, 30.

4. Ralph T. Whitelaw, *Virginia's Eastern Shore: a History of Northampton And Accomack Counties* (Richmond, VA: Virginia Historical Society, 1951; reprint, Gloucester, MA: Peter Smith, 1968), 214–219 (hereinafter: Whitelaw).

5. In 1608, Thomas Savage had been left with Chief Powhatan by Captain Christopher Newport in a mutual exchange of youngsters as a gesture of diplomacy and friendship. Savage lived with Powhatan for about three years.

6. Northampton County Court Records, *Orders, Book 7, 1657–1664*, folio 189.

7. Hotten, *Lists*, 174, 236; Nugent, *I*, 9. Ann Addams was noted to be a servant in Hamor's household. Her ship and arrival date were not listed. Elkington Ratclife was also in both counts, listed each time among Hamor's people.

8. The question may surface about whether or not a woman who paid her own way would be anyone's servant. The answer is that all people—men and women—pulled their weight in some capacity or other. Contracts in exchange for passage were usually seven years of service. Contracts for people who paid their own passage were individualized. It would have been rare in those years for any person, particularly a single person, to pass their time in the colony as a person of pure leisure.

Chapter 5

First Known African Inhabitants of the Eastern Shore

The Accomack/Northampton court records are the oldest continuous court records in North America.[1] However, despite their antiquity, these records provide only fragmentary information about what was happening each day in the early Eastern Shore settlement. Also, while they are the earliest continuous records, they did not begin until 1632. The Accomack settlement had taken root at least twelve years earlier. Though the records are renown, they provide information reflecting only a small percentage of what was happening in the settlement and almost no information about the first dozen years. Be that as it may, to tell the stories as accurately as possible, the records are our guide. At times, they tell us exactly what we want to know, but more often, they reveal only enough to tempt a theory or a guess.

To identify the first Eastern Shore inhabitants who came from Africa—either directly or by way of the Caribbean—we have only the court records to help. No other documentation has surfaced; therefore, we are left to guess that the names given below are indeed the first Africans.

This information was revealed on May 4, 1635, when Charles Harmar sat as a member of the Accomack court for the first and last time. Harmar had been an original appointee to the Accomack court in February 1631/32, but the only time he participated in formal leadership before then was when he served as a burgess for the 1632 Grand Assembly session.[2]

Harmar had come to Virginia in 1622 when he was twenty-two years old. How much schooling he had is not known, but his brother, John Harmar, was a well-educated Greek and Latin scholar at Oxford. Their uncle had also been a professor at Oxford, and in 1604, Uncle John Harmar, by King James's appointment, had been "one of the translators of the New Testament."[3]

Harmar was sent to Virginia by Lady Dale to correct her finances in the colony, as she had suspected that her Virginia people were cheating her. At the time of his Accomack court attendance, Harmar had been living in the county since the days of William Epps's command. It may be remembered that Harmar was the witness who accompanied Epps to Thomas Savage's door and watched as Epps accused Savage of slander. By 1627, Harmar was working for himself and soon acquired the first land tract to be leased outside the bounds of the original Accomack settlement. He lived south of Old Plantation Creek in the area that today is known as Arlington Plantation site.

That Harmar was present for that May 4th court probably surprised no one because he had some court business to be handled. First, he wanted Richard Tomson and Phillip Taylor questioned regarding the beaver skins that Captain Claiborne had bought the previous fall at Susquehanna in a ship called the *Affryca*. The significance of this to Harmar was not stated in the records, and nothing further appears in later records.

The second item of business was a court order certifying to the colony's governor and council that nineteen people were Harmar's servants. Eleven people were named and eight were noted to be "Negroes." The minutes did not name these servants, but the other eleven servants were named.[4] When Harmar traded his certificate for land a month later, on June 4, 1635, all the servants were named. The eight African servants were: Alexander, Anthony, Sebastian, Polonia, Jane, Palatia, Cassanga, and John. These eight men and women were the first African people recorded in the old records. It was unusual for the records to identify anything about headrights, but in Harmar's case, the court certified that they were all servants belonging to Harmar.

With the nineteen headrights, his own headright, and his wife's personal adventure, Harmar received 1,050 acres.[5] His tract was on the bayside, south of Old Plantation Creek's mouth, and north of "the deepe ditch" pond. The tract likely included Harmar's original 100-acre lease, north of Magatty Bay Pond (now Costin Pond). It is a guess that Alexander, Anthony, Sebastian, Polonia, Jane, Palatia, Cassanga, and John actually lived and worked on Harmar's bayside plantation, but it is the best guess we have.

Harmar's wife, Ann Southey, had come to Accomack from James City. She originally hailed from Rimpton, Somerset, England, and arrived in Virginia with her parents and five siblings in the summer of 1622, a most unhealthy time. Ann's father, Henry Southey, and all of her siblings died within their first two years in Virginia. Only Ann and her mother survived those years, and it may be that Ann left Jamestown only after her mother died in the late 1620s. Harmar was Ann's first husband.[6] Her second husband would be Nathaniel Littleton.

In 1640, Ann sold a servant, John Negro, to Garrett Andrews for 1,200 pounds of tobacco. Ann's husband at that time, Littleton, certified the sale to the June 1640 Accomack court.[7] Ann had made the agreement with Andrews; however, the law required her husband's assent to the sale.

It is possible that John Negro was one of the eight Africans who were claimed as Charles Harmar's headrights. That this was a sale into slavery is probable. The document reads as a deed of sale with no consideration for John's years of service as would have been seen for a contract servant.

Twenty-one years after Harmar certified his headrights, Ann Southey Harmar Littleton died. In her will, she named several "Negroes." It is apparent in this will that all persons referred to as "Negroes" were enslaved, although the word "slave" was not used. Among the enslaved persons were Old Tony (who may have been Anthony), Cossango (who was surely the same as Cassanga), and Fallassa (who may have been the same as Palatia). Cossongo and Fallassa were married with children. Old Tony had one son, maybe two.[8]

Almost a year after Harmar had certified his servants and claimed his land, Nathaniel Littleton freed a man named

Anthony Longo (Longoe, Longee) from servitude. Four years later, on July 30, 1640, Longo asked Littleton to give him papers that would prove his freedom. Littleton wrote a lengthy, thorough, and formal release, witnessed by the court clerk. He identified Longoe as "the Negro being [formerly] my servant and soly and propperly belongeing unto mee."[9]

That Longo needed papers to prove his freedom is probably significant in terms of the changing behaviors toward people of African descent. Papers were important for any former servant, but it seems that a European man's freedom was taken for granted unless someone could prove otherwise. Anthony Longo's actions suggest that he foresaw the beginnings of the hard times that were coming.

Over the next dozen and more years, the records show Longo on the court docket for typical debt issues. The clerk (or others) did not consistently identify him by race, a factor that suggests an uncommon regard. In 1655, the court would certify 250 acres to "Tony Longo Negro" for the headrights of five people, including himself and Hannah Longo. He later sold these headrights and did not claim land in his own name.[10]

It is not known how long Tony Longo had worked for Littleton or when he came to the Eastern Shore. However, the year of his release surely puts him into the mix among the first Africans to live and work on the Eastern Shore and perhaps the first African to be termed as "free."

Thirty-three years after Longo received his freedom, he petitioned the governor to be "eased of his great charge of children." The governor referred the matter to the Accomack court. This court referred to Longo as "Anto: Longo negro." Apparently, the Accomack court justices had a low opinion of Longo; they referred to his life as "lazy and evil" and his behavior as "slothful." The court stated that the children were likely to become the same as their father if left with him, so it approved apprenticeships for each of the three children. The younger girl would go with Captain Edmund Bowman and the older girl would go with Captain George Parker, each girl assigned to learn housewifery. The boy was to go with Colonel Edmund Scarburgh to learn shoemaking. Each child would stay in the apprenticeship until twenty-four years of age. Additionally, the court discharged Longo from paying taxes.

The next month, Longo was back to petition the court, "desiring Liberty to keep his children." This suggests that he never meant to give them up but perhaps meant only to be relieved of taxes. The court allowed him to keep his older daughter, but the other two were to go as previously ordered. In the meantime, he had placed his son with William Chase. The court ordered Chase to appear at the next session to answer for going against the court's previous order. It may be that Longo had put his son into service with Chase, hoping the court would allow it in lieu of service in Scarburgh's shoemaking operation.[11]

The tax lists show that Longo had no tithable workers over the years other than himself. That the court relieved him of taxes suggests that he may have become disabled and, no doubt, in need of the help his oldest child could provide. Longo may have died not long after this, as he failed to appear in court twice and then was not mentioned again in the Accomack records.

Imagining the lives of men and women such as Anthony Longo is nearly impossible. Little information was recorded;

few, if any, snippets of behavior were described. We are unable to see cultural customs that perhaps led European justices to use words such as "lazy," "evil," and "slothful." We rarely see an occupation or skill revealed. For the most part, the records reflect little about African people, especially those who were enslaved. It was as though their existence mattered only as a tithable commodity. Even so, tithable meant valuable.

It is a glorious thought that many people living today are descendants of Alexander, Anthony, Sebastian, Polonia, Jane, Palatia, Cassanga, John, or Anthony Longo. It is a heartbreaking thought that we will probably never know for certain if this is true. However, hope endures that further research will bring us closer to knowing more about the many early Eastern Shore ancestors whose lives, though hidden, were as remarkable as any other.

NOTES, Chapter 5:

1 To understand why these earliest records bear both county names, refer to **Accomack/Northampton** Records in the Glossary.

2 Ames, *1632*, 33; Hening, *Statutes I*, 170, 179.

3 Reginald M. Glencross, "Virginia Gleanings in England," *The Virginia Magazine of History and Biography* 29, no. 1 (January 1921): 38.

4 Ames, *1632*, 35. The named eleven servants were: Evan Jones, Thomas Cole, James Courtney, Lazarus Manning, Thomas Davis, Richard Wryth, John Symons, Richard Newton, Elizabeth Bennett, Rebecca Slaughter, and Mary Chester.

5 Nugent, *I*, 28. Ann Harmar's "personal adventure" meant that she personally held the right to that certificate, but her husband was exchanging her headright for land in addition to the headrights that he owned.

6 Ames, *1632*, 33-35; Hening, *Statutes I*, 170. Leslie Stephen and Sidney Lee, editors., *Dictionary of National Biography*, Vol. XXIV (New York, Macmillan and Co., 1890), 412-413; Nugent, I, 28; Martha W. McCartney, *Virginia Immigrants and Adventurers: A Biographical Dictionary, 1607-*

1635 (Baltimore: Genealogical Publishing Co., 2007), 364–365, 654–655 (hereinafter: McCartney, *Immigrants*); Whitelaw, 77.

7   Ames, *1640*, 4.

8   Northampton County, Virginia, *Deeds, Wills, &c, No. 7–8, 1655-1668*, fol. 22–fol. 24.

9   Ames, *1640*, 32. Longo's release had been given on March 16, 1635/36. See Appendix II.

10 Ames, *1640*, 32, 84, 249; Mackey, Howard and Marlene Groves, Editors, *Northampton County, Virginia, Record Book, Orders, Deeds, Wills &c, Volume 3, 1645-1651* (Rockport, ME, Picton Press, 2000), 155, 209 243 (hereinafter: Mackey, *Vol 3*); Mackey, *Vol. 6, 7 & 8*, 60; Nugent, *I*, 380.

11 JoAnn Riley McKey, *Accomack County, Virginia, Court Order Abstracts, 1666-1670*, Vol. 2, (Bowie, MD, Heritage Books, Inc., 1996) 170, 172; Accomack County, Virginia, *Orders, 1666-1670*, 151, 152, 154. It is interesting that Longo originally petitioned the governor rather than the local court. Perhaps he knew that the local court had a low opinion of him and hoped to avoid its interference. In 1663, Virginia's Eastern Shore was divided into two counties. Longo lived somewhere in the new county, Accomack.

Chapter 6

First Minister

Some early writers were led down the wrong path regarding the identity of the Eastern Shore's first minister. As is the case with most mistakes, it was an easy one to make.

Historians Jennings Cropper Wise and Ralph Whitelaw each concluded that Reverend Francis Bolton was assigned to the Eastern Shore's church. Some historians have called Bolton "the first rector of this first church," but the records do not support this assumption.[1] This idea seems to have originated from a Virginia Governor and Council order that directed the Eastern Shore to pay Bolton's 1623 salary.[2] Interpreting this order to mean that Bolton lived and worked on the Eastern Shore is certainly a reasonable theory, but it is not the most fitting possibility. Events over the two years preceding that order and the symbiotic relationship between the Eastern Shore and Elizabeth City reveal an interpretation very different from that of Wise and Whitelaw.

In the fall of 1621, when Sir Francis Wyatt joined the colony as Virginia's new governor, two "sufficient preachers" came with him. The first sufficient preacher was the governor's brother, Mr. Hautt Wyatt, who would live with the governor and serve as James City's preacher. The second sufficient preacher was Mr. Francis Bolton, who was assigned to Elizabeth City where he would live with Captain Thomas Nuce.[3]

As described in *An "Uncertaine Rumor" of Land*, the Eastern Shore settlement at the time of Governor Wyatt's arrival consisted of the Blowers, John Wilcocks, and the Secretary's tenants. In the following summer, Sir George Yeardley took an unknown number of people to the Eastern Shore as an element of his commission to prepare a place for 300 to 400 colonists in the wake of the March 22nd Indian attack that killed a quarter of the English colonists. By September, Yeardley's Eastern Shore commission was replaced by a commission to fight the mainland Indians, and the Eastern Shore plan was abandoned. As we saw in Chapter 1, the Company apparently saw the plan as a unilateral decision to desert the James River plantations. Fearing that investors would pull their money if the old plantations were abandoned, the near-bankrupt Company sent strong words to the Virginians, including heavy intimations of treason.

The Virginians quickly backed away from the Eastern Shore plan; in fact, they reported that they never gave it serious consideration. They had merely suggested, they said, a survey and the planting of a small party. The Company sent word to the governor and council, ordering that settlers be allowed to go back to their James River plantations. The governor and council did as they were ordered, but not without some lingering resentment. All their efforts had been for the safety and security of the people; how could such actions be judged as traitorous from an ocean away by people who had never stepped foot on Virginia's soil?

By the fall of 1623, Reverend Francis Bolton had been in the colony two years, but his second-year salary had not been paid. On November 21, 1623, Governor Wyatt and the council wrote an order, directing that Bolton's salary be paid by the Eastern Shore plantations. Every "Planter and Tradesman" who was above sixteen years of age was to pay ten pounds of tobacco and one bushel of corn to Captain Epps, the commander of the said plantations.[4] Epps then was to pay Bolton.

This warrant led some historians to assume that Bolton was the first minister of the Eastern Shore. That assumption, while not accurate, has a thread of truth. Bolton was assigned to Elizabeth City.[5] Most of the first Eastern Shore people hailed from Elizabeth City. In fact, the Eastern Shore was still considered a part of Elizabeth City as late as 1625.[6] Bolton was likely the first minister to visit the Accomack settlement.

The theory that seems more fitting begins in 1622, when Yeardley was planning to execute his commission to place 300 to 400 colonists on the Eastern Shore. One of his first thoughts for settlement planning would have been a church. All else—the town fields, an ordinary, storehouses, cow pens, and trade shops—would evolve around the church and its graveyard.[7] Yeardley had enough experience in the colony to know the features that were necessary for a church site: drinking water, accessibility by foot and water traffic, nearby landings for boats, suitable grounds for burials, and convenient woods for fuel and fencing. Even so, he would have understood the need for a minister's eyes and mind to envision the altar. Most importantly, he would have known that greater success followed people who were inspired in their endeavors. Among believers, there is no greater inspiration than God's blessing.

Yeardley likely invited Reverend Bolton to join his commission, at least for the first stages. On the Eastern Shore, Bolton would have lodged with Captain Wilcocks, a man he had met in Captain Nuce's house. By the time of Yeardley's commission, Wilcocks had lived at Accomack for a full year. He would have been an excellent advisor for envisioning a town to serve hundreds of settlers.

Imagine, if you will, Bolton rising before daybreak to walk to the site that Yeardley and Wilcocks had suggested for a church. With a mallet and stakes in hand, his purpose would be to select the place for the end wall of the church, the wall that would face the east.[8] Later, after Yeardley's approval of Bolton's work, word would have been sent down to Blower and to all tenants then living on the shore, informing them that Reverend Bolton would conduct divine service on the next Sabbath day. Everyone was expected to attend. For that matter, everyone wanted to attend. Gathering together was a rare opportunity, and for the devout, celebration of the Eucharist was a life-renewing experience.

After conducting that divine service—the first on the Eastern Shore—Bolton would have returned to Elizabeth City upon the first fair winds. He was a Company appointment. While the people at Accomack were among his congregants, they were not his primary charge. The mainland colonists were doing all they could just to remain alive day by day. Reverend Bolton was needed where people were suffering, not on the other side of the bay where people were safe and prospering.

After the Company raised such a fuss about the Eastern Shore commission, the Virginia leadership likely did not encourage Bolton to take the time and expense to return to the Eastern Shore. His Elizabeth City host, Captain Nuce, died by the following April, leaving Mrs. Nuce and her baby in very poor circumstances.[9] Bolton had not received his salary by that time, so he also was likely strapped for resources.

In the meantime, at Accomack, the church site remained staked but not built. This early in the time of the Accomack settlement, no one had the time or the resources to put toward building a church. The Company especially would have disapproved of any resources diverted from improving the James River plantations. Even so, it is a comforting thought that Reverend Bolton might have taken advantage of fair winds and following seas to visit Accomack at least once more. Soon after arrival, he would have performed the Eucharist, and he would have preached a sermon for those who had been laid to rest since his last visit. The graveyard grew while the church remained a staked pattern in the earth.

Later in 1623, when Bolton prepared to leave Elizabeth City for a new appointment in Isle of Wight, his second-year salary had not been paid. For Elizabeth City to pull together enough tobacco and grain for Bolton's salary was not possible. Another year would pass before the colony's corn harvest was plentiful enough that the governor and council could say Virginia "hath worn out the scars of the massacre."[10] However, throughout these years, Eastern Shore workers remained healthy, and their crops were bountiful.

When framing the warrant for Bolton's salary to be paid, one may imagine that the governor and some council members felt a good measure of self-satisfaction. Among all the Elizabeth City plantations—even of all the colony's corporations—only the Eastern Shore was viable for such a levy. Paying Bolton's salary in this way was as good as saying, "Treason, ha! Thank God for the Eastern Shore!"

NOTES, Chapter 6:

1. Jennings Cropper Wise, *Ye Kingdome of Accawmacke, Or, The Eastern shore of Virginia in the Seventeenth Century* (Richmond, VA: Bell Book, 1911), 253–255 (hereinafter: Wise, *Ye Kingdome*); Whitelaw, 1393–1394; M. C. Howard, "Hungars Church, Northampton County, Virginia," in *Colonial Churches in the Original Colony of Virginia: A Series of Sketches by Especially Qualified Writers* (Richmond, VA: Southern Churchman Company, 1908), 288

2. Kingsbury, *VCL-4*, 404.

3. Kingsbury, *VCL-3*, 485. In these early records, Bolton is referred to merely as Mr. Bolton; subsequent records reveal his name as Francis. Some historians have called him "Richard" Bolton; however, Richard Bolton was a planter in the colony, not a minister. (See the next footnote for an explanation of this confusion.) Subsequent records show that Francis Bolton was at Bennett's plantation in today's Isle of Wight in 1624. By 1628, he was rector of James City parish (McIlwaine, *Minutes*, 44, 98, 115; McCartney, *Immigrants*, 143).

4. Kingsbury, *VCL-4*, 404. The warrant named him only as "Mr Bolton minister." Later editors of the records numbered and named the warrant as "CDXIV. Governor in Virginia. A Warrant Granted to Richard Bolton." This was an error; it is known that the minister was Francis, not Richard.

5. Nora Miller Turman, *The Eastern Shore of Virginia 1603 - 1964* (The Eastern Shore News, Onancock, VA,1964), 9 (hereinafter: Turman, *Eastern Shore*). Turman concluded that Bolton continued to live in Elizabeth City. She called him "a circuit-rider by boat."

6. In the 1624/25 muster, the Eastern Shore was identified as part of the Elizabeth City Corporation.

7. For a discussion of the meaning of "ordinary," please see the Glossary. The word "tavern" would be used years later.

8. Churches of England were oriented so that the congregation faced the east. This was based on Matthew 24:27 ("For as the lightning comes from

the east and shines as far as the west, so will be the coming of the Son of Man").

9   Kingsbury, *VCR-4*, 107. One may question whether it was proper for the minister to continue to lodge in the home of a widow. Bolton was probably one of several lodgers, including male and female servants. It is likely that the house had one or two rooms with a loft. Sexual impropriety was governed by stringent laws. Offending servants could have additional years of service added to their contracts. Offending free men and free women could be punished with stringent fines and public humiliation. The colony experienced a shortage of shelter; privacy was rare. Today, we would be wide of the mark to apply our present-day social and cultural standards to the early Virginia colonists. How they dealt with their conditions is vastly different from how we would manage if suddenly we were transported back in time. For example, my first question would be, "Where's the ladies' room?" No doubt, I would be met with blank stares.

10 McIlwaine, *Minutes*, 71.

This image appears on the historical marker in the foreground of the photograph below. It is a conjectural image of the Second Church drawn by Sidney E. King (1906–2002). The Eastern Shore's first church at the Town (Kings Creek) likely had a similar appearance.

Historical markers at the site of the "Second Church at Kecoughtan," Hampton, Virginia. Photograph by Devry Becker Jones, 02/06/2021, CC0 (HMdb.org). This church site is currently undergoing extensive archaeological study at the direction of St. John's Episcopal Church, which owns the site.

Chapter 7

First Church, First Glebe, First Parsonage

As discussed in previous chapters, Sir George Yeardley appointed Captain William Epps as commander of the new settlement at Accomack River in the summer of 1622. Likely at that time, Yeardley selected the sites for a church and for a fort; however, the records indicate that only the fort had been built by the time of the 1624/25 muster. Yeardley had been forced to quit his commission three months after it began, and it appears that no Company resources were allotted to continue building a new settlement on the Eastern Shore. When Yeardley left to take up his next commission—to fight the mainland Indians—only a small Company party was left at Accomack settlement, in addition to the three original cohorts: Blower, Wilcocks, and the secretary's tenants.[1]

In the 1623/24 and 1624/25 musters, no church or ministers were listed as present on the Eastern Shore.

Sometime between the 1624/25 muster and late 1632, the Eastern Shore's first resident minister came to live at the Accomack settlement. Precise information is not available before 1632, the year the local court records began. These early records reveal that the first minister was William Cotton. He was present on the Eastern Shore at least by January 1632/33, although a year would pass before his name was written in the records. When ink was put to the first page of the records, the Accomack settlement did not yet have a parsonage, but it did have a church. By May 1634, the Accomack church had been standing long enough to need a roof repair and daubing.

The word *daub* in the records may have led at least one early writer to imagine the first church as a log cabin. This writer (named merely as "an early chronicler") wrote that the first church was "constructed of roughly riled logs, cemented loosely with wattle."[2] Because no description of the early church has been found, the chronicler's portrayal was likely inferred from the word daub. That the chronicler decided the job was put together "loosely" is unjustifiable. All indications are that the early Eastern Shore settlers were as skilled as anyone in building houses, possibly better than most. Perhaps rather than an actual log cabin, the chronicler meant to suggest that the early structure was made of wattle and daub, a reasonable idea. Wattle is woven sticks or branches, and daub is plaster made of mud. Such materials can last a goodly number of years when applied with skill and maintained with care.

The August 1626 General Assembly allowed eight months for each of the colony's settlements to build a church or a meeting room. Before this, the Accomack settlers had probably been meeting for prayers within their own households. Without a designated minister, a church had not been essential. This new law for building a church or a meeting room had the purpose of ensuring a sanctified place to worship, but it also had a secular role. King Charles firmly believed in the divine right of kings, so when the people came together in the name of God, Charles saw them as coming together in his name also. If worship could be regulated and uniformly practiced—including the use of England's church doctrine—the people would be better regulated. While the earlier laws had required attendance at Sunday's divine service, the newer law required taking names. One cannot very well keep track of who is present at Sunday services without a designated place for meeting.

Knowledge of the Eastern Shore's first church and burial ground has been lost. To imagine this church, one might consider its sister church built at Kicotan (Elizabeth City) in 1624. The Kicotan church was clapboard, twenty-three feet by fifty-two feet, with an eight-foot by nine-foot entryway. The foundation was made of cobblestone and brick.[3] The building survived many years, serving the Elizabeth City community as a church until 1667. Today the building is called the Second Church at Kicotan. It was abandoned in 1667 because of a fierce hurricane storm surge. After the storm, the parishioners built the Third Church two miles away, outside the area of flooding. The Second Church continued to be used as a chapel for funerals and perhaps other community meetings until 1698 when it was razed.[4] This clapboard structure survived at least three-quarters of a century.

Like the church at Kicotan, Accomack's first church stood as a place of divine worship for perhaps as many as fifty or sixty years. That being said, it does seem possible that the site may have had two successive church buildings within those years, but it is also possible that it had only the one.[5] As noted above, the Accomack church (at least the first one) was likely made of well-constructed wattle and daub rather than of clapboard.

Whitelaw deduced that the church was on the Secretary's Land, an area close to the mouth of Kings Creek.[6] For all intents and purposes, the site of the church was the settlement's geographic center at that time. After the building of this first church, its immediate area seems to have acquired a most practical name: the Town.

As noted, Accomack inhabitants probably modeled their church after the one at their sister plantation. The Elizabeth City or old Kicotan church would probably have held about 100 people by today's standards, not counting anyone in the entry and behind the altar. The early colonists sat on forms (benches) and surely crowded in a bit more than today's codes would allow. In the 1624 muster, the Accomack population was about twenty percent the size of Elizabeth City's population, therefore the Accomack church surely would have been smaller. If one had to guess, sixteen by twenty-four feet would have been a generous size.

That being said, Accomack's first parish house was undoubtedly as large as any parish house in the colony, so it stands to reason that the church was comparable to any other church in the colony. Hopefully, the church site will one day be discovered, and archaeology can reveal the church's dimensions and features.

On September 14, 1635, Minister William Cotton brought an order to the Accomack court from the James City court. For the minister to deliver an order was unusual, but Cotton was particularly interested in this one: it called for the construction of a parsonage upon a glebe.[7] The Accomack court referred the matter to the vestry. Perhaps it was only then that the court realized that a vestry had never been appointed, and so, it appointed a vestry.

Prior to this time, issues of the parish had been handled by churchwardens or by other appointees. However, the Assembly had passed a new law—the Vestry Act—that required the parishes to choose "the most sufficient and selected men" to work with the minister and the churchwardens as a vestry. Ten years later, the vestry would be elected by free male inhabitants of a parish, but for now, they were chosen by the court.[8] The Accomack court referred the matter to the vestry, and then appointed the vestry. They appointed themselves along with several others.

This first Accomack Vestry consisted of Minister William Cotton, William Andrews, Thomas Graves, Obedience Robins, John Howe, William Stone, William Burdett, John Wilkins, Alexander Mountney, Edward Drew, William Berryman, and Stephen Charlton. Seven were court members and five—Cotton, Mountney, Drew, Berryman, and Charlton—were not.

Two weeks later, the newly appointed vestry (minus Cotton, Wilkins, and Charlton) devised specifications for a parsonage to be built upon the glebe. They gave themselves until "Christyde next" to complete the project, meaning that they had almost three months.[9]

The 100 acres they chose for the glebe were on Old Plantation Neck, about a half mile up the bay shore from the Sanders-Blower land and just north of Thomas Graves's plantation.[10] These early patents and leases stretched from the beach into the woods. For example, Graves's 200 acres fronted 100 poles (1650 feet) of beach. Sanders's fifty acres fronted twenty-five poles (412.5 feet) of beach. The glebe would have had fifty poles (825 feet) on the beach. Each of the tracts stretched a mile eastward to the woods. It seems safe to suggest that the east–west direction of today's Old Cape Charles Road would have paralleled the east–west boundary lines on each of these early tracts.[11]

The court directed that the parsonage was to be forty feet by eighteen feet with ceilings nine feet high. The chimneys at each end were to have small rooms for study and storage. The kitchen and "the chamber" were to be divided by a partition near the middle of the house with a passage between them. One door from outside would allow entrance to the kitchen and another door would lead directly into the chamber.[12]

At the time of its construction, the parsonage was surely the finest house in Accomack. It may have been one of the finest in the colony, as the standard Virginia house at that time was smaller at twenty-five feet by sixteen feet.[13] No records exist to tell what sorts of houses other Accomack vestry members built for themselves, but surely this was the house to which they all aspired. The exact location of this first parsonage has been lost. One hundred eleven years would pass before a new glebe was designated and the old one was sold.[14]

NOTES, Chapter 7:

1   Wilcocks left to fight with Yeardley. His laborers had been Company tenants hired from a Company officer (probably Nuce), a practice that the

Company soon banned; therefore, Wilcocks's small plantation may have been empty of people while he went to war. He did return.

2. "Early Episcopacy in Accomack," *Virginia Magazine of History and Biography* 5, no. 2 (October 1897): 128. This "chronicler" was also noted in Wise, *Ye Kingdome*, 254–255. Many writers who have quoted the "early chronicler" also subscribed to the theory that the first church was a chapel on Old Plantation Creek. The Eastern Shore's first church was, without doubt, on Kings Creek. The "chapel" was paired with the second burial ground, as will be discussed later in this book. Regarding log cabins, it is thought that the first in the new world were built by the Swedes who came on the *Kalmar Nyckel* and the *Fogel Grip* in 1638 and settled near present-day Wilmington, Delaware (Amanda Casper, "Log Cabins" (The Encyclopedia of Greater Philadelphia) philadelphiaencyclopedia.org.

3. Eleanor Sayer Holt, *The Second Church of Elizabeth City Parish, 1623/4–1698, An Historical-Archaeological Report* (Hampton, VA, 1985), 61–62. The ratio of cobblestones to bricks was 3 to 1, with the foundation corners being made of brick. The stones and bricks were "dry-laid at random on the top of the ground level. The stones were carefully selected and placed to form a foundation uniformly 12 inches in width." The site of this church is on the campus of Hampton University, Hampton, Virginia; it is preserved for visitors, but currently closed for archaeological research.

4. Lyon Gardiner Tyler, *History of Hampton* (Hampton, VA, 1922), 22. "This Is Hampton, Virginia," *Bringing History to Life*, www.VisitHampton.com.

5. On August 2, 1641, three men were sentenced to cut weeds and clear paths to the church. Some writers took this to mean that a new church had been constructed at this time. An alternate theory is that the community was preparing for Reverend William Cottons's funeral.

6. Whitelaw, 1394.

7. A glebe was land provided specifically for the support of a minister.

8. Arthur Pierce Middleton, "Anglican Virginia: The Established Church of the Old Dominion 1607–1786," *Colonial Williamsburg Library Research Reports Series - 0006* (Colonial Williamsburg Foundation Library, 1990): 31–32; accessed 2017-12-12 via www.research.history.org.

9. Ames, *1632*, 31, 39, 43. The Virginia Company had ordered each region to set aside 100 acres for a glebe for the support of the minister. Christide means Yuletide, the Christmas season of twelve days.

10   Nugent, *I*, 13–14. John Blore was the first resident of Old Plantation Neck. His widow married Roger Sanders (Saunders) who claimed fifty acres adjoining Blore's 140 acres. Thomas Graves had a long history of service in the colony, having arrived with the Second Supply. He was Commander of Accomack after Epps.

11   The beach dimensions are found in the early patents. For comparison, today's Cape Charles Natural Preserve has a beachfront of about 675 feet. The Old Cape Charles Road takes a dogleg curve about a mile inland from what would have been the early shoreline. The glebe's beachfront was about a half mile south of the beachfront at today's preserve.

12   Ames, *1632*, 43; Whitelaw, 142–143. The first vestry meeting was 09/29/1635.

13   Henry Chandlee Forman, *Virginia Architecture in the Seventeenth Century* (Charlottesville, VA: The University Press of Virginia, 1957), 40. The standard house was 25 feet by 16 feet.

14   In the February 1745/46 General Assembly session, the local vestry received permission to sell the old glebe (noted to be 87 acres) and to build a new parish house on the new glebe land (1600 acres bequeathed by Stephen Charlton). The vestry was told to use the sale money to purchase slaves for the use of the new glebe (Hening, *Statutes V*, 390–391). William Burton purchased the old glebe; it was located on the bayside of Old Plantation Neck.

Chapter 8

The Second Burial Ground

An "*Uncertaine Rumor*" *of Land* showed that the Eastern Shore's first permanent English settlers were the Blowers, Captain John Wilcocks, and the tenants belonging to the Virginia secretary's office. These three cohorts lived within four miles of one another on Accomack Neck and Old Plantation Neck, the two necks that are separated by Kings Creek.[1]

One of the secretary's ten tenants died in November or December of 1621.[2] Who made the decision about where to locate this first grave? As no minister had yet been assigned to the Eastern Shore, was the burial service performed by fellow tenants and neighbors?

We are likely never to know the answer to those questions, but we can guess that Captain Wilcocks—as the only person with a military title—may have taken charge and decided how and where the burial would be performed. At the time the man died, a plan did not yet exist for an Eastern Shore community, so it is doubtful that the decision was made with any forethought for the eventual placement of a church and its graveyard.

As discussed previously, Sir George Yeardley traveled to the Eastern Shore a half year later with a commission to populate the area. It was most likely that the church site and its accompanying graveyard would have been chosen at this time. Did Yeardley give a nod to the tenant's burial site? Is this why the first church and graveyard were eventually built on the secretary's land?[3]

As noted in the previous chapter, Accomack's first church was probably built in 1626 or 1627 after the General Assembly ordered all settlements to build a place of worship. By this time, Accomack had been in existence no less than five years. Imagine the number of graves that may have been necessary even for a small settlement over that time span. Then further imagine the number of graves added to that over the next ten years. By 1636, Accomack found itself in need of a significant change.

During its first sixteen years, Accomack's population had grown and expanded across the lower Eastern Shore. The extent of growth prompted the vestry to designate a new graveyard. It was not within the vestry's authority to order a new church, but it could order new ground for burials.

On May 20, 1636, the Accomack vestry (consisting of William Cotton, William Stone, William Burdett, John Wilkins, and Stephen Charlton) was joined by two new members: John Neale and Henry Bagwell. On this day, the vestry created the position of parish "Clarke" (clerk). This clerk would be paid an annual salary of one peck of corn and two pounds of tobacco from every tithable person. Additionally, estates were to pay the churchwardens fifty pounds of tobacco for each burial. From that amount, the parish clerk would receive ten to fifteen pounds of tobacco for arranging the burial, and the sexton would be paid for digging the grave and tending the churchyard.

To accommodate the Accomack inhabitants who lived a distance from the church, the vestry established a second burial area. The page that records these changes is badly damaged; however, it appears to say that the new burial area was to be used for those who lived "at the old plantation from the land of mrs. Graves unto Magoty Bay" and to the head of Old Plantation Creek. These bounds kept the parsonage within the area designated for burials at the churchyard. The new area would have encompassed all of the Eastern Shore south of a line drawn from the beach (just over a mile south of today's Cape Charles harbor) to the head of Old Plantation Creek (near where south Parsons Circle meets Route 13). For this southern region, the vestry designated that burials would be on a part of the land belonging to William Blower.

The map (Figure 8A) shows how the line for the second burial area essentially divided the English-occupied land into two sections, the upper and lower. The more northern dot shows the church burial area, and the more southern dot shows the second burial area, on the Blower land.

This burial-ground order is the seed of a misbelief that I call "the Fishing Point myth." It has led some of the early historians astray about the location of the county's second graveyard. The order directed that the people living in the remote area (south of the line as noted) "shall bring [the] bodys to be buried on part of the land of Wmll Blower where

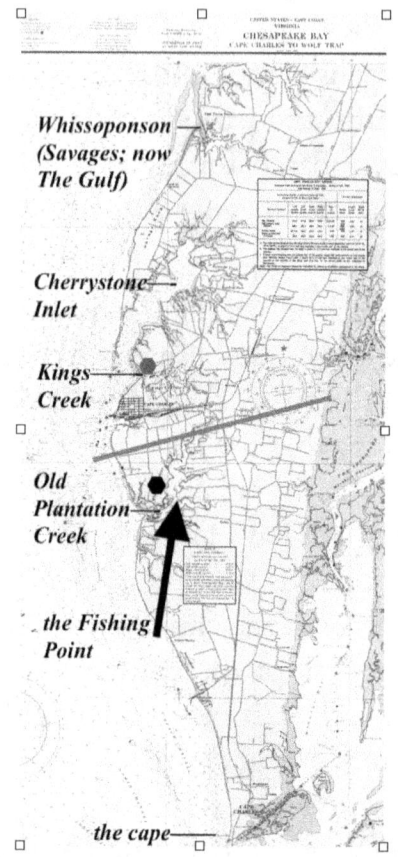

Figure 8A: (www.historicalcharts.noaa.gov)

[now] Wmll Berriman liveth" (bracketed words are in the damaged part of the page).⁴ The order is clear. However, apparently because William Berriman had lately patented land at the Fishing Point, some writers concluded that the court must have meant that burials were to be at the Fishing Point.⁵

A widely cited 1940 article has perhaps led many astray regarding the Eastern Shore's first church and the formation of a second burial area. In George Carrington Mason's article, "The Colonial Churches of the Eastern Shore of Virginia," Mason cited the 1636 local court order that formed the new burial area; however, he noted only that the "place selected for burial purposes was on the land" where Berriman lived. He failed to add the part about the place being on William Blower's land.

Mason then said that Berriman's land was located "immediately southwest of Fishing Point neck." Further, he reasoned that "the first graveyard was evidently adjacent to the church, which also seems to have been on Berriman's land." Mason cited a 1698 deed that carved out an acre for the "church or chappell," and he then identified that site as where the Eastern Shore's 1623 church stood and where Magothy Bay Church was later built.[6]

Apparently, Mason did not know of references that showed the first church to be on Kings Creek. He assumed that the second burial area was on Berriman's patent. He further assumed that the church must have been adjacent to the burial area, and thus, on Berriman's land. He then concluded that the site of the later Magothy Bay Church must have been the same as that of the first church. It was an unfortunate series of assumptions. Surely if Mason had not been led astray as to where Berriman lived when the 1636 order created the second burial area, his reasoning would not have jumped the creek. Mason's interpretation was a misstep that came to masquerade as a fact when it was repeated more than once.

In a 1669 will, Christopher Stribling asked "to be buried before the Chappel of Ease at the Old Plantation Creek."[7] Stribling's will is the only reference to a chapel on Old Plantation Creek. As he could not direct a burial on land he did not own, his will also reveals that a public burial ground edged the chapel. Therefore, because the burial ground was on Blower's land, it is known that the chapel was there also. William Blower's land was the land of his father, John Blower. John Blower had held the first Eastern Shore patent, 140 acres on Old Plantation Neck.[8]

The line of reasoning that led some writers to think that the burial ground was at the Fishing Point caused them to miss the fact that William Berriman did not immediately go to the Fishing Point to live after he patented his land. In fact, when the court gave the second burial-ground order, three quarters of a year had passed since Berriman received his patent. Had he sent laborers to clear and plant the land, or was he using it for cattle? Perhaps he preferred to dwell on the settled side of the creek while he prepared his patented land on the unsettled side.

This bit of information is interesting because it reveals that patent dates cannot be relied upon to pinpoint a patentee's occupation of the land. Traditionally, research has indicated that occupation usually preceded the patent, but here we see Berriman living nearby but not on his patent.

Berriman was a vestryman. Perhaps he had expressed an opinion about Blower's land as a good place for a new burial ground. Vestryman Henry Bagwell no doubt had a favorable opinion of the idea, because he lived nearby. In fact, within three years, Bagwell would patent 250 acres on Old Plantation Creek across from Blower's land. Vestryman William Burdett lived on Blower's land and—as stepfather to William Blower—he probably had the last word on the decision (after clearing it with his wife, Frances, who was William's mother).

The records are silent as to each man's opinion; however, it is certain that the vestry's decision for the new burial area was not random. These men most likely chose this area as a step toward development of a new commerce and government center located at the southern end of Old Plantation Creek. They perhaps envisioned that a grand church would one day stand beside that burial ground.

In this exercise of conjuring motives from 400 hundred years beyond, consider the mistress of old plantation, Frances Blower Sanders Burdett. We met Frances in *An "Uncertaine Rumor" of Land* (with her name spelled as Blore). She and her husband, John Blower, as two of the earliest settlers, had lived on the Eastern Shore for at least six years before the first church was built. It is likely that someone in their household died in those years, perhaps a servant or, more likely, a child. Without a church and rules for burial, where did the grieving parents decide to bury their child? I suggest that they wanted the child close by.

Given that the records tell us that the second burial ground was on William Blower's land where William Berriman lived, I further suggest that Berriman may have lived in Frances and John's first dwelling on the Eastern Shore. In *An "Uncertaine Rumor" of Land*, the idea was put forth that the Blowers inhabited quarters that had been left by the earlier fishermen and salters. The Blowers would have repaired and freshened the house for habitation, and once they knew the land well, they probably built a new home in a more suitable location. Once they were in the new house, the old house could have continued to house any servants or others who had joined the Blowers. After time, it may have become a rental house. In the meantime, Frances would have tended any family graves that preceded the building of the church and the Assembly's rules for burials. The county's choice for the second burial area most likely was the same ground where Frances had buried her loved ones, perhaps even her husband John Blower.

The available evidence from the record shows that the second burial ground was on the creek side of Blower's land. Evidence also indicates that the burial ground was probably across the creek from "the fishing point." In *An "Uncertaine Rumor" of Land*, this point was described as being within feet of the creek's channel at a nine-foot-deep hole. This had probably been a gathering spot for Native people, a tradition that carried over to the English.

Consider that the records show men having conversations "at the point" over pipes of tobacco as early as 1635.[9] Then in 1636, the second burial area was chosen. In 1638, the Accomack court arranged for a new ferry to transport people across Old Plantation Creek.[10] In 1640, Anthony Hoskins received a license to keep an "Ordinary or victuallinge howse." This license was Accomack's first, and it permitted Hoskins to sell beer, ale, wines, strong waters, and other liquors. (Whitelaw said this ordinary was at "the Fishing Point" and became known as "the Point House."[11]) A year later, Hoskins was designated as keeper of the Old Plantation Creek storehouse, an official county position for receiving and storing tobacco prior to shipping. Within the next few years, the Point House ordinary became an established, favorite meeting place of the Northampton court.

Undoubtedly, the area had indeed developed into a new center of commerce and government. It was thriving in these years and held great promise to evolve into a bona fide town. Nevertheless, this promise was never realized, as one essential feature was never granted to the Fishing Point. That missing feature was a parish church.

The Eastern Shore's only official parish church continued to be the one on Kings Creek until about 1647 when a second church, the Upper Parish church at Hungars, opened for divine services. The Grand Assembly had made the decision to create this new parish and church in 1642. That decision injured the dream that men such as Berriman, Burdett, and Bagwell had held for Old Plantation and "the Fishing Point."

In the six years between designation of the second burial area (1636) and the Grand Assembly's creation of the second parish (1642), the Eastern Shore's population had shifted northward.[12] This shift may have come as a surprise to men such as Berriman, Burdett, and Bagwell who had watched the early growth of Accomack stretch southward to the cape. And then three prominent men—William Stone, William Andrews, and Argoll Yardley—established homes in the Hungars region. Many settlers followed their example and pushed to the north.

When the Grand Assembly created the second parish on the Eastern Shore, it placed the upper parish and the lower parish boundary at the northward side of Kings Creek (see black line in the map Figure 8B).[13] When the new upper parish church at Hungars was completed (see gray star in the map Figure 8B), the Assembly moved the boundary northward to Savages Creek (see the gray line in the map Figure 8B).[14] Hence, during the five-year process of raising funds and building the new church, the old church—the original church (see black dot on Figure 8B)—was within the bounds of the upper parish. Perhaps the purpose of that first boundary had

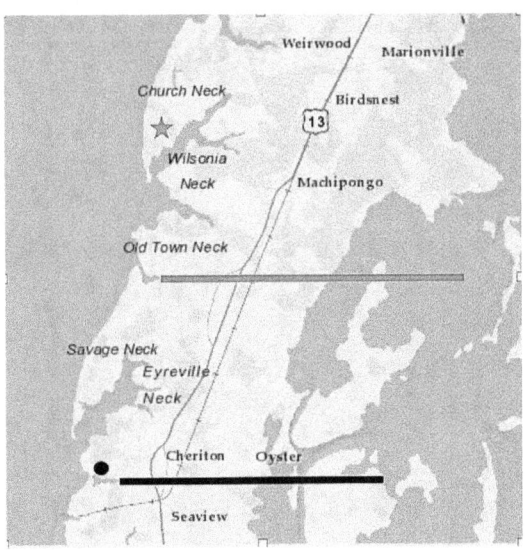

Figure 8B

been to allow sufficient tithes to be collected to build the new church at Hungars.

Before the new church had been authorized, the Hungars inhabitants made a private arrangement with the minister to conduct divine services once a month in their community. It may be that the first boundary put an end to that arrangement so that all upper parish money could be funneled to the new church. And if that were so, perhaps the lower parish arranged a separate divine service at a place of its own choosing during the five years that the upper parish subsumed the original church. Was that place the chapel of ease on Old Plantation Creek? The records do not shed any light on this subject. (In Figure 8C, the gray hexagon represents the chapel of ease; the black dot represents the original parish church; and the gray star represents the new, upper parish church).

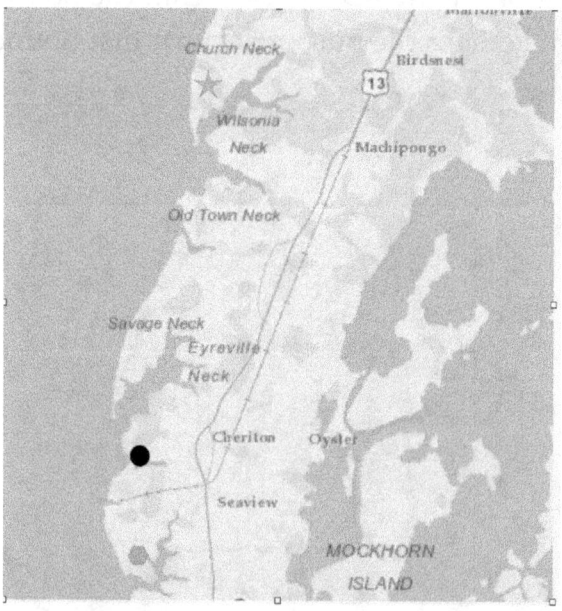

Figure 8C

Into the 1650s, the local court would continue meeting at the Point House ordinary alternately with other county locations. As long as the court's presence brought business into the area, hope for a town likely survived. Perhaps that hope endured until the last funeral at the second burial ground. No one knows when that was, and the site of that ground is lost to us.

NOTES, Chapter 8:

1   Jenean Hall, *An "Uncertaine Rumor" of Land*, (Independently published, IngramSpark and KWE Publishing, LLC, 2022).

2   Kingsbury, *VCR-3*, 585.

3   In a January 1621/22 letter to the Company, the Virginia council stated that only nine of the twenty tenants belonging to that place remained. In the previous fall, Secretary Pory had said only ten tenants were provided to him (see Smith, *Generall Historie*, 274); however, the council's letter indicated that the other ten tenants may have been provided. Pory did make a second voyage soon after he placed his ten tenants, therefore, it is possible that he had received his other ten tenants and placed them. If that is so, it means that not just one tenant died within those few months, but eleven! Eleven graves would certainly make an unmistakable graveyard.

4   Northampton County Court Records, *Orders, Book 1, 1632-1640*, 73. In the record, "on" was spelled as "one" (which was standard for the day). I modernized the spelling in this passage. "Wmll" is an abbreviation of William with the two "lls" written in superscript. William Berriman's name also appears spelled as Berryman in the early records. Accomack's parish name was not used in the records until several years later. Following the pattern for other counties, this parish would have had the same name as the county. Whitelaw stated the same (Whitelaw, 1394). Turman concluded that the burial ground was "at the head of Old Plantation Creek" (Turman, *Eastern Shore*, 31). However, from mention of Blower's land in other patents, it is known to have been more to the south on Old Plantation Neck.

5   In 1640, George Carrington Mason promoted the idea that the burial ground was on Berriman's land. (George Carrington Mason, "The Colonial Churches of the Eastern Shore of Virginia." *The William and Mary Quarterly* 20, no. 4 (1940): 454. https://doi.org/10.2307/1919927).

6   George Carrington Mason, "The Colonial Churches of the Eastern Shore of Virginia." *The William and Mary Quarterly* 20, no. 4 (1940): 454–456. https://doi.org/10.2307/1919927. Mason was a prolific, colonial-church researcher. He was also the editor for Ralph T. Whitelaw's two-volume set, *Virginia's Eastern Shore*.

7   James Handley Marshall, *Abstracts of the Wills and Administrations of Northampton County, Virginia 1832–1802* (Camden, ME, Picton Press, 1994), 82.

8   William Blower was the son of John and Frances Blower. When John died, Frances remarried, but John's estate was protected for his son by a bond. William died during his mother's lifetime. When his mother wrote her will, she invoked the bond for whatever could still be claimed; she also cited the 140 acres as still intact. That 140 acres was John's original Eastern Shore patent. It was located between the bay and Old Plantation Creek toward the southern end of Old Plantation Neck, an area now occupied by luxury golf courses and upscale housing. If the reasoning of *An "Uncertain Rumor" of Land* is correct, that John Blore (Blower) claimed his land before George Yeardley and Thomas Savage met with the Laughing King to negotiate for their patents, then it stands to reason that Blower held the first patent.

9   Ames, *1632*, 52.

10 Ames, *1632*, 128–130.

11 Whitelaw, 121–122.

12 Hening, *Statutes I*, 249.

13 Hening, *Statutes I*, 249

14 "Acts, Orders and Resolutions of the General Assembly of Virginia," *The Virginia Magazine of History and Biography* 23, no. 3 (1915): 249; http://www.jstor.org/stable/4243447. Today Savages Creek is called The Gulf.

Chapter 9

The Chapel of Ease

Christopher Stribling's 1669 will is the only surviving record that mentioned a chapel of ease on Old Plantation Creek. As indicated in the previous chapter, determining the sequence of events that led to the building of that chapel is very much like trying to put together a jigsaw puzzle. The task is all the more difficult because most pieces are missing and many of the existing pieces are damaged. In the case of the chapel, the task boils down to giving it our best guess.

A chapel of ease was exactly what the name suggests. It was a worship space built for the ease or convenience of the people. It was not a sanctioned church. Only the Grand Assembly or the governor and council could sanction a new church or a new parish.[1]

When a local person died in the remote area of Accomack, someone was to notify the minister and provide him a means to attend and to "bury the dead." If anyone refused "such decent and christianlike" burial, they would answer to the vestry. (Such orders were aimed at survivors, as the dead would not be answering.) People were to give timely notice to the parish clerk of "all such dead people," so that the graves could be made ready.[2]

In 1636, when the court ordered the creation of the second burial area, it instructed the churchwardens to acquire a pulpit cloth, a pillow, other altar items, and a chest.[3] Some writers have interpreted this to mean that these items were for the chapel, and thus, that it was built at this time. Because a chapel was not an official church, it is not likely that public funds would have been used to support it in any way, so those items were probably for the official church at Kings Creek. Still, then as now, people had a way of bending rules. The chest could have doubled for storage and transport, in case the construction of a chapel was anticipated. We do not know.

The local court made no mention regarding the chapel, but we can draw from the neighboring community of Lower Norfolk County to see what may have been similar factors for constructing a chapel of ease. On May 2nd, 1641, the Lower Norfolk County court recorded an order granted by the governor and council, directing the county commander to build the county's parish church at Sewell's Point. The county inhabitants were to pay for the construction of this church. Additionally, the order allowed for a chapel of ease to be "built in Elizabeth River at the charge of particular families situated in the said river by reason of the remote plantations from the aforesaid" parish church. The order stated clearly that the chapel was not a parish church. Also, at no time was a separate vestry to be chosen for the chapel; however, the parish church vestry was to attend equally to the administration of both the church and the chapel. Also, the parish vestry was never to meet in the chapel. Additionally, all tithable people were to be taxed for the transportation of the minister to the parish church every other Sunday. In other words, the Elizabeth River residents would privately fund the minister's travel costs for the Sundays when he preached at the chapel, and they would also be levied for the alternate Sundays when he preached at the parish church. On at least two occasions, the Lower Norfolk court sentenced transgressors to public shaming during the time of divine services in the chapel of ease at Elizabeth River. For example, in 1643, in front of the congregation, a man was required to ask forgiveness of a woman whom he had accused of adultery; in 1645, a man who had committed "whoredom" was required to wear a white sheet while he asked God's forgiveness in front of the chapel congregation.[4]

Regarding the Eastern Shore's chapel of ease, we know only that it was probably built after the second burial ground was created and before Stribling mentioned it thirty years later. To make a reasonable guess about when it was built, it is helpful to consider who had a motive to build it. A bit of what follows is a repeat of discussion from the previous chapter.

The second burial area was on William Blower's land. This was the 140 acres that had belonged to his father, John. When John died, his widow, Frances, married Roger Sanders. Frances and Roger had a son together. They named him John. When Roger died, Frances married William Burdett who had a son named Thomas. Frances and Burdett had a prenuptial agreement when they married in 1633 to protect the rights of her children. Over the following eight years, both William

Blower and John Sanders died. It is not known if either or both of Frances's boys died before the second burial area was created. The fathers, John Blower and Roger Sanders, probably would have been buried at the churchyard (assuming the churchyard existed by that time), so Frances may have buried each of the boys near his father. However, given that Frances stated in her will that she wanted to be buried next to her younger son, John, one may wonder if she had the boy's grave made in the second burial ground, a place that was very near their home.

The second burial area was created on Blower land where William Berriman was living at the time. Berriman probably lived in a laborer's cottage while Frances and her family lived in the main dwelling. In her will, Frances gave life rights in the house to her husband William Burdett, and after his death it was to become the property of her stepson, Thomas. If Thomas did not have heirs, the dwelling would revert to Frances's siblings. This line of succession could not have been possible unless the land and house belonged to Blower's original 140 acres.

Frances probably had the greatest motive for building the chapel of ease. My first thought about this was that after a few too many mourners drifted over to the Burdett house for refreshment, Frances might have suggested that a chapel would be nice for wakes and services. My second thought was that Frances's grief for young John had been so great that she did not rest until a chapel was built in his honor to give other families a more worshipful place for wakes and services.

A third possibility is that the chapel was a part of the plan from the beginning. The Burdetts may have offered the site and promised to convert Berriman's dwelling into a chapel for the use of mourners. That would have been an attractive offer and one that could help to shift the county seat of power toward the southern end of Old Plantation Creek. The county leadership would have seen that Fishing Point was developing into a commercial area, a fact that presaged the possibility of a new town. A new town presaged a church, and a church was the centerpiece of a town. As we saw in the previous chapter, that church never came to be.

We are likely never to know who built the chapel of ease at the Old Plantation burial ground. Because Frances Burdett controlled the Blower land during a time when women had few rights and little power, it is a compelling idea that the burial ground and chapel were created at her direction. It is also a compelling idea that this burial ground on Old Plantation Creek was Frances's final resting place, next to that of her son John.

NOTES, Chapter 9:

1   (The Assembly's name was changed from General Assembly to Grand Assembly in 1631/32.)

2   Ames, *1632*, 54; Northampton County, Virginia, Court Records, *Order Book No. 1*, 73.

3   Ames, *1632*, 55.

4   Alice Granbery Walter, *Lower Norfolk County, Virginia, Court Records: Book "A" 1637–1646 and Book "B" 1646–1651/2*, (Baltimore, MD: Genealogical Publishing Co., 2002) 60, 146, 192. The Elizabeth River chapel was located on the grounds of St. Paul's Episcopal Church in what today is the City of Norfolk, Virginia.

An original bond, written about a hundred years after the Burdetts lived. This bond addressed the promises of Neech Eyre to run a ferry from Northampton to York and Hampton. It is included here as an example of a local, original document. Few (if any) mid-seventeenth century, original bonds have survived within the county. The seals are bright red. This document is maintained in the office of the Clerk of the Circuit Court, Northampton County, Virginia. Photograph by the author.

Chapter 10

Burdett's Prenuptial Promise and Frances's Last Will and Testament

Frances Blower Sanders Burdett figures prominently in the early English history of Virginia's Eastern Shore. Prior to the publication of *An "Uncertaine Rumor" of Land*, her role in colonial history was mostly unknown. In the present book, her character is explored beyond her role as that of a "first settler." Because the only documents she left behind were Burdett's promise to her and her own will, these documents are included here in a chapter of their own. I considered placing them in an appendix because they will seem supplementary to some readers; however, these two documents—especially the will—are the marrow to understanding Frances. Some of you may skim through the following documents. For those of you who read the words one by one, prepare yourself to know Frances better than most people ever knew her.

[Mr. Burditt his Guift]. Know all Men by these presentes that I William Burditt Gentleman doe binde my selfe not to take or meddle with any of the goodes of Frances Sanders which shee now enjoyeth, or with any of her Chrildrens portions which they now have, but that shee shall quietly and peceably enjoy them without the lett molestation or hinderance of him, or any other by his meanes. Provided that hee the said William doth promise to manage the Cropps and other Affaires belonging unto the said Frances, or her Children In Witness whereof I have heerunto putt my hand and seale this present day being the sixtenth of September. Anno Domini 1633.

William Burditt,
his seale

Sealed and delivered in the presence
of us.
Henry Carsly, William Strong

The Last Will and Testament of Frances Burditt being in perfect memory this 23th of March 1640 [/1641].

[Frances Burdett, her Will]. First I bequeath my bodye to Christian buriall, and my sowle to the Almighty God. It is my desire that Edward Lake and Richard Lake and Jane Lake and Margarett Lacke and Ellinor Lacke I freely give the Estate of William Blower of what can be demanded by the bond and one Plantation of one hundred and Forty acres of Land scituate and lyeing on the North side of the old Plantation Creeke in the County of Acowmack, And when this Estate is paid to the aforementioned partyes there is more three Fetherbedes,

and Fower pairs of sheetes, and halfe of the goates and halfe of the servantes now remayning in the Custodye of Mr. William Burditt and all my wearing Clothes Lynen or Woolling made, or unmade and all that does belong to mee, one Beaver hatt, Fower gould Rings two silver bodkins, one silver thimble, two scarfes onely one of my best pettycoates, and owt of the Estate of William Blower which I freely give unto Peirce Scott, more I give unto my aforementioned brothers, and sisters two Rugges, six pillowes and six pillowbeers, Five gould Wrought quoifes and two dresclothes, and all the rest that is my trunck, Peirce Scott to have her Clothes, the trunck to be nayled up and to be delivered to my brothers, or sisters, or to theire Assignes. Likewise I Freely give to Edward Daniell one heiffer with Calfe to be delivered owt of the Estate of William Blower. Likwise it is my desire that when I have departed this Mortall lyfe, that Thomas Stanton and John Tompkin shalbe my Overseers to take these goodes afore mentioned and the Cattle of William Blowers Estate into theire possession, and to keepe them Male and Female upon the Land of William Blowers or where they shall appoint, untill they the said Thomas Stanton and John Tompkin have delivered the whole Estate up unto my aforementioned brothers or sisters. Further it is my desire that if I have ever a brother or sister come into the Country that my Overseers shall deliver his or theire deu share of the Estate aforementioned either in Cattle, or goodes. Further it is my desire that they the said Thomas Stanton and John Tompkin shall have sufficient satisfaction what two men shall judge for theire paines taken. Further it is my desire that the now dwelling howse which I am in freely give unto Thomas Burditt after his Fathers decease, with *all moveables, or unmoveables Cattell or Chattells and all that thereunto belonges and if in Case that the said Thomas Burditt should dye before hee have any issue that then the said Estate to be delivered unto the said Thomas Stanton and John Tompkin for the use and sole benifitt of my aforementioned brothers and sisters. It is my desire that I may be buryed by John Sanders. Likewise for the making over of the Estate of William Blower that the bond makes mention of James Bruse hath the testimony of it. This I leave as my Last Will and Testament. In Witness thereof I have heerunto sett my hand and seale this 23th day of March 1640 [1641]. Before the sealing of this Will It is my desire that the Pinnace should be sould to pay Men theire deu.*

The marke of
Frances Burdett
her seale

Signed and Sealed in the
presence of
William Cropp
Signum Garrett Andrewes, Edward Daniell.[1]

In the record book, the clerk copied Frances's will first and then William's "guift." The bond for William Blower's estate was never copied into the record. That Frances said James Bruce had "the testimony of it," probably means that she had lost the paper and relied on Bruce as a witness. Frances noted that the estate included "what can be demanded by the bond and one Plantation of one hundred and Forty acres of Land..." The bond had probably been Roger Sander's promise to protect Frances's son's inheritance upon Frances's second marriage.

The bond may have promised repairs and maintenance of the property or even construction of such improvements as a storehouse or a fence. It could also have involved goods such as livestock or tools.

Frances did not mention a bond in relation to her son John Sanders; therefore, it is not likely that he had a substantial inheritance. His father, Roger, a mariner, had been an indentured servant in Elizabeth City before moving over the bay where he married Frances and was selected to be one of the first court commissioners. He was also chosen to be a burgess to the 1632/33 Grand Assembly.[2] Roger never patented land, but he did obtain a lease for fifty acres just to the north of the Blower land. He sold that lease to George Travellor.

The outstanding factor that impelled a bond for the Blower land is that it was a patent, and thus it provided shelter, sustenance, and a future for any Blower heirs. Frances had been diligent in obtaining bonds for the protection of her children, but as it turned out, she left no descendants.

NOTES, Chapter 10:

1 Ames, *1640*, 126–127. Peirce Scott was one of the Eastern Shore's first babies. When Frances died, Peirce was about seventeen years old. In the 1624/5 muster, she was listed as "Percis," child of Walter and Apphia Scott. The Scotts and the Blowers were among the seven known couples of the first Eastern Shore census. (The others were Epps, Ball, Wilkins, Williams, and Powell.) After Apphia died, Walter married Alice, mother of Elizabeth Carsley. After Walter died, Alice married Henry Wilson. At some point, the Scott children (Peirce and Samuel) were taken into others' homes. Obedience and Grace Robins took Samuel, and Frances and William Burdett took Peirce. Dr. Ames (Ames, *1640*, 222–223) transcribed the name as *Pervis*, but it appears as *Percis* in the original record (CCR-2, 116). Whatever her name may have been, she seems to have liked it; when she had children, she named a daughter *Percy*, shortened from *Pearice* (MilesFiles 22.2, accessed 31 Dec 2022).

2 McCartney, *Immigrants*, 142, 622; McIlwaine, *Minutes*, 95.

Jan Gossaert (1478–1532), Portrait of a Merchant, (possibly Jan Snouck Jacobsz), c.1530, courtesy of The National Gallery of Art, Washington, D. C., public domain.

This famous portrait puts me in mind of an early clerk, taking notes as he listens to the cases brought before the court. In the case of John Jones (as follows in Chapter 11) the clerk was George Dawe (substituting at this time for Henry Bagwell). Surely even the most circumspect of clerks occasionally had difficulty listening to the drama unfolding around him without appearing to be on the verge of an opinion.

Chapter 11

Shameful Politics

Frances Lake Blower Sanders Burdett must have been considered "a catch." Before she married Burdett, wagers were made on whether or not she would marry him. George Scovill bet ten pounds sterling that the match would never happen. In fact, he was so sure that Frances would not marry Burdett, he raised his wager to forty pounds sterling![1] Burdett so much wanted the marriage that he put his intentions in writing, in the agreement you just read in the last chapter. He promised not to meddle with any of Frances's possessions nor those of her children. Also, he pledged to manage their crops and other affairs. Frances and William married in 1633. Scovill lost his wager.

Frances was likely the first English lady of the Eastern Shore. As the first lady and as the wife of two court commissioners, she probably provided a guiding voice behind many county decisions. For these reasons, she merits our recognition and remembrance.

That being said, stories in the records do show a darker side to Frances's character. The major case in point involved a court action that was apparently carried out in vindication of Frances's reputation. Unexpectedly, the event tarnishes our esteem for members of the court, as well as for Frances. However, in another light, it also shows how emotion can skew an otherwise rational mind to do things that are monstrous. This was truly monstrous.

Frances and William Burdett had been married five years. They lived at the Blower house on Old Plantation Neck. The second burial ground near their home had been in use for two years. A ferry ran people from one side of Old Plantation Creek to the other. People gathered at the Fishing Point across the creek from the Burdetts, but the ordinary there had not yet been licensed; that would come within a couple of years.

William Burdett held the responsible job as Lady Dale's local agent for her Eastern Shore assets. After Lady Dale died in 1640, it would be said that her pen contained no less than eighty-five cattle (cows and bulls) along with uncounted calves.[2] No one has determined where the pen was located, but it probably was on the south end of Old Plantation Creek, in the area of Burdett's 1638 patent, the same ground where John Custis would build Arlington Plantation over thirty years later.[3]

The event at issue came to light in court on August 13, 1638, with Nathaniel Littleton presiding and William Stone, William Burdett, William Andrews, William Roper, and John Wilkins seated to hear the cases brought before them. After about twenty cases were considered, the court heard two depositions about what John Jones had said about Mrs. Burdett.

Elizabeth Keltridge told the court what she had heard John Jones say. Thomas Lee was next and said merely that he had heard the same thing Elizabeth Keltridge just said. It is not known who Keltridge, Lee, and Jones were; however, Jones may have worked for Burdett, perhaps as one of Lady Dale's cattlemen or perhaps as a laborer on the Blower land.

According to Keltridge, Jones said that Mrs. Burdett told him to get a woman to wash his clothes and dress his victuals. This apparently did not sit well with Jones, as he had given her something (perhaps a handkerchief) for the service. Jones then told Keltridge that Mrs. Burdett had washed and starched a Mr. Saunders's clothes in England. Further, he said, Mrs. Burdett had a bastard by this man, and so came to this country. "I told her as much to her face," Jones boasted.

Keltridge rebuked him, saying, "I thought that they were then married."

"No, by god, no more than you or I," Jones replied.

After Thomas Lee affirmed Keltridge's testimony, the court ordered "that the said John Jones shall have thirty lashes on the back presently and twenty more next Sabbath and twenty more the Sabbath following." Also, he was "to ask Mrs. Burdett's forgiveness in the church" and he was to provide surety for his good behavior. [4]

In total, the court ordered seven whippings that day. Four were for twenty lashes, two were for twelve. Jones's sentence was extraordinary. Thirty lashes was harsh enough, but it was unheard of to follow a week later with twenty more and then twenty more a week after that. Two and a half months later, the twenty-two-year-old John Jones was dead.

It is not known, of course, that the sixty lashes killed Jones, but the likelihood of anyone surviving such an ordeal was slight, as infection likely set in. If he died because of the punishment, how could it be viewed as anything but murder? Whether he died of the whippings or not, the punishment was heinous, reckless, unconscionable—even for those days. A comparable punishment is not evident in the old records, especially not for slander or defamation of character.

John Jones had said that Frances Burdett had a child outside of marriage before she came to Virginia. It appears that Jones said the father of the child was the man Frances married after John Blower died, Roger Sanders (also Saunders). Frances's third husband, William Burdett, was one of the court members sitting that day when Elizabeth Keltridge told what she had heard.

We have no information about how this information came to court. Did Keltridge just show up, asking to be heard, or had she and Lee been summoned? If Jones had indeed told Frances "as much to her face," did she react then, or did her reaction come after hearing that Jones was repeating the story in the community?

Frances had been the first lady of Accomack for eighteen years. Such scandalizing gossip could not be tolerated; however, the imbalance of the punishment tells us this was vengeance, not justice. Frances was not a county official, yet her presence in the community predated that of all the local court commissioners. Her previous husband had been one of the first court commissioners. Her current husband was presently a court commissioner. She probably had more clout than we can imagine, or maybe the court commissioners would have done the same for any of their wives.

Consider the next glimpse we have of Frances. It was Christmas of 1638. Frances's servant Joan Stockley told her that Roger Moye, "being in drink," and four other servants had killed a hog and roasted it at creekside. Since all these folks lived in the lower area of Old Plantation Creek, that is probably where this party took place. Upon hearing the story, Frances marched over to the quartering house and, in an effort to find the culprits, confronted the men who were working there. Arthur Rayman, John Allen, Thomas Lawson, Thomas Browne, and Patrick "the Irishman" were at work pulverizing grain at the mortars. Frances addressed Rayman first.

"Art thou a true man?" she asked.

"I am," Rayman replied.

She then forced the pestle from Rayman's hand, saying, "I will give you a spell." Her behavior must have stunned the men because they stopped work. Frances then turned upon the others.

"I will hang you all if it cost me forty pounds," she said.

John Allen turned to his fellow worker, "Come, Tom, let us make the mortar ring, for if my mistress hangeth us she will want two of her beaters."[5]

The undersheriff came to investigate, and Frances told him she was afraid that her servants would run her over. When John Allen figured out what he was accused of, he told the overseer that he would not go back to work until his name was cleared. The outcome was never revealed, but no one was taken to court for the theft.

The quartering-house glimpse suggests that Frances had an unbridled temper. Her threat of hanging was extreme; punishment for such a crime was usually a lashing and a fine, not death. John Allen was right to want his name cleared; an angry Frances Burdett had proven to be a danger to life and limb.

It certainly appears that Frances may well have had a hand in what happened to John Jones. Does this render her and the court members to be unworthy of our regard and remembrance? Do we expect perfection from our forebears? John Jones's fate was certainly a tragedy of judgment, but the greater tragedy may be that, these 400 years later, we are no more perfect than those who came before us.

NOTES, Chapter 11:

1   Ames, *1632*, p. 11.

2   Ames, *1640*, pp. 133 - 137; p. 176; p. 203; pp. 250 - 251. (The number of beasts were determined by a cursory counting of the sales showing in the records.)

3   This John Custis is known as John Custis II; however, he was the first of that name in a series of three. The mistake in numbering came about when an early researcher assumed that this first Eastern Shore John Custis was the son of a man named John Custis. (Actually, his parents were Henry and Joan.) The mistake in numbering has continued because the use is so widespread. Trying to change it will merely cause more confusion than already exists. To recap: John Custis II was the first and he built Arlington. (He is buried there, but his is not the famous tomb.) John Custis III was the second and he lived at today's Wilsonia Neck. John Custis IV was the third and he spent most of his life in Williamsburg; his tomb is the famous one (near that of his grandfather, John II).

4   Ames, *1632*, 118, Northampton County, Virginia, *Court Records Book No. 1*, 148.

5   Northampton County, Virginia, Court Records, *Orders, Deeds, Wills, Etc., No. 2, 1640 - 1645*, fol. 106. Allen's instruction to Tom, "to make the mortar ring," refers to the sound that the large metal mortars and pestles made when a person pulverized the grain with a good, steady rhythm. His comment seems to suggest that if they showed themselves to be good workers, Mrs. Burdett would not want to hang them.

Chapter 12

Argoll Yardley

Argoll Yeardley, son and heir of Sir George Yeardley, was hardly more than twenty years old when he and his bride, Frances Knight, sailed to Virginia from England. Upon arrival, young Yeardley wasted no time claiming as much land as he could prove he had a right to own. On February 6, 1637/38, he claimed a patent for 500 acres in Upper Norfolk County on Dumpling Island Creek of the Nansemond River. (Today this is within the city of Suffolk.) A hundred acres were for his "personal adventure" and his wife's "personal adventure," and 400 acres were for the passage of eight people, including "Andolo and Maria 2 Negroes."[1] Argoll's efforts to settle his land at Nansemond are not known. Given his almost immediate involvement in colony government, he and Frances probably lived in or near James City.

On September 6, 1638, Argoll Yeardley received a patent for 3,700 acres in Accomack. This had been his father's claim, and it had lain dormant of English activity for about sixteen years. Soon after, Argoll patented land at Tyndalls Neck on today's York River.[2] He recorded his Accomack patent at the March 1639/40 local court.[3] His reason for waiting eighteen months to have the patent recorded is not known.

Between the time of his return to Virginia in 1637 and his visit to the Eastern Shore in 1640, Argoll settled on a new spelling of his surname. He dropped the first e to render the name "Yardley." This change no doubt corrected the pronunciation and cut down on the tendency to mistake the name as "Early" or "Yearly" (renditions that show in the early records).

When Argoll Yardley first visited his Eastern Shore land, surely he heard stories about the Native people who lived on the tranquil creek that today is called Mattawoman. This creek no doubt gained its name from Mattawombes, the waterside town that Native people still inhabited when Yardley visited. Twenty years had passed since the Laughing King named the boundaries of George Yeardley's and Thomas Savage's tracts. At that time, the English people's northern border was Mattawoman Creek. All land north of that creek was Indian land.

William Stone ventured north of that bound in June 1636 when he patented land at what was then called Hungars on the neck north of Yeardley's gift. Perhaps with Stone's move into Hungars, some Native people of Mattawombes drifted south, back over the creek to land that had once been a part of their old town. This was George Yeardley's land, essentially vacant until the heir came to claim it.

It seems that the Indians of Mattawombes town had become an isolated group here, separated from their people who had moved northward to Occohannock, Nandua, Wachapreague and beyond. The Indians who remained at Mattawombes were likely from the tribe of the great man, the Laughing King. Mattawombes may have been his last home.

Almost ten years earlier, the Grand Assembly had singled out the Native people of Mattawombes for especial treatment with "all good termes of amitie."[4] At that time, these Indians were visiting the English and receiving visits from the English. Their proximity may have prompted a certain deference, but the home of the great werowance would also have warranted such treatment. The Eastern Shore people had not forgotten the great man's protection during the 1622 attack. And from all accounts, he had been generous providing corn, especially when Thomas Savage was the main trader. The werowance's formal name was written only twice in the English records, but the legend of his kindness continues to this day under the sobriquet "the Laughing King."[5]

By the time Argoll came to view his Eastern Shore patent, the man known as the Laughing King had likely died. If the Laughing King had been in poor health, the possibility exists that Argoll had been advised to wait until the old king died before attempting to settle the land. If that were indeed the case, the tribe members who remained on the creek would have been family and others who had cared for the great man in his last days. Some writers have suggested that the Laughing King lived to become the Great King of the Eastern Shore named Wachiowamp, or even the Great King of the Eastern Shore named Debedeavon. (Some have said that he was both of these leaders.) Nevertheless, I suggest that if the Laughing King had still been a vital Eastern Shore leader when Argoll came to claim his father's land, the subsequent history of the Indians at Mattawombes would have been a markedly different story than what you are about to read.⁶

On October 28, 1640, Argoll Yardley walked upon his land that later would bear the name "Old Town Neck." He was accompanied by a party of men, including William Andrews who had known and been with Sir George Yeardley when Yeardley came to the Eastern Shore. The party probably had gathered at William Stone's house on the neck between Hungars Creek and today's Mattawoman Creek; although, it is possible that they started out at Andrews's home just across from Stone at the mouth of Hungars Creek. Among the group were Nathaniel Littleton, Nathaniel Eaton, Thomas Stampe, William Stone, George Dawe and, of course, Yardley and Andrews.

Stampe was from James City, but his role at this gathering has not been discovered. Eaton would become a local church clerk and marry the minister's widow (the younger sister of Stone's wife). However, at this time, Eaton was a fugitive from New England. He had recently fled Massachusetts to escape a church trial for beating his assistant and students at Harvard.⁷ (Whether or not the other men were aware of Eaton's past is not known.) Littleton was the local county commander. Stone and Andrews were court commissioners and neighbors of Yardley's patent. Dawe's presence signifies that an official writing was anticipated, either in his capacity as the Clerk of Court or as an experienced scribe. Dawe's presence here and his subsequent actions suggest something odd; this will be discussed later in this chapter.

No one recorded that any women attended this event, but if Frances had accompanied Argoll, then surely Ann Southey Littleton, Susanna Andrews, and Verlinda Graves Stone were also present, if not for the tour, certainly enjoying the host's home. Properly planned, this gathering could have been Accomack's social event of the year. Fashion would have been at its highest with bright colors, linen collars and cuffs, shiny buckles, brilliant capes, and broad-brimmed hats. And that was just the men.

William Andrews, now forty years old, would have welcomed Argoll with a warm, paternal greeting. Andrews had come to the Virginia colony in 1617 and had lived at the Accomack plantation since at least 1623. Andrews, William Stone, William Burdett, and John Wilkins had been appointed to the Accomack court, all on the same day in 1633. Their longevity as local leaders was surpassed only by Obedience Robins.

Argoll Yardley had been about ten years old when Sir George died thirteen years before. Surely he had memories of his father, but to hear someone else's stories of the man—to walk the very ground he had walked, and to gaze upon the ridges and coves where his father had hoped to dwell—would have touched all but the coldest of hearts.

Later that day, Argoll put the facts to paper. What he wrote, Whitelaw quoted wholly in his book, *Virginia's Eastern Shore*.[8] Andrews told Argoll that when Sir George came here, the Indians all lived together on the land now inhabited by Captain Stone. The creek at that time "was then and since hath bene called Hungers Creeke." The Indian town split by the creek there was called Mattawombes. According to Andrews, Sir George had intended to settle his plantation at this place.[9]

In his written account that day, Yardley appointed Edmund Scarburgh to survey the land. He directed

Scarburgh to begin at the northern point of the land and from there go all along the main creek southeasterly. Argoll said that his land "shall Bee and aboutt on and uppon the Mayne Creeke Afforesaid and noe further."[10]

When Argoll heard that Indians inhabited a part of this land, surely his first thought was that they should remove themselves. However, in his conversations with Andrews and others, he would have learned that this was a special group of people. Based on subsequent actions, Argoll seems to have understood that the colony's leadership had more or less lionized the Indians of Mattawombes. And from a personal point of view, these were the people of the man who had been his father's Eastern Shore benefactor. Any remaining family of the legendary werowance was to be carefully considered.

That day, the touring Englishmen most likely pointed to and extolled land features that supported Argoll's domestic and business interests. The Indians' presence would not have fit with visions of English cultivation and shipping. Littleton likely advised Argoll that he would assist to devise a plan to remove the Indians from Mattawombes. Also, he would accompany Argoll to present the plan to Governor Wyatt and the council.

Following that October gathering, Court Clerk George Dawe did something that seems odd. (Historian Dr. Susie Ames noted this oddity in her transcription of the court records.) He rewrote the minutes of the previous February's court and copied them into the official court book preceding the entry of Yardley's Mattawombes paper. When a researcher sees previous minutes rewritten into the record, it signifies that those minutes may have been a copy used as evidence in another case. Here, it may be that the previous

February minutes and Yardley's paper were used as exhibits when Littleton and Yardley made their presentation to the governor and council about the Indians of Mattawombes. The February minutes included a court order to survey the property of Ensign Thomas Savage, deceased. This order included instructions about payment for Savage's survey. Yardley's paper then followed, authorizing and directing Edmund Scarburgh to survey the Yardley property.

When Littleton and Yardley made their presentation in James City about moving the Indians, the governor and council would expect "to scan the business" (a term that essentially meant "to view the official court minutes"). Page 17 and folio 17 as they now exist in Order Book No. 2 make a persuasive exhibit. Unusual for Dawe, he began the account of Yardley's meeting with a flourish, an affectation that draws one's attention to that particular item on the page. (See Figure 12.) If these pages are what the governor and council viewed to make their decision, the information (exhibits) would have been copied into the record along with the governor and

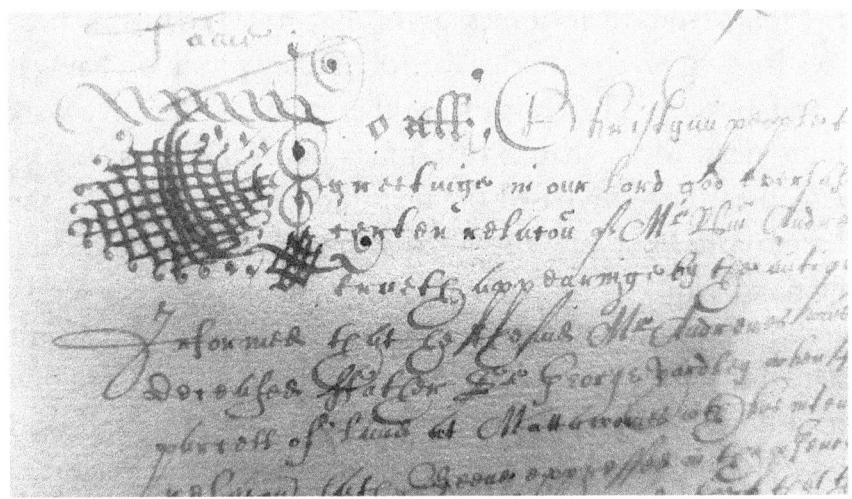

Figure 12 (Author's photograph)

council's decision. Thus, the February minutes (at least the relevant parts) can be found twice in the book. (It turns out not to be so odd as it first appeared.)

On December 15, 1640, Nathaniel Littleton and Argoll Yardley addressed Virginia's Quarter Court to propose a relocation plan for the Indians of Mattawombes. The proposed new home for the Indians was a tract on the Eastern Shore's seaside. Not everyone was pleased with this option. Phillip Taylor claimed that 200 acres of the tract belonged to him.

The Quarter Court approved the plan and granted 1,500 acres "upon the easternmost shore of the seaboard side to the Indians of Accomack." It ordered Littleton and Yardley to have a new survey completed and to ensure that Taylor's right to his 200 acres was not violated. Further, the court ordered a land patent to be drawn up for the use of the Indians.[11]

Within the next few weeks, Littleton, Yardley, William Stone, William Andrews, and William Roper viewed the tract. To reach this seaside land, the men probably walked four or five miles from their homes. Some may have traveled by boat to a landing on the south shore of Yardley's neck on Savages Creek (today's The Gulf); from that point, a four-mile walk came next. More than a year and a half would pass before Argoll Yardley purchased the first horse known to be on the Eastern Shore, so any supply carts may have been pulled by men or oxen.[12] Workmen may have been sent ahead to set up a camp so that the party could have a rendezvous point with a fire for warming and a table for viewing maps and making field notes. The party's purpose was to determine the land bounds for the Indians' tract while ensuring Taylor's rights.

Argoll Yardley attended the Accomack court on January 11, 1640/41. He was listed just after Commander Littleton, signifying that his rank exceeded that of all the other court members. Not only that, but Yardley carried the honorary title of Esquire, the same as Littleton. For both men, the honor would have been a nod to their knighted fathers, but in Virginia, all council members were given that title. Littleton presently sat as a member of the colony's Council of State. Apparently, the king had listed Yardley as a potential councilman, but Yardley had not yet been called to take the oath. Littleton was now thirty-five years old; Yardley was no more than twenty-three.

Yardley's local court attendance would be sporadic over the next year. He and Frances had a baby girl at home, so until adequate housing could be built in Accomack, they may have continued to reside at their home over the bay. Yardley's sale of his land at Tyndalls Neck on the York River no doubt placed him in good standing to purchase whatever he needed.[13]

The January local court received the report that the Indians of Mattawombes had been relocated to the seaside tract. Regarding Phillip Taylor's claim, the viewing party had determined "that if the Indians be displaced of the 200 acres of land which the said Mr. Taylor doth laye clayme to they in noe wise can subsist." In other words, the Indians needed the disputed 200 acres in order to survive. This means that those particular acres provided access to fresh water, access to timber, access to a landing, or a combination thereof. The viewing party had determined that Taylor's rights were not violated, because his plantation was on the other side of the creek from the Indians. And besides, no one had cleared any land there, so surely no Englishman's rights were being trampled. Taylor had probably already voiced his displeasure with the decision, as the January Accomack court began its report with an order to Taylor. It said that he was not "to disturbe or molest the Indians formerlie seated att Mattawomes Creeke neither for anie Cause or reson."[14]

The Indians' patent was supposed to be 1,500 acres; however, the land allocated to them never approached that amount. Whitelaw noted that the Indians' patent was not devised until April of the next year; however, that document has never been found.[15] Subsequent transactions over the next two hundred years would reveal that the Indians received only 650 acres, less than half of what had been ordered.[16]

At the time of Yardley's machinations to clear his land of all inhabitants, Phillip Taylor lived at Cherrystone, on what today is Eyre Hall Neck. Three years later, Taylor patented 1,000 acres to the south of the Indians' land. It is doubtful that he ever resided at his seaside patent as he died soon after receiving it and his son sold the land in that same year.[17]

When Argoll Yardley came to the Eastern Shore, he probably found a few Englishmen living on his land without permission. The Accomack court would address this issue for Savage's land when Savage's widow, Hannah Cugley, died in the early spring of 1641. At that time, the court appointed a guardian to Thomas and Hannah's son, John, and gave that guardian the right "to call in question all such person, and persons as are seated upon the said land without Order." A few months after Hannah's death, during efforts to determine who was on the Savage land by permission, it would be reported that Hannah had said William Munns had a fully paid lease on sixty acres for twenty-one years. This lease allowed Munns to run his hogs and cattle anywhere on the

Savage land and to have timber for his own use from anywhere on "the Greate divident of Land." Munns had been one of John Ward's servants who were rescued by the Epps brothers after the Indian attack nineteen years before. Without doubt, William and Jane Munns had been among Hannah's oldest and dearest friends.

Notwithstanding that the Savage and Yardley lands were the legacies of two beloved Englishmen, a greater legacy loomed here. When the Laughing King bestowed these gifts upon the Englishmen, it had been as a sacred pledge of community. The return of a portion of this land to the Native people in the form of a protective, English patent was surely a nod to this pledge and perhaps a commitment to sustain it. That is a grand thought, but—if true—the promise was miserably short-lived.

NOTES, Chapter 12:

1 Nugent, *I*, 81.

2 Nugent, *I*, 96, 126.

3 Ames, *1632*, 166; Northampton County Court Records, Order Book No. 1, 216. In a footnote, Dr. Ames said this was the 3,700 acres of George Yeardley. Dr. Ames noted that the court clerk had misspelled Yardley's name as "Mr. Early." Argoll Yardley was referred to as "Mr." at this time, not as "Esquire," the title that would soon be added to his name.

4 Hening, *Statutes I*, 167. The reference to Mattawombes was made in February 1631/32. The spelling of Mattawombes evolved to Mattawomes in the county court book. The first spelling has been used here for consistency.

5 In 1635, Hannah Savage patented her husband's land at what we call Savages Neck. In this patent we find the following words: *...which said parcell of land was granted unto her husband Ensigne Thomas Savage by the King of the Easterne shoare as by a deed under his hand calling himself Esmy Shichams...* Two years later, the man's name was again written into the record. Most people miss this second recording of his name, but in

1637 Thomas and Hannah Savage's son, John Savage, renewed the patent. (See Chapter 13 for a discussion of these names.)

6 I have been asked what the Laughing King might have done had he been alive at this time. Given what I know from the records, I believe that he would have been invited to meet with Argoll's party of men, and that afterward, he would have led his own people to a safe location, away from the English patented lands. It's just an opinion.

7 Eaton had recently fled New England after being forbidden to teach children ever again in the Massachusetts colony. He had been charged for cruelly beating his assistant and his students. (His wife also had been required to answer accusations, such as whether or not she had flavored the hasty pudding with a bit of goat's dung.) The Massachusetts civil court had found Eaton guilty, and Governor John Winthrop authorized a church trial (which threatened excommunication); Eaton fled. He left such a mess behind him that Harvard closed for a year to recover (Arthur Bernon Tourtellot, *The Charles* (New York: Farrar & Rinehart, New York, 1941), 127–138). The complaint against Mrs. Eaton had no sound basis, and she remained in Cambridge when her husband fled to Virginia. Later, when she and most of their children left by boat to join him, they were apparently never heard from again. Eaton remarried in Virginia in the early 1640s.

8 Whitelaw, 288.

9 The creek they spoke of as Hungars is now Mattawoman Creek. Apparently, this creek was considered a branch of Hungars Creek for many years.

10 Ames, *1640*, 33–34; McCartney, *Immigrants*, 86, 775. The phrase, "and noe further," suggests that Argoll Yardley never intended to claim land that would later be disputed between Argoll's son (Argoll II) and Thomas Savage's son (John). This dispute will be discussed in Chapter 14.

11 McIlwaine, *Minutes*, 478.

12 Ames, *1640*, 250.

13 Nugent, *I*, 555.

14 Ames, *1640*, 56. As the creek had been known as a part of Hungars roads, this may be the beginning of when it was called Mattwomes Creek which eventually was altered to "Mattawoman" Creek.

15 Whitelaw, 281–286. Almost immediately, harassment of the Indians began. Ten years later, Governor Berkeley would issue a warning that no land was to be taken from the Indians known as the "Laughinge Kinges Indyans" (Northampton County Court Records, *Orders, Book 3, 1645-*

1651, 207). That would be the second of many court rulings regarding this seaside tract. (The first was the local court's warning to Taylor.)

16 The records do not reveal how the Indians reacted to being moved. Over the next 173 years, they would occasionally petition the English courts to complain about land encroachment. From time to time, rumors of plots would be reported. At least one English posse was formed to quash rumored plans for attack; however, no physical battles were ever reported in the Northampton County records.

17 Mackey, *Vol. 3*, 48; Whitelaw, 206. Figure 1A of this book depicts what may have been an early understanding of the line that separated Yeardley's land and Savage's land. If the original southern boundary of the Indians' patent was intended to be along such a line, it would have cut through land that Phillip Taylor later patented (see Whitelaw, 206). Edmund Scarburgh had not yet surveyed the land when the Indians were moved from Mattwombes. Scarburgh surveyed the land in 1643, at which time Yardley disclaimed the line running off Sugar Run. He apparently approved the line that ran off the next branch to the north of Sugar Run. (This left that triangular tract that ran off lines coming from the two branches in limbo for a few years, until John Savage was able to secure it by about 1667.) The year that Scarburgh surveyed the lands (1643) is the same year that Phillip Taylor patented his 1,000 acres.

John White (English, −1593), *An aged, Native man from Pomeiock (outer banks region of North Carolina), full-length portrait, facing front, wearing winter garment; landscape scene with village in the background,* 1590, courtesy of Wikimedia Commons, public domain.

Chapter 13

The Laughing Kings

In the previous chapter, we read about the shutdown of Mattawombes town and the removal of its people to a seaside location. The records give little to no information about the Native people's reaction to this event, although within ten years, their complaints would be heard by the colony's governor. In the present chapter, we will explore how the English records reveal that the people of Mattawombes town were none other than the Native people known as "the Laughing Kings" Indians. We begin this exploration in 1650 when Virginia's governor, Sir William Berkeley, wrote to the Northampton County court commissioners. After being told that the Indians' land was being taken from them through dishonest means, he wrote the following:

> Having been frequently informed by the testimony of diverse of undoubted credit that the Indians commonly called by the name of the Laughinge Kinges Indians have

been ever most faithful to the English, and particularly that neither they nor their King in the last bloody massacre could be induced to engage with our enemies against us. And so by consequence kept the remoter Indians at least neutral in a time when a general commotion against us had been, if not ruinous, at least of insupportable prejudice to us in that conjuncture; and considering that we cannot reasonably hope for the like efforts of their friendship in case we should again need it, which God knows how soon it may be, unless we abstain from acts of rapine and violence which they say we begin to do by taking away their land from them by pretenses of the sale of a part. My desire therefore to you is, and I make it in the name of the peace & safety of the country, that you suffer no land to be taken from them but what shall be allowed both in justice & convenience by the full court, and in case the commissioners disagree in their opinions that you refer the whole matter to be considered by a full court at Jamestown. / Your Humble Servant, William Berkeley[1]

That Governor Berkeley instructed Northampton to involve "the full court" is interesting. Ten years before, when the Indians of Mattawombes town were moved, the full court had not been involved. Berkeley's directive implies that the local court commissioners were not seeing eye to eye on this issue.

Northampton's court commissioners in 1650 consisted of Nathaniel Littleton, Argoll Yardley, Obedience Robins, Stephen Charlton, William Roper, Thomas Johnson, Edward Douglas, Edmund Scarburgh, and the recently appointed John Stringer. Upon receiving Berkeley's directive, the court—consisting of Yardley, Robins, Charlton, and Johnson—announced a meeting on May 7th at "the house of Walter Williams" for the purpose of determining "the business concerning the Indians about land."[2] All commissioners were present at the May 7th meeting except Douglas and Scarburgh. The only issue regarding Indians recorded this day was a complaint from "Wachiwamp," King of the Occahanocke Indians, against Richard Hill, overseer for Edmund Scarburgh. While Wachiwamp had been hunting, Hill had "presented a gun" at the man's breast. The court noted this to be an "unadvised practice" and directed that no Englishmen were "to disturb, molest, or act anything against the said Indian King to hinder him in his hunting."[3] Given the gravity of Berkeley's dispatch, it is interesting that the local court issued no additional directives. We can be certain that they acknowledged the governor's words, but their tacit silence implies less than whole-hearted agreement.

Four years later, officials at James City would again take up the issue of the Indians' land. In November of 1654, the Grand Assembly's legislative Act IV gave the Northampton commissioners permission to allow the Indians in their county to sell their lands if the Indians wished to do so, but only if they had "the consent of the major part of the town." If such sales took place, the court was to send its "proceeding" to the governor and council who would allow the sales "unless they shall see cause to the contrary."[4] It appears that no such proceeding was ever sent to the governor. The land was now protected by the tribe's decisions, not by the decisions of the court commissioners. Still, the pressure to sell or vacate the land would continue.

In his 1650 instruction to Northampton, Governor

Berkeley may well have used the term "the Laughinge Kinges Indians" to reference all Virginia Eastern Shore Indians, including those at the seaside patent; however, based on the subsequent and on-going conflict, it is believed that he was referring specifically to those of the seaside patent. His knowledge of these Native people would have come from men such as Littleton, Yardley, Robins, and Scarburgh. Berkeley's use of the name, the Laughing Kings, is the last time that name shows in the old records.

I propose that Laughing King was indeed the name of that most famous group of Indians who were led by the great werowance known as the Laughing King. I believe it was the name as heard and pronounced by the Jacobean English ear and tongue. To explore this idea, note the following history of the name "Laughing King" in the English records:

- In 1621, John Pory, secretary of the colony, first used the term in a report he wrote about his Virginia travels.
- In 1624, the werowance known as "the Laughing King" was with Ensign Thomas Savage to verify a corn shipment.
- In 1633 or 1634, the werowance known as "the Laughing King" visited Obedience Robins, according to a later report from William Jones.
- In 1636, Obedience Robins testified to the local court that some Indians "from the laughing king" had come to Daniel Cugley's house.
- In 1650, Governor Berkeley cautioned the Northampton court not to allow land to be taken from "the Laughinge Kinges Indians" without full court agreement.

The name appeared only these five times in the English records. I propose further that a word or words, sounding similar to Laughing King, was the tribal name, whereas words such as Mattawombes and Gingasscount referred to towns. Mattawombes had been this tribe's bayside town. Gingasscount (later Gingaskin) was their new town on the seaside.

No issue is taken with the fact that the Eastern Shore Indians were early identified as Accomack Indians; however, this appears to be related to the location of their habitation at the time they received visits from the English who then wrote about it. For example, in 1621, Pory called the great king "this Laughing king at Accomack."

The personal name of the great werowance was written twice into the patent records. First, when Hannah Savage recorded her husband's patent, the name was written as Esmy Shichams. And when Hannah's son, John, renewed the patent, the werowance's name was written as Lui Shichoms.[5] (See Figures 13A and 13B.)

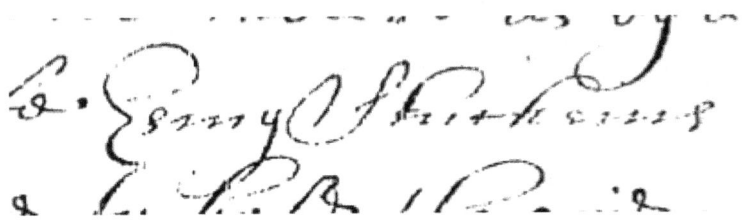

Figure 13A: (Land Office Patent)

Figure 13B: (Land Office Patent)

Just as Wahansnechav was called by his tribe's name, "Powhatan," it is likely that Esmy or Lui Shichams was called by his tribe's name, "Laughing King." However, "Laughing King" was the English version of that name. What was the version given by the Native people?

The only English, documented instance of the name given in the voice of the Native people themselves was swept away from serious consideration by an early anthropologist who deemed the name "a mistake." This anthropologist—who was likely swayed by the longstanding English tradition of the name— evidently did not think twice about his decision. However, his gesture of dismissal apparently led researchers astray for over a hundred years. This one documented instance of the name came in the form of a petition to the Virginia House of Delegates in 1786. Some Northampton white inhabitants had been petitioning the legislature to do something about the Indians' land, and the Indians wrote a petition of their own. In this petition, they called themselves "The Tribe of the Lingaskin." One hundred and twenty-one years later, the anthropologist said this was a mistake in the reading, that it should have said Gingaskin, but he cited no evidence for his conclusion, and none seems to exist.[6]

Even in modern, American English, the sound of "Lingaskin" is remarkably close to the sound of "Laughing King." Now, imagine the first seventeenth-century Englishman who attempted a conversation with a member of this Native tribe. Perhaps he turned to his English companions, saying something like, "Methinks he said, 'Laughing King.'" Perhaps it was Pory himself. The name was catchy, and the sobriquet took hold. That the werowance was an exceptionally peaceful, welcoming man may have bolstered the Englishmen's use of what seems a genial nickname.[7]

Moreover, I suggest the word "Gingaskin" derived from a blend of the tribe's name and its name for the new seaside town. They had called their old town something that sounded like "Mattawombes" to the English ear. The new town's name was first recorded in the English records in 1643 as "Gingasscount."[8] Robert Beverley in 1720 wrote it as Gangascoe.[9] Other versions of the name show as Gingaskin, Gingas King, and Chincoskin.

THE PETITION OF THOMAS LYTTLETON SAVAGE, A CONFOUNDING DOCUMENT

On October 26, 1787, the great-great-great-grandson of Ensign Thomas Savage petitioned the Virginia House of Delegates, asking that the land on which the "Gingas King" Indians lived be returned in whole or in part to him as the rightful heir. In his petition, he gave a history of how the Indians came to be on the land; unfortunately, his understanding of this history was incomplete.

According to Thomas Lyttleton Savage's petition, the Gingas King Indians had applied to Governor William Berkeley and the Virginia Council in 1674 for an allotment of land on which to settle as they were being disturbed by "a certain John Kendall." In consequence, the governor and council "directed that 650 acres of land should be laid off for the use of the said Indians out of Capt. John Savage's Land then held under the aforesaid patents."

Mr. Savage went on to say that his ancestor had surely submitted to the grant only because he had held such a large quantity of land at that time and it had been of low value. Mr. Savage felt "humbly confident" that his ancestor expected the land "of which he had been so unjustly devested [sic]" would be returned to him upon the extinction of the Indians. This is particularly true, he said, because his ancestor never received any compensation for the land. Mr. Savage felt that the decision to provide the land had been arbitrary. He felt that "the spirit and meaning of the Grant thus made is now entirely defeated, the Indians of the Gingas King Tribe being at this time almost extinct." He thought no more than two or three Indians remained and that the land was "entirely occupied by Mulattoes and free Negroes from the adjacent parts who are every day settling on the Land and are become a nusance [sic] and Injury to the people of the County."[10]

When Mr. Savage wrote this petition, he apparently thought that the Indians had a 113-year history on the seaside patent where they resided. Actually, they had a 147-year history on that patent by that time. The petition certainly gives the impression that Mr. Savage was not aware of the true history of the land that he claimed should be his. Perhaps he had relied on old family stories that stretched back only to the time of Great-Great Aunt Susanna who married John Kendall. The Kendalls' home had been on the land at what today is called Poplar Hill, adjacent to the Indians' patent.

Mr. Savage said it all started in 1674 when the Indians complained about John Kendall's harassment of them and asked Governor Berkeley for an allotment of land. It is true that the Indians complained about Kendall at that time and that a committee of men looked into the matter, and Captain Southey Littleton even drew a plat.[11] In the year before, in 1673, the Indians of the seaside patent had complained that Thomas Harmanson had "runn within their bounds." The General Court ordered the Accomack surveyor to lay out the 650 acres of land "belonging to the Chingoskin Indians," and if Harmanson encroached on their property, he was "to be turned out."[12] In 1660, the issue still was not resolved. The "Indians of Accomack" complained that they were "very much straightened for want of land, and that the English seat so neare them, that they receive very much damage in theire corne." The governor ordered that two or three gentleman and a surveyor who was not affiliated with the Eastern Shore lay out "such a proportion of land for the said Indians as shall be sufficient for their maintenance with hunting and fishing excluded." Further, the governor ordered that the land was to be "so secured to the Indians that they may have no power to alienate it, or any part of it hereafter to the English."[13] Twenty years later, under Governor Culpeper, the patent for the Gingas King Indians was recorded in the James City patent book. The 650-acres patent began at Angoods Creek (now Indiantown Creek) and touched on Harmanson, Savage, and Colonel Kendall's lands. The patent noted that the Indians had been possessed of the land since the year 1641 "as appeares by an Antient Pattent or Record in the same yeare."[14] Thirty-two more years passed before that patent was finally recorded in the local court records on December 16, 1712.[15] Thomas Lyttleton Savage missed or failed to understand that the patent was supposedly immutable, to be protected.

Thomas Lyttleton Savage became Northampton County's Clerk of Court three years after he wrote the petition, and he held that office for twenty-two years. In his last year as clerk (1813), the General Assembly passed a law "to eliminate the Gingaskin reservation and divide the land between the official members, deeding the divided plots to individuals. These individuals would then own their land in the same way as other Virginians owned land. This was the first instance of a legal allotment of reserved lands being terminated. It is also believed to have been the first instance of detribalization by law in United States history."[16]

LAST OF THE LINGASKINS

Whether called Laughing King, Lingaskin or Gingaskin, their land lost its identity as a protected patent when it was divided into individual plots. A committee had been appointed under the authority of the General Assembly's "act authorizing a division of the land of the Gingaskin tribe of Indians." This committee of four white men met several times "on the said lands, made inquiry & examination of the titles of said Indians, their numbers, families and connections." The committee's determination was that the "land ought to be divided among those of the tribe who are of proper age to be housekeepers."[17] The committee directed the county surveyor to divide the land among the twenty-seven adult people whom the committee determined to be the totality of the tribe (not including minors). These twenty-seven, in addition to their underage children, are the only people we know through whom to trace the "Laughing King" Indians. Whether or not my theory about their tribe's name is correct, the undisputed history of the land upon which they lived can leave no doubt that this was the tribe that Virginia's governor and council protected in the colony's early decades. The beneficent character of the great werowance, the Laughing King, merited that protection.

In genealogy circles, we occasionally hear people excitedly exclaim a new discovery, such as, "I can trace my family to Charlemagne!" or "I go all the way back to Rurik!" Those are indeed exciting finds, but on Virginia's Eastern Shore, to be able to trace one's lineage to the Lingaskin is as remarkable a find as that to any other royal lineage, if not more so. The twenty-seven people through whom this lineage can be traced with a fair degree of certainty are listed below.

Edmund Press, Thomas Baker, Betsey Baker (wife of said Thomas), James West, Rachael West, Molly West, Nancy Carter, John Carter, Sophia Jeffery, Stephen Jeffery, Peggy Bingham, Susan Beavans, William West, Betsey Collins Senior, Betsey Collins Junior, William Drighouse, Thomas Jeffery, William House, Betty Drighouse, Anne Drighouse, Molly Beavans, John Bingham, Molly Press, Tabby Francis, Littleton Jeffery, Solomon Jeffery, and Ebby Francis.[18]

NOTES, Chapter 13:

1   Mackey, *Vol. 3*, p. 402. (Spelling and some punctuation have been modernized.) While Berkeley said, "the last bloody massacre," it is suggested that the stories told to him referred to the legendary behavior of the Laughing King in 1622. The colony had experienced another attack in 1644, and the Eastern Shore Indians apparently did not participate in that attack either. While it is tempting to think that Berkeley was referring to the Indians at the seaside tract, he probably was referring to all Eastern Shore Indians who were being pressed by the Englishmen for land. As noted in the last chapter, the seaside tract was originally ordered to contain 1,500 acres, but 850 of those acres eventually fell into the hands of Englishmen, perhaps by "rapine and violence."

2   Ibid, 405. Walter Williams' house was the public house (or ordinary) on the north side of Hungars Creek.

3   Northampton County, Virginia, *Orders, Vol. 3, 1645-1651*, 212.

4   Hening, *Statutes I*, 391. As no other Indian town is known to have existed in Northampton in these years, the town is believed to be none other than the one that was called Gingasscount (later Gingaskin).

5   Nugent, *I*, 30, 75; Library of Virginia, *Virginia Land Office Patents and Grants, No. 1 (1623-1643), Vol. 1 & 2)*, 275-276, 499-500. The two recordings took place in 1635 under Hannah Savage's name and two years later in 1637 under John Savage's name. Both recordings refer to

a deed, but this deed has not yet surfaced. In each patent, the man was called "the King of the Eastern Shore." If the recorder transcribed directly from the deed, it is interesting that he had such a different interpretation of the first part of the name; however, just as today, it is not an uncommon occurrence. Venturing a guess as to what the name really sounded like, it would be "[blank] e Shichams." Whether the name began with "Esm" or "Lu" seems unknowable without further documentation.

6   James Mooney, a historian writing in the *American Anthropologist* ("The Powhatan Confederacy, Past and Present," Vol. 9, No. 1, Jan-Mar, 1907, pp. 122-152) wrote in a footnote: "The name is given as Lingaskin by error of reading" (p. 142).

7   John Pory noted that the Indians ruled by the Laughing King were "... the most civil and tractable people we have met with...." (Smith, *Generall Historie*, 277).

8   Ames, *1640*, 235.

9   Robert Beverley, "The History and Present State of Virginia" in The History and Present State of Virginia, ed. Robert Beverley: (London: R. Parker, 1705), 232-233.

10 Library of Virginia (https://www.lva.virginia.gov), *Legislative Petitions*.

11 This plat has not yet surfaced; it may not have been saved.

12 McIlwaine, *Minutes*, 353.

13 Hening, *Statutes II*, 13–14.

14 Library of Virginia, *Virginia Land Office Patents and Grants, Vol. 7 (1679-1689, Vol. 1 & 2 p. 1–719)*, 49–50. It appears that Southey Littleton's plat has not yet surfaced in any documents of colonial Virginia. In the patent of 1680, the year 1641 has an ink splat over the word "forty," making it difficult to decipher. This "Antient Pattent" of 1641 also has never surfaced in the surviving colonial Virginia documents.

15 Northampton County, Virginia, *Order Book No. 15, 1710-1716*, 86.

16 Sarah Nerney, "The Gingaskins of Virginia," November 18, 2011, (Library of Virginia, The Uncommonwealth: Voices from the Library of Virginia) https://uncommonwealth.virginiamemory.com. After the land was divided into plots to be owned by individuals, the land was no longer a factor holding together the tribal identity. According to Kirk Mariner, this process of detribalization was realized by the end of 1831 when "nearly all the lands of the old reservation were in the hands of whites, the result of 'tremendous pressure' put on the non-whites to leave" (Kirk Mariner, *Slave*

and Free on Virginia's Eastern Shore (Onancock, VA: Miona Publications, 2014), 175).

17 "Housekeeper" in this context means "house owner."

18 Northampton County, Virginia, *Order Book No. 35, 1808-1816*, 416. The names listed here are in the narrative report of the committee. When the official plat was drawn and labeled, William Drighouse and Molly Beavans were not listed; however, Samuel Beavans was listed on the plat at Lot No. 19, and Nathan Brickhouse was listed at Lot No. 18. Also on the plat, "Mac:" was noted to be Betsey Collins, Jr.'s husband.

Adriaen van de Velde (Dutch, 1636–1672), *Three Cows*, c. 1657/1659, courtesy of The National Gallery of Art, Washington, D. C., public domain.

By the time Thomas Cowdrey sold his ordinary to Henry Mathews in 1679, Northampton had been a home to cattle for at least fifty-seven years. What do you suppose happened to all those horns? Imagine, if you will, that Cowdrey, in a clever effort to mark his ordinary, hung a bunch of those horns from a signpost, or maybe piled some at the roadside corner. For the mostly illiterate population, the horns would signify the ordinary. Cowdrey's thought process might have been something like: Cowdrey/cow/horns/ordinary; the horns = the ordinary. (It's a theory.)

Chapter 14

The Horns

Jennings Cropper Wise, an early twentieth-century writer, noted that *horns* was another word for creek *branches.*[1] According to Wise, this was therefore the reason that a seventeenth-century Northampton ordinary was called "the Horns." I will not dispel that theory any further than to say "horns" was not a word that the early court used to describe the side streams. "Branches" is the word they used. Thus, when the early settlers referred to this particular ordinary as "the Horns," it is more likely that they were referencing something other than the branches. Perhaps a mass of horns or antlers were dangled from a rope in a nearby tree, or were stacked in a pile near the road. Such a feature would serve as a signboard, identifying the house where one could purchase a meal and an ale. A definitive answer about this has not yet been found in the old records.

The more pressing question about the land between the two middle, head branches of Whissoponson Creek (later Savages Creek and now The Gulf), has to do with ownership. Argoll Yardley disclaimed this wedge of land at a time when most folks thought it was his.[2] After he disclaimed it, the logical owner would have been John Savage, but perhaps John was too young at that time to prevent claims on the land Yardley gave up.

The first claim came in late 1640 when John Angood, a merchant from London, took possession of the land between the two branches. By the following March, Angood fell ill and sold or mortgaged the property to Edmund Scarburgh. This included 1,000 acres and a house, twenty-four hogs, all his corn, his moveables, a boat, an ox, and a yearling heifer. Angood died in August of 1641, and Scarburgh relinquished the plantation to William Hawley for 1,650 pounds of tobacco (unstripped). Payment was due in November 1642.[3]

William Hawley had acted as governor of Barbados from 1638–1639 in the stead of his brother Henry Hawley. Their brother Jerome Hawley had been a former Treasurer of Virginia. William Hawley received a land certificate for 1,100 acres, but he never used it to claim the land he had by way of Scarburgh. By mid-century, Hawley was living in Maryland.[4] After Hawley's occupation of the land in question, it appears that John Savage firmly claimed the area as his own, as a part of his father's great patent

In 1667, John Savage promised what had been Angood's and Hawley's land (minus what had been determined to belong to the Indians of "Gingas King") to his daughter Susanna upon her marriage to John Kendall. This gift ran from what today is known as Indiantown Creek at Poplar Hill toward Whissaponson Creek's headwaters. The gift would be finalized in Savage's last will and testament.

In 1677, John Savage gave a life interest in the 100-acre triangle at Whissaponson's headwaters to William Cowdrey, the ordinary keeper.[5] Two years later, Cowdrey sold this interest to Henry Mathews who continued to run the ordinary.[6] Upon Mathews's death, Colonel Kendall purchased the interest at auction. In 1687, Kendall's son sold the life interest to the rightful heir, Susanna Kendall. (Her grandfather, John Savage, had left it to her.) Around 1690, young Susanna married John Harmanson. Her land, including her parents' land at Indiantown Creek, was retained by the Harmanson family for over half a century.

In Chapter 1, a theory about this land was introduced, suggesting that the colonial furnace found near Indiantown Creek could have been built here under Sir George Yeardley's instructions. That furnace is on the land that belonged to Angood and then to Hawley, so these two men are in the mix of candidates for who built the furnace. After Angood and Hawley, the Savage-Kendall-Harmanson family joined the club of candidates. Surely at least one of the people named in this paragraph built that furnace. The old records have been of no help in giving up the answer. Archaeology remains our best hope for knowing.

In summary, the Horns was the name of the house where Henry Mathews operated an ordinary. Its name is a fact. The origin of that name is still unknown, although I have shared my theory (a cluster of horns and antlers) as well as that of Mr. Wise (the branches). In late 1677, Northampton County freeholders voted to hold court meetings at Mathews's ordinary. The Northampton court then met at this house for thirteen years. The actual site of the ordinary remains a matter of speculation; however, no one doubts that the Horns was the means by which Northampton's county government came to be where it continues today in the Town of Eastville.

NOTES, Chapter 14:

1   Wise, *Ye Kingdom*, 48.

2   Mackey, *Vol. 9*, 152–153. Argoll Yardley's disclaimer was reported on July 8, 1667, when Urmstrong Foster, Richard Patrick, and William Satchell testified to their knowledge of earlier surveys of the Yardley and Savage lands. It is interesting that Yardley disclaimed the middle branch (Sugar Run) as the line separating his and Savage's lands. This decision was made after he had worked with others to move the Indians of Mattawombes onto land that would have been included in that triangle. [See TBI.]

3   Perhaps Hawley planned to claim this land by patent, but he never did. It was not unusual for men to occupy land prior to claiming it in an official manner.

4   William Betham, *The Baronetage of England, Vol. 4*, (Ipswich: Burrell and Bransby, 1804), 298. William Noel Sainsbury et al., *Calendar of State Papers, Colonial Series, [America and West Indies] 1574–1660* (London: Longman, Green, Longman, & Roberts, 1860), 313. Whitelaw, 274–275.

5   Northampton County, Virginia, Court Records, *Deeds &c, No. 11, 1668-1680*, 158.

6   Ibid, 200–201.

Chapter 15

A Petticoat War

Bridgett Severne stepped off the boat at Captain Samuel Mathews's landing on Warwick River and practically marched up the pathway to the captain's house. Phillip Taylor, fast on her heels, tried his best to step in front, but she was having none of it. A short distance behind, Alexander Wignall and Mrs. Neale kept pace as best they could. The year was 1640.

The story is found in the old records of Northampton County. (At the time of this incident, the county was still called Accomack.) The chain of events is fragmented (thus many of the details written here are fictional); however, enough information is present in the old records to piece together a fascinating tale.

It appears that these four had been in James City where they had attended the colony's Quarter Court to address Mrs. Severne's lawsuit against Mr. Taylor. The suit was heard in

James City rather than in Accomack because the value of the disputed items was greater than twenty pounds sterling. The law required that suits of such value were to be settled by the governor and his council. What happened in the Quarter Court is not known; however, by some means, the litigants wound up in Captain Mathew's manor house, seeking arbitration.

Captain Mathews's plantation, Denbigh, was in what today is the City of Newport News. Sailing southeast on the James River, a boat captain would round Mulberry Island to enter Warwick River, and the plantation landing would have been practically straight ahead. Once ashore, the walk to the manor house was about a fifth of a mile up a gradual incline.

At that time, Samuel Mathews was probably the most powerful man in the colony, aside from the governor. He had built a twenty-one by fifty-one-foot, two-story house about fifteen years earlier. It was the seat of one of Virginia's finest plantations at that time.

Alexander Wignall was Accomack's Undersheriff (what we call "deputy sheriff"). As an official of the court, Wignall would have carried the court's order as they all rushed up the path. This order apparently allowed Mrs. Severne to receive a legacy left to her in the last will and testament of Mrs. Anna Dunne, who had been a resident of Accomack. Mrs. Neale was probably present as Mrs. Severne's companion, and all probably knew her as the wife of John Neale, the merchant.

Phillip Taylor was administrator of Mrs. Dunne's estate; as such, he was either a kinsman or Mrs. Dunne's major creditor. Either way, he had refused to give the legacy items to Mrs. Severne. His legal reason for doing so might have been because he thought Mrs. Dunne's debts took precedence over a mere gift. Whatever his reason, Mrs. Severne did not agree. She felt strongly enough about it that she did something few women of her era did: she used the local court proceedings to ensure that her voice was heard equally to that of a freeman.

Bridgett Severne was not your average colonial woman, and Phillip Taylor was not your average colonial man. Bridgett Severne was the wife of John Severne, a chirurgeon (an archaic word for "surgeon") who was trained to dress wounds and make cures.[1] She was the niece of Dr. John Pott, who had served as an interim governor in Virginia. She had come to the colony with her uncle, Francis Pott, who had served time in Fleet Prison for his part in Governor John Harvey's expulsion from Virginia. Two years before this suit against Taylor, Bridgett had prevailed in court against the future Mrs. John Custis II, who had called her a thief. All this to say, Bridgett Severne and her family were known for their pluck.

Phillip Taylor was a planter, businessman, and mariner of Accomack. In Chapter 12, we saw him speaking up for his land rights. He would soon be elected as a burgess and he would serve as a court commissioner and as High Sheriff of Northampton. Taylor was no doubt clever and popular.

Captain Mathews probably knew each person of this Accomack party through his years of Virginia civil and military leadership. In particular, he had known the Pott family well; in fact, he had appointed Mrs. Severne's uncle Francis to the Point Comfort fort command in the early 1630s.

When Captain Mathews received the party, a discussion of the particulars ensued. After "much communication," Captain Mathews turned to Mr. Taylor.

"Give Mrs. Severne any content in reason you shall think

fit that she may have no further trouble," Captain Mathews said.

"Captain," Mrs. Severne interjected, "I ask that you put your hand to that order."

"What need it?" Captain Mathews asked. "This man and this woman is witness sufficient," he said, gesturing toward Mr. Wignall and Mrs. Neale.

The problem had begun at least four months before when Phillip Taylor asked the November 1640 Accomack court to order an appraisal of the deceased Mrs. Dunn's goods. The identity of Anna Dunn has never been determined, but from subsequent events, it seems that she had at least a modest wealth and may have lived in James City before spending her last days in Accomack. One of the clues suggesting that Mrs. Dunn's estate was sizable is that the Accomack court assigned two court commissioners to the group of four appraisers. Such a party denotes some prestige.

On March 8, 1640/41, the case came back to Accomack's court. Undersheriff Wignall gave his report, including an account of Captain Mathews's ruling. The Accomack court then ordered Phillip Taylor to deliver a watchet (pale blue) satin petticoat and a silver-laced waistcoat to Mr. John Severne for Severne's wife, "immediately upon sight hereof."[2]

Bridgett Severne had prevailed.

NOTES, Chapter 15:

1 See Glossary for further information regarding "Chirurgeon."
2 Ames, *1640*, 269, 446. Perhaps Mrs. Dunn's will was proven in a court between August and November 1640, a time period for which Accomack Court minutes are missing in the records book. William Roper, Stephen Charlton, James Perrin, and Daniel Baker were the appraisers.

Chapter 16

A Curious Sequence of Events: the "False Raid"

On May 10, 1651, the Northampton County Court (consisting this day of Argoll Yardley, Obedience Robins, William Andrews, and Stephen Charlton) ordered the sheriff to arrest fifty men. These men were to be kept in custody until they gave bond to appear before Virginia's governor and Council of War in James City eleven days later, on May 21st. The charge was that they had broken the law and the League of Trade with the Indians two weeks before, on April 28th, by marching "among the Indians with a resolution to take or kill the Queen of Pocamoke." It was said that these men "shot at Indians, slashed and cut their bowls, took Indians prisoners, and bound one of them with a chain." Further, the actions of these men "caused the Indians to gather themselves together in great numbers to invade the county, to the great danger of our lives and estates." Among the fifty charged were Edmund Scarburgh, Thomas Johnson,

Richard Vaughan, Captain John Dollinge, John Robinson Toby Norton, Richard Baily, Ambrose Dixon, Richard Hill, and Jenkin Price.[1]

The court selected county court members Argoll Yardley and William Andrews to prosecute the case in James City. To prepare for the voyage, the court directed the sheriff to press a sufficient boat into service and equip it with three men and provisions. An announcement went out to the county inhabitants, cautioning them to be vigilant of any Indian plots and conspiracies.

Commander Nathaniel Littleton met with Yardley and Robins the next day. Their purpose seems to have been to stave off any retaliatory, Indian uprisings. Toward this end, they instructed William Andrews to send 100 arm's length (perhaps 100 yards) of Ronoke to the Queen of Pokomoke, ten wooden hoes to the King of Matomkin, a coat to each of the two Indians who were bound, and twenty arm's length of Ronoke to the Indian whom Toby Selby's wife shot. Andrews, they said, would be compensated for the Ronoke.[2]

Before examining that fateful trial in James City, a few clarifying factors are worth noting. First, the law that the fifty men were accused of breaking was probably the 1646 treaty that had ended the Third Anglo-Powhatan War.[3] A great, coordinated attack had resulted in the deaths of about 400 mainland colonists in 1644. In the ensuing war, the Indian leader Opechancanough was captured and then killed while in English custody. Necotowance succeeded Opechancanough and gave assent to the treaty. Edward Douglas and Thomas Johnson had been Northampton's burgesses at the time of the treaty signing. Thomas Johnson was now among those fifty charged with breaking the treaty.

Second, in the summer before, on July 25, 1650, the Northampton "Councell of Warre" had met to hear a report from Robert Berry. Under oath, Berry told the court that James Onnamus, an Indian, had visited him about two weeks before and told him that the Gingaskoyne Indians were going to poison the English. Also, he said Indians from over the bay had been hired to come and fight the English. The court also heard from Phill Mongum and Domingo Mathews who reported that King Tom was conspiring with the Nanticoke Indians against the English. As a result of these reports, the court ordered the Northampton inhabitants to "stand upon their own defence." Also, the court ordered that any commissioner had the "power to raise a considerable party of men to go out amongst the Indians and make inquiry and to give report to the court".[4]

The Nanticoke Indians were based in Maryland, a fact that brings us to the third clarifying factor about what was happening in the spring of 1651. That factor concerns the place where the raid supposedly took place. Our only clue to knowing the location is that the alleged target was the Queen of Pocamoke. Some writers have suggested Pocamoke meant the Maryland river by that name, but at this time in the history of Northampton, "of Pocamoke" referred to a branch known by that name. Today this is known as Taylor Creek, a branch of Pungoteague Creek.[5] At that time, this area would have been at the edge of Northampton County's northern reaches. Except for the "Gingaskoyne" people of the seaside patent, all native Eastern Shore towns were now to the north of this area.

After Northampton's "Councell of Warre" met, the reports of an impending attack seem to have graduated in urgency—from the local Native people at the seaside patent, to mercenaries from over the bay, to the Nanticokes of the north—yet the Northampton court commissioners had apparently not been concerned enough to do anything about it. Now, upon hearing reports of a fifty-man raid into the northern territory, the court was alarmed that the Indians to the north might attack.

Not even a month had passed since the alleged raid when, on May 21, 1651, Argoll Yardley and William Andrews stood before the colony's Council of War in James City to prosecute Edmund Scarburgh and Thomas Johnson, the supposed ringleaders of the fifty-man raid.

The colony's Council of War consisted of Governor Sir William Berkeley, Colonel William Bernard, Colonel George Ludlowe, Colonel Francis Morrison, Colonel Edward Hill, Colonel Richard Lee, Lieutenant Colonel Walter Chiles, and Major William Taylor. The James City court clerk recorded the court's findings, and the Council of War ordered the report to be published. This meant that the report was to be placed into the official colony record and into Northampton County's court record. The report was as follows:

> *Whereas Edm: Scarburgh gent. Tho: Johnson gent. with divers others were bound upp to this Court by the County Court att Accomacke to answer for Raising of forces & going in a Hostile Way upon the Indians & doing them outrage which (upon Scanning of the business) is found to be altogether false: And the said Scarburgh & Johnson & the rest are cleare from the things they are accused of And therefore the Court doth clear them therefrom Concerning they did (as Honest & careful men ought to have done in such a Case as they did it). And do order that this be published.*[6]

In summary, the accusation was determined to be false. All of the fifty men were cleared of any wrongdoing.

Most historians who have written about the event seem to have ignored the word "false," deciding that the deed was done and that James City's great men looked the other way. For example, in *Ye Kingdom of Accawmacke, Or, The Eastern Shore of Virginia in the Seventeenth Century*, Jennings Cropper Wise described the event as a result of Scarburgh's plan "to capture or kill the King [sic] of Pocomoke." Wise concluded that the result of the Council of War's trial was that "the raid was justified by the facts." He went on to suggest that Governor Berkeley was indeed unconcerned regarding Scarburgh's actions, as he immediately wrote out an order to gift two ewes to Scarburgh's young daughters.[7] This gift has at times been used to suggest that Scarburgh was found not guilty due to cronyism. However, the problem with this interpretation is that Berkeley's gift to the Scarburgh girls was actually made a full year later.[8]

Nora Miller Turman, in *The Eastern Shore of Virginia 1603-1964*, also reported the raid as a reality and said that the men were acquitted.[9] James R. Perry, in *The Formation of a Society on Virginia's Eastern Shore 1615-1655*, said too that the attack took place. Perry suggested that the court charge was either brought too quickly or the defense presented a better argument.[10]

Perhaps the most distressing interpretation of the event was that of Henrietta Dawson (Ayres) Sheppard, who reported that the fifty men had "slashed and cut" the Indians' bowels. (This surely would have added murder to the charges.) Additionally, Sheppard characterized Yardley, Andrews, and Robins as "timid" and the fifty men as "brave fighting men," leaving no doubt about where her allegiance lay.[11]

Wise, Turman, Perry, and Sheppard appear to have missed a crucial piece of evidence. This oversight led them to a conclusion quite different than the one I draw. The conclusion I suggest is that the event was less a raid and more a staged rumor designed to impel the governor's intervention.

Consider that the reason for the acquittal is plainly stated in the report: "...which (upon Scanning of the business) is found to be altogether false..." After many hours of reading in the old records, one discovers that the phrase "scanning of the business" means that the court looked at the written records. The pertinent business, in this case, would have been the Northampton County Court Orders for April 28, 1651, the day that Scarburgh, Johnson, and the others were said to have perpetrated this attack. The April 28th court minutes show that court commissioners Mr. Edmund Scarburgh and Mr. Thomas Johnson were present in court on that day along with Mr. William Andrews and Mr. Stephen Charlton. This was exculpatory information. How did Argoll Yardley and William Andrews miss it?

Given the scant bit of information we have, the answer to that question may always elude us; however, the record itself offers some clues. These clues are apparent when researching in the Northampton court records of those years. The experience is a bit like finding one's way through a random maze. Court Clerk Edmund Mathews's clerking style seems to have been to attend to it when he could. Court minutes, deeds, sales, and other legal instruments would perhaps be stacked, and Mathews would work as time allowed to copy items, one by one, paying little attention to chronology. I suspect that few people used the official books in those years, and no one was checking the clerk's work. Such oversight had not yet been introduced to the clerk's office.

To illustrate the problem, we can look in Order Book No. 4. The April 28th court minutes are recorded on all of folio 21 and part of the next leaf, page 22. The rest of page 22 contains the recording of the May 21st James City Council of War. Following the May 21st court recording are the minutes from October of the year before. Not until page 40 and folio 40 do we find the Northampton court record of May 10 and May 11, 1651, when the court ordered the arrest of the fifty men.[12]

It appears that Mathews saw his job as using the spaces on the pages to record legal transactions and court orders. For those of us who wish to follow events as they happened, it is a chaotic mess.

That the documents from April 28th and May 21st were copied into the book together is a clue about what happened. Most likely, a defendant asked Mathews to make a copy of the April 28th minutes for use in James City and this copy is what begins on folio 21. The original April 28th minutes begin on folio 17, but in those original minutes, Scarburgh was not present at the beginning of the meeting. It is documented that he arrived late, but his name was not listed with the other attendees at the beginning of the meeting in the original minutes. On folio 21, his name is very neatly included with all the rest: this is the copy provided in James City.

To add more drama to the event, let me suggest that Clerk Mathews himself was present in James City to provide the copy when called upon by the defendants. The copy became evidence in James City. Upon returning home, Mathews "published" the papers from the Council of War as he was told to do; therefore, he copied the evidence and the orders into the official record. It was his job to do so; and thus, we have two accounts of the Northampton court meeting on April 28th, the day that the alleged raid took place.

Turning now to the words of the James City Council of War, its decision stated that the fifty men had done something: "Concerning they did (as Honest & careful men ought to have done in such a Case as they did it)." The attack was determined to be false, so what was it they did "as careful men ought to have done in such a case"?

To answer this question, let us return to the Northampton Council of War that was held the summer before, on July 25, 1650. On this day, it was ordered that any commissioner had the "power to raise a considerable party of men to go out amongst the Indians and make inquiry" [spelling modernized]. Scarburgh and Johnson were court commissioners, so it follows that they had this power to "raise a considerable party."

It is apparent that a great deal of information is missing, but events that happened after the James City trial indicate that the precipitating problem had been a refusal of resources. Scarburgh and Johnson had no problem raising a "considerable party," but they did have a problem providing the resources needed for such an expedition. Why would the Northampton court have refused to cooperate?

The answer to that question is no doubt multifaceted. The most credible facet is William Andrews's commission to trade with the Indians. Andrews would have been reluctant to give support to a posse whose actions could threaten his trade relationships. He had rushed out to give "ronoke" to several local werowances in an effort to ensure peace after hearing that fifty men had been on a raid. Such hasty behavior from Northampton's senior leadership may have hampered what should have been a thorough investigation prior to setting out for a trial in James City.

Another facet of the answer is that men who owned valuable horses, equipment, and weapons were reluctant to loan them to men who may or may not return them in good condition. Perhaps a prejudice was at play in the perception of the men who were pushing against the northern boundary; they may have been viewed as rough, lawless, and incendiary.

Back home and freshly validated by the outcome of the James City trial, Scarburgh and Johnson set into motion what seems to have been their plan all along. On July 20, 1651, Stephen Charlton, Edmund Scarburgh, Thomas Johnson, and John Stringer met as a court. They noted a probability that the Indians had formed a confederacy to inflict a massacre on Northampton inhabitants, and in the hope of preventing this, a "party of horse" was ordered to be formed. The sheriff was ordered to press horses into service, as well as saddles, bridles, ropes, pistol carbines, and short swords. As they needed able riders, the owners of the horses were not necessarily on the list for this party. (Owners were not necessarily good riders.) The court ordered that the party was to set out from Richard Bailey's house at Nuswattocks about three or four o'clock in the afternoon on the following Monday. Each man was to bring provisions for one week and a half pound of gunpowder with shot and bullets.[13]

Four days after the July 20th court meeting, Charlton, Scarburgh, and Johnson wrote a letter to Commander Littleton. The letter stated that a possible confederacy of Indians was suspected of planning a sudden massacre and that a "party of horse" was needed "to discover and prevent the threatened danger." They stated the need as an emergency and asked that Littleton authorize the pressing of men and horses. Littleton's response was immediate.

> *Gentlemen, I have received your letter and I think it fitting that you all meet at Mr. Charltons upon XXX of this month and there unto give Mr. Yardley and Mr. Andrews notice of the meeting and what you shall there agree (for the good and safety of the County) I do willingly consent to, I pray you be careful and not to engage us in a war but upon good grounds, not else but God directing you I rest. Your servant, Nath. Littleton.*[14]

Notice that Commander Littleton injected Yardley and Andrews into the plan. The court met again with Charlton, Scarburgh, Thomas Johnson, and John Johnson. An order and warrant (under Littleton's signature) authorized the enlisted horsemen to make inquiry and take arms for "the service intended." The warrant allowed for the borrowing of "saddles, ropes, pistols, carbine, swords, girths (or any other equipment necessary for the present employment and service against the Indians)."

In the meantime, an additional court meeting had taken place on July 28th, probably at the county's southern meeting site. This court consisted of Charlton, Edward Douglas, Peter Walker, and John Johnson. The business on this day was the usual assortment of cases. Nothing was recorded about a threat from Native peoples. Keep in mind that the southern part of the peninsula was a fair distance (twenty miles and more) from the county's northern border. Beyond the northern border, the land was occupied by long-established Indian communities.

The "party of horse" apparently rode out and completed its mission, but we know this only because William Andrews later reported that he had lost a whitish-gray or stone horse that had been pressed into service but had not been returned to him. Testimony was heard from someone who saw a troop of horses run by and recognized two of Andrews's horses among them. The court of October 29, 1651, ordered that Andrews be paid for his horse at levies from the next crop. Fellow court commissioner Thomas Johnson did not approve. He must have insisted that his dissenting vote be recorded, as it is written in the margin: "Mr. Tho: Johnson dissen:." Also present that day were Littleton, Yardley, Douglas, and Stringer, but only Johnson dissented.[15]

We hear no more about the party of men who rode out to make inquiry among the Indians. Other than the disagreement about the horse, nothing noteworthy happened. For all intents and purposes, it was a nonevent (for the Englishmen, if not the Indians).

Unless some long-lost document is found, we will never know for certain what the fifty men did to prompt their arrest. My theory is that a number of men did indeed meet. They probably gathered at Scarburgh's son's newly acquired property on the north side of Occohannock Creek. These men would have discussed taking a party into the Indians' lands to the north; however, without enough horses and arms, they could not reasonably protect themselves from the unknown. Even though the Northampton Council of War of the previous year had approved the formation of exploratory parties, Scarburgh and Johnson, as court commissioners, had failed to convince the senior leadership to provide the resources for such a venture. The only way that they would obtain the resources was if a higher authority approved their plan. The next highest authority in the colony was the governor, but without Littleton or Yardley's cooperation, an audience with the governor was out of the question. Perhaps one of the fifty men then said something like, "Ha! The only way the likes of us'll get to see the governor is if we murder someone!"

Some people are gifted with the ability to see strengths and weaknesses in others. When such a gift is paired with an uncommon ability to provoke and manipulate others' behavior, heaven help the target! I am not the first person to suggest that such a mind existed among those fifty men. Even this early in his career, Edmund Scarburgh had become a personality that some people loved to hate. He would have used this sentiment in his planning, and men who felt threatened by him would have hastened to bring him up on charges, especially in front of the governor. Thomas Johnson's presence among the fifty merely enhanced the likelihood of hasty charges, because Johnson was known to be trustworthy and honorable. No one would ever suspect Johnson of subterfuge.

The story of the raid would have been strategically fed into the community just days before the James City Council of War met. An investigation would take time, and Argoll Yardley and William Andrews could not afford time if they were to be ensured of a place on the Council of War's docket and of a means to travel to James City.

In James City, when Scarburgh and Johnson had their turn to speak to the governor and council, they told the truth. The raid did not happen. They revealed an official document as an alibi for their own whereabouts on the day in question. They revealed the county's failure to support its own Council of War's decisions. And finally, they confessed to having planted a false story in the community. That Northampton's leadership had failed to properly investigate the story only bolstered the men's position that no one was listening to them, and therefore the ruse was essential in order to have an audience with the governor. The Council of War cleared them "therefrom Concerning they did (as Honest & careful men ought to have done in such a Case as they did it)." Within a few short months, the county outfitted a party of fifty men to go and make inquiry among the Indians to the north. Scarburgh and Johnson had prevailed.

[Please note that the scenario of subterfuge as presented above is a theory. The records reveal only the charges, the trial and acquittal, and the subsequent formation of a sanctioned and equipped posse. It is as good a theory as any, better than most.]

The story in James City did not end there. Later that day at the Council of War in James City on May 21, 1651, the council declared that Palmers Island (north of today's Baltimore) was within Virginia. Further, it gave the trade commission at Palmers to Edmund Scarburgh. What the council did next certainly must be connected to what had happened over the previous weeks in Northampton. See for yourself:

The court does think fit and accordingly orders that Mr. William Andrews be permitted to trade no more with the Indians in the Bay but that hereby his commission be made void.[16]

It appears that this decision was made after a break, perhaps the court's break for the midday meal. During that break and in the presence of one or more council members, did someone express doubts about Andrews's suitability for the commission? Essentially, upon hearing about the raid, Andrews—instead of investigating—had rushed out and needlessly given away 120 arm's length of Ronoke, ten wooden hoes, and two coats. Had he lost his edge? Was he no longer proficient in trading? These questions will never be answered. The court gave no explanation for taking the trade from Andrews.

Andrews likely went home crimson with embarrassment. He had lost his commission, and he and Yardley had failed—in front of the governor and council—to secure convictions against Scarburgh and Johnson. Would the events of May 21, 1651, have any damaging, carry-over effects as to how these court colleagues—William Andrews, Argoll Yardley, Edmund Scarburgh, and Thomas Johnson—would deal with one another in the future? We have already seen how Andrews and Yardley appear to have shunned meetings for organizing the horse troop until the commander included them. And we have seen Johnson vigorously dissenting to Andrews's reimbursement of a horse said to have been lost on that expedition. It is all as fleeting shadows through the gossamer window of ancient words. Yet, it seems crystal clear: these were—and would continue to be—strained relationships.

NOTES, Chapter 16:

1. Northampton County, Virginia, *Orders, Deeds, Wills &c.*, No. 4, 1651-1654, 40. No other men of the fifty were named.

2. Ibid, page 40–folio 40. Ronoke (sometimes spelled as Roanoke) was Indian money made of certain shells. An arm's length is considered from shoulder to the tips of one's fingers, approximately three feet. Toby Selby's wife had shot an Indian six months before this event, and at that time, the court (consisting of Charlton, Johnson, Douglas, and Stringer) had authorized surgery performed on the man at the county's charge.

3. Hening, *Statutes I*, 323–326.

4. Mackey, *Vol. 3*, 418–420. King Tom was a local Indian. (Spelling was modernized.)

5   Walczyk, Book IV, p.159. When Gov. Bennett granted Thomas Teagle 350 acres, the location was described: "...at Pungoteagg Creek, beginning at a little beach issuing out Pocomocke Branch; bounded on the eastern part by the said Pocomocke Branch which is a main branch; on the south side of Pungotegg Creek, on the northern and southern part by two right lines and running west southerly into the woods..." (Northampton County, Virginia, Court Records, *Orders, Deeds, Wills &c, Book No. 4, 1651-1654*, p. 186).

6   Northampton County, Virginia, Court Records, *Orders, Deeds, Wills &c, Book No. 4, 1651-1654*, folio 21. (Spelling was modernized. However, it should be noted that false was spelled as "falce," since it is a key word in this story.)

7   Wise, *Ye Kingdome*, 117–119.

8   Northampton County, Virginia, Court Records, Orders, Deeds, Wills &c, Book No. 4, 1651-1654, p. 67. The occasion of Berkeley's gift to the Scarburgh girls was that he was leaving office due to the Virginia government's surrender to Parliament.

9   Turman, *Eastern Shore*, 52.

10 James R. Perry, *The Formation of a Society on Virginia's Eastern Shore, 1615-1655* (Chapel Hill: The University of North Carolina Press, published for the Institute of Early American History and Culture, 1990), 211.

11 Henrietta Dawson (Ayres) Sheppard, *Ayres-Dawson and Allied Families, Volume 1, Recording the ancestry of Richard Johnson Ayres Jr. of Accomack County, Virginia and of his wife Elizabeth Hack Dawson of Loudoun County, Virginia* (New York, The American Historical Company, Inc., 1961), 195.

12 Northampton County, Virginia, Court Records, *Orders, Deeds, Wills &c, Book No. 4, 1651-1654* fol. 21–p. 22, p. 40–fol.40. While the records show numerous examples of Clerk Mathews's disordered style, the juxtaposition of the April 28th local court minutes and the May 21st James City court meeting actually demonstrate the point that the April 28th minutes were used as evidence in the James City court trial. This is discussed within the text of this chapter.

13 Walczyk, Frank V., transcriptionist, Northampton County VA, Orders, Deeds, & Wills, 1651 - 1654, Book IV (Peter's Row, Coram, NY, 1998), 27–28. Northampton County, Virginia, *Orders, Deeds and Wills, No. 4, 1651–1654*, fol. 36." Shot" in this sense was balls or pellets of metal used as charges from guns.

14 Northampton County, Virginia, Court Records, *Orders, Deeds, Wills &c, Book No. 4, 1651-1654*, p. 36. The phrase,"upon XXX of this month," means the 30th.

15 Northampton County, Virginia, Court Records, *Orders, Deeds, Wills &c, Book No. 4, 1651-1654*, p. 57; fol. 57.

16 Northampton County, Wills, *Vol. 4*, 1650 - 1654, p. 22–fol.22. Some sources have read the date for Andrews's decommissioning as May 20; however, the date is given in Roman numerals as "xxjth of May 1651," which translates to May 21st. (At that time, i and j were still used as interchangeable letters.) Spelling was modernized in this passage.

Chapter 17

Scarburgh's Brother

Historian Ralph Whitelaw had two suggestions to explain how Edmund Scarburgh walked away free and clear from the trial as described in the previous chapter. First, Whitelaw said that Scarburgh may have talked himself out of the charge about the alleged raid; and second, he suggested that Scarburgh's brother may have "used his influence to have a directive sent to the Governor."[1] Edmund Scarburgh's brother is said to have been Dr. Charles Scarborough. Whitelaw was not alone in this thought. Many writers have suggested that the great doctor's influence with King Charles II may have paved the way for Edmund Scarburgh to slip past laws that otherwise would have called him out on questionable behavior.

As you consider this possibility, keep in mind that Dr. Charles Scarborough, in 1651, was Reader of Anatomical Lectures at the Barbers-Surgeons Company, Monkwell Street,

London.[2] He had been appointed to this position in 1649 and held the position for nineteen years. He probably did not meet Charles II until 1660.[3] All this to say, it is highly unlikely that Edmund Scarburgh received any help in the matter of "the raid" from anyone in high places.

It is interesting that Charles Scarborough would become a physician to the king and also to Governor Berkeley's brother, Lord John Berkeley.[4] Indeed, if the genealogical sources are correct that Charles and Edmund were brothers, Edmund could have been influential to the career of his brother Charles rather than vice versa. By the time Charles Scarborough attained a position with enough influence to assist a brother in Virginia, Edmund was already decades into a public career that included titles such as Surveyor General, Court Commissioner, Burgess, Speaker of the House, and Colonel.

NOTES, Chapter 17:

1   Whitelaw, 629. Twenty-two days passed between the alleged raid and the trial; this was not enough time to solicit and receive help from anyone in England.

2   As "reader," Dr. Scarborough was a university lecturer of the highest degree below that of "professor."

3   Burton Chance. "Charles Scarborough, An English Educator And Physician to Three Kings: A Medical Retrospect into the Times of the Stuarts." *Bulletin of the History of Medicine* 12, no. 2 (1942): 274–303. http://www.jstor.org/stable/44446270.

4   Ibid, 277, 285.

Chapter 18

The Event in Hack's Old Fields

On June 11, 1653, what was to be a peaceful gathering in Northampton County quickly mushroomed into a rebellious throng. Some of the local leadership considered the event so menacing that they reported it to the Grand Assembly later that month. The Grand Assembly then ordered the governor and state councilmen to travel to the Eastern Shore. Their purpose would be to restore peace and to punish the offenders.

It is a fascinating sequence of events, yet relatively few people know about it. Furthermore, many who have heard of the incident mistakenly confuse it with an event that happened the year before.

The event that happened that year has come to be called "the Northampton Protest." Essentially, this protest was a paper written on March 30, 1652. That day closely followed Virginia's official surrender to the English parliamentary government and preceded the first Grand Assembly under this new government. The paper was written to instruct the county burgesses when they attended this Assembly session. It was signed by one court commissioner, Stephen Charlton, and five freemen: Living Denwood, Jonathan Nuthall, John Ellis, William Whittington, and Stephen Horsey.

Some writers have depicted the March 30, 1652, paper as a unique protest, stating that the reception of this paper in James City resulted in punitive measures toward the men who had signed it. This is not true. The punitive measures that have been cited were actually inflicted a year later on the men who participated in the June 11, 1653, event. Several reasons can be found for the confusion. One is that Stephen Horsey figured prominently in both events. Another is that each event produced a paper criticizing leadership practices. A third reason has to do with the odd order of reports within the records themselves.

Having told you that the two events are separate, I am going to leave the first event, the Northampton Protest, for later discussion. We will focus now on the second event, the one that happened on June 11, 1653. Discussing these events out of sequence will hopefully help to differentiate the real story from the myth. The second event is most often noted by a rather colorless and unimaginative title: "the event in Hack's old fields." What happened that day was anything but colorless and unimaginative.

The setting is the simplest aspect of this story to explain. "Hack's old fields" was land owned by Dr. Peter Hack. The land was located west of present-day Franktown, off Warehouse Creek in the area of Cedar Cottage. Dr. Hack had owned the fields for less than two months at the time of this event, so it was not called "old" in relation to him. "Old fields" were fields that had been cleared and planted by Indians but later traded to the English, as the soil was depleted and unable to bear corn without "an extraordinary deal of sap and substance to nourish it."[1] Before Hack's ownership, the fields had belonged to William Berryman. Upon Berryman's death in 1645, Thomas Johnson was certified as one of Berryman's estate administrators.

Thomas Johnson was the central character of the event in Hack's old fields.[2] By this time, Johnson was a member of the parish vestry, a court commissioner, and a captain in the local militia. That he was popular among the people is clear in that he had been elected as a burgess four times in the previous seven years. In the most recent election, William Melling and Stephen Horsey joined Johnson as burgesses-elect.

In the spring of 1653, Northampton freemen were keyed up, waiting to hear if taxes were to be raised as a result of a local court action. The seed of this irritability was a maritime event that had occurred a full year before. That was the tangible cause that riled Northampton inhabitants; however, another factor no doubt played a part in the general discontent. Just fifteen months before, Virginia had surrendered to parliament. Parliament had prevailed in the English Civil Wars, giving Oliver Cromwell control over the country. In March of 1651/52, almost every Northampton freeman had signed a promise to be loyal to "the commonwealth of England as it is now established without King or house of Lords."[3] No colonist in his or her lifetime had known life without a king. Imagine how difficult it would be to trust the government that had just chopped off the head of your king. Leadership across the colony was no doubt still finding its legs.

The maritime event that upset the county inhabitants took place off the Eastern Shore bay waters on June 13, 1652. In response to the Navigation Act of October 1651 (which required that goods be brought in only in English ships), Captain Richard Husbands intercepted and took possession of a vessel in Northampton's jurisdiction. His license to do this was provided by a commission granted by The Keepers of the Liberties of England, which apparently was a no-frills (yet lengthy) name for the authority of the new, parliamentary government. Captain Husbands declared that the vessel was from Rotterdam, unlicensed, and therefore, free prize.

Four days later, Captain Walter Chiles of James City petitioned the Northampton court, saying that his vessel, the *Fame of Virginia*, had been illegally taken by Husbands. His ship, Chiles said, had sailed from Virginia in January. It had made its voyage and returned to Virginia in June when it was seized while setting sail out of Accomack road toward the port of James City. Chiles demanded the return of his vessel as well as restitution for lost goods and lost time, all to the value, he said, of £2,000 sterling. The Northampton court acknowledged that Captain Husbands's crew was in possession of Captain Chiles's ship, holding it in Hungars road. It ordered Husbands to release the ship to the court.

On June 18, 1652, the Northampton court conceded that Chiles was an inhabitant of the colony, sole owner of the ship and goods, and that he was loyal to the new government; therefore, the ship was not a legal prize. The court declared that it would detain Husbands until his men released the *Fame of Virginia* and its goods to Chiles. Husbands's men sent word that they were waiting for their captain to be on board to give them orders. Also, they reported, no goods were on board except "a little drink," half of which had been consumed.

Husbands disagreed with the court's determination. He insisted that the ship was from Holland and therefore a legal prize. He demanded satisfaction. With arbitration from court members Nathaniel Littleton, Argoll Yardley, William Andrews, and Stephen Charlton, Husbands agreed to surrender the ship to the court on the condition that Chiles discharge him from all manner of suits, actions, debts, dues, or demands.[4] The court then released Husbands. The following day, Husbands sailed out of Hungars road and, to the court's dismay, took Chiles's ship with him.[5] Northampton now had no ship to return to Chiles and no means to chase Husbands. The capture, the appeal, and the arbitration had taken place under the authority of the Northampton court. Questions began to circulate as to whether or not Northampton would be held responsible for the loss.

A year passed, and no minutes or orders were written into the official Northampton court book regarding the court's dealings with Husbands and Chiles. Rumors abounded. With no official word from the court commissioners, who knew what to think? The court—especially Littleton, Yardley, Andrews, and Charlton—seemed to be sitting on their hands. Perhaps they reasoned that if no documentation existed, no lawsuit could happen.

Chiles's ship had been detained in Hungars road for at least five days and then had been edged away while in the custody of Northampton court. Some said the ship carried papers proving it belonged to Rotterdam and thus was a legal prize; but the officials had said it belonged to Chiles, a Virginian. Would Chiles sue Husbands and, if so, would Husbands sue Northampton? Or, would Chiles sue Northampton, leaving it up to Northampton to sue Husbands? If any legal action came from this, would the people of Northampton be culpable? In the eyes of some of the county inhabitants, the court commissioners should have handled the situation in a manner that protected the citizens from culpability. Many thought that the ship was a prize and that the court should have stood with Husbands. Others thought it wasn't a prize, and thus, the court should have ensured that the ship was returned to Chiles. Now a lawsuit against the county seemed likely. The idea of raising taxes was infuriating. For the small farmer, it was food from his table and clothes from his back. Each man, rich and poor, paid the same tithes. The commissioners were all wealthy; why should the costs of their ineptitude be passed on to the people?

The absence of official information served merely to fuel fear and anger within the Northampton community. This went on for a year. One way or another, something had to be done.

In the meantime, in the months preceding the event in Hack's old fields, Northampton's court commissioners grappled with other fallout from English policies toward the Dutch. England had declared war on the Netherlands on July 10, 1652. The following January, Parliament wrote to Virginia's governor, requiring Virginia to be on the defensive against the United Provinces, to seize any Dutch ship that came into harbor, and to "dispose of them to the public use."[6] Anti-Dutch sentiment was on the rise, and the local citizens had already seen what could happen to a ship that was thought to be Dutch. In February, seven members of Northampton's court penned a letter to the governor, noting that they had received a petition from Northampton's Dutchmen who were concerned for their safety. The letter endorsed the honesty and loyalty of these Dutch inhabitants and asked that the governor issue an order to ensure their safety.[7]

In April 1653, Deputy Governor William Claiborne replied to Northampton, allowing the Northampton court to protect the county's Dutch inhabitants. Immediately upon receipt of Claiborne's reply, the court issued an order that no one in the county should molest or trouble any county, Dutch-nation inhabitant. Additionally, all militia members were ordered to do their best to suppress any seizures of Dutchmen or their properties.[8]

In June 1653, Court Clerk Edmund Mathews finally copied the information about Husbands's capture of Chiles's ship into the official court record. Unusual for a clerk, Mathews included several personal observations about the origin of this information. His notations are discussed in Appendix III, but for now, we will look at what happened just after the information was officially available to the public.

The upcoming meeting of the Grand Assembly no doubt spurred the timing of these entries into the court book. The burgesses' usual practice was to collect the local inhabitants' concerns to present to the Grand Assembly so that laws could be created or adjusted to remedy grievances. The Northampton court had waited until the last minute to submit the entries regarding the Husbands/Chiles debacle for inclusion into the official court record.

On June 11, 1653, Thomas Johnson took a copy of that record to Hack's old fields, and he proceeded to read it to the people who had gathered there. This was not a spontaneous event. For all intents and purposes, this was a "town hall meeting," arranged by the current burgesses to gather the people's concerns. In this particular year, before hearing the people's concerns—which undoubtedly included the Husbands/Chiles debacle—it would be necessary for the people to know what the official court record said. Belated though this record was, the leadership and the people all needed to be on the same page. The governor, the council, and the body of burgesses would always defer to the official written record. So what did the official written record say?

The ink was hardly dry in the books when Thomas Johnson took that copy to Hack's old fields. When I envision that day, it begins with Johnson walking up from a landing on Warehouse Creek. A well-worn leather folder is tucked tightly under one arm. The folder contains a copy of the official court record as well as freshly sharpened quill pens, a flat (portable) bottle of ink, and several blank papers. Johnson, usually a friendly fellow, today wears a steely visage of chilling seriousness. Some people perceive this as earnestness, others as anger. (Johnson might have used the word "disgust" and mumbled something about his colleagues who created this mess.) A fair number of people have gathered. They give him a wide berth as he makes his way to a low ridge.

It is a lovely spring day. As Johnson approaches the ridge, he hears the voice of Stephen Horsey. Horsey is talking politics, dragooning his distrust of the court commissioners. Johnson is a court commissioner, but his role today is dual: court commissioner and burgess. He is not offended by Horsey's zeal. He knows such zeal spurs people's interest, but he also knows that zeal must be tempered if it is to be useful.

When Horsey spies Johnson's approach, his words trail as he walks to greet his fellow burgess. He trusts Johnson. Johnson is a transparent man. He says what he means. He does what he says he will do.

A hush weaves through the crowd as Johnson unties his folder and takes out a folded, coarse sheet of paper. The paper is densely stained with inked words. Johnson passes the folder to Horsey so as to be unencumbered as he reads. For a few seconds, the only sounds to be heard are the harsh shrieks of roving gulls. And then Johnson speaks.

We know what happened that day from the eyewitness reports of two young men, twenty-two-year-old Thomas Harmanson and nineteen-year-old John Severne. Both were later deposed by Severne's stepfather, Stephen Charlton. Perhaps the young men had ventured over to the fields together and then later hurried to Charlton's home, knowing that he would relish the information as to what had just happened. Severne and his stepfather did not have a genial relationship, so this may have been an opportunity for young Severne to impress his stepfather with stirring details. Does that mean he embellished the story to impress Charlton? Probably not. The facts did not need embellishment. Upon hearing what the two young men had to say, Charlton no doubt summoned William Andrews. Andrews would have sent word to Argoll Yardley, and Yardley would have sent word to Nathaniel Littleton.

If Johnson had maintained his composure as a court commissioner, rather than acting on his role as a burgess, perhaps events that day would not have happened as they did. According to Harmanson, Johnson began reading the court's account about the clash between Husbands and Chiles. Johnson paused in his reading and asked, "Is there any man here who is able to judge whether the ship were a prize or not?" With this question, he was reflecting on the actions of Littleton, Yardley, Andrews, and Charlton when they declared that Chiles's ship was not a prize.

Johnson surely meant those words as a rhetorical comment, not as a question to be answered. However, according to Harmanson, Stephen Horsey answered. "I know no man in that court able to judge her a prize," Horsey was reported to say, "but through their wrong, they did detain the man's right, like a company of villains." Young John Severne, in his deposition about what happened, added a bit more flame to that fire. He said he heard Horsey "revile against some of the magistrates of this county (saying) the county would be ruinated by a company of asses and villains."[9] These were inflammatory words, attacking the integrity of the commissioners. Horsey's sentiments were clear: he felt that the commissioners had stepped on the rights of Captain Husbands. If this was the sentiment of most people who gathered that day, it means that they were in opposition to the court commissioner's decision.

Johnson had only himself to blame for the tone that shaped the grievances that were put to paper that day. As burgesses, he and Horsey did their job by gathering and recording the people's concerns to take to the Assembly, but Horsey's comments apparently inspired words that surpassed the pale of decorum. The actual paper (what I call "the Hack's old fields paper") is now lost, but its contents will surface in the many official reactions to it, as will soon unfold.

Nathaniel Littleton, Argoll Yardley, William Andrews, and Stephen Charlton received the reports on what happened that day and responded with collective indignation. These four men then put their heads together and drew up a petition to Virginia's governor and council, complaining specifically that Horsey had scandalized them with his insults and incited mutiny against them as magistrates. They demanded reparation and vindication.[10]

When the issue came before the Grand Assembly in the next month, the contents of the grievance paper became enmeshed with the commissioners' complaints against Horsey and also with an issue involving Edmund Scarburgh that actually had nothing to do with the event in Hack's old fields. Consider the Assembly's first instructions regarding their understanding of what had happened in Northampton:

> *"Whereas the paper subscribed by name of the inhabitants of Northampton county is scandalous and seditious and hath caused much disturbance in the peace and government of that county, it is therefore ordered by this present Grand Assembly, That all the subscribers of the said paper be disabled from bearing any office in this country, and that Leift. Edmund Scarbrough who hath been an assistant and instrument concerning the subscribing of the same be also disabled from bearing any office until he hath answered thereunto, and the honourable Governour & Secretarie be intreated to go over to Accomack with such assistants as the house shall think fitt, for the settlement of the peace of that countie, and punishinge delinquents."*[11]

It is interesting that the Assembly viewed Scarburgh as a sideline culprit of the Hack's old fields event. It is doubtful that Scarburgh had anything to do with it. In fact, later in the session, the Assembly would revise its understanding and omit Scarburgh's name as a player in the event. (The Assembly had issues with Scarburgh, but they were separate and not related to the Hack's old fields paper.) The General Assembly's journals do not reveal how much time elapsed between the Assembly's first directive to Northampton and its second. Cooler heads apparently prevailed in the interim, and the Assembly then refined its concerns about Northampton.

Note this later entry:

> *"According to an order of this Assembly, upon the petition of Coll. Nathaniel Littleton, Coll. Argoll Yarley [sic], Major William Andrews, and some other commissioners of Northampton county, Master Speaker, Left. Coll. Edward Major, Left. Coll. Geo. Fletcher, Coll. Thomas Dew and Left. Coll. Rob't Pitt are nominated as assistants to attend the Governour and Secretarie for the settlement of the peace of that county, and the punishment of delinquents there according to their demerrits, the appointment of all officers both for peace and warr, the division of that county, and the hearing and determineing of the business of damages between Capt. Daniel How and Left. Coll. Edm'd Scarbrough, As also between Capt. John Jacob and the said Edmund Scarbrough, with all other matters and things necessary and incident for the preservation of the peace of that place, For which this shall be their commission. The charges which the said commissions shall be at, both in goeing staying there & returneing, to be levied upon those persons that occasioned their repair thither."*

The issues had been honed. The "delinquents" were those who had created and signed the Hack's old fields paper. Scarburgh had problems, but they were not those spilling out from Hack's old fields. (Scarburgh's issues are not a concern of this essay.)

No more than two weeks after the Assembly adjourned, Governor Richard Bennett, Secretary William Claiborne, Speaker William Whitby, and Colonel Thomas Dew sailed to Northampton County. Along with the local leadership (Colonel Nathaniel Littleton, Colonel Argoll Yardley, Lieutenant Colonel Obedience Robins, Major William

Andrews, Captain John Stringer, Captain Edward Douglas, Captain Stephen Charlton, Mr. William Whittington, and Mr. William Jones), they met as a joint court. (Note that Edmund Scarburgh and Thomas Johnson were not among their colleagues.) From among the decisions made by this extraordinary court over the three days they met, we can have a better sense of the issues as they finally shook out from among high-flying egos and personal passions.

Before looking at this court's work, imagine the setting that could provide for this large, venerable court. For some years, the Northampton court had been alternating its meetings between Point House on Old Plantation Creek and Walter Williams's house on Hungars Creek. However, by this time, commerce at Old Plantation Creek had diminished, and investment of repairs to Point House had likely ceased. This joint court no doubt met at Walter Williams's establishment in the Hungars/Nuswattocks community. The homes of petitioners Yardley, Andrews, and Charlton were nearby, but perhaps of greater weight, the "delinquents" who had caused all the hullabaloo lived in the northern reaches of the county. Walter Williams's establishment was large enough to accommodate the court and close enough for the northern inhabitants to attend. The mid-summer's heat and humidity probably drove them to meet and break early. Cooking for their meals would have been removed from the house so as not to add to the heat inside the court's room. Neighbors helped to cater and serve. The Eastern Shore—then as now—would have provided incomparable hospitality.

Some may wonder why Yardley or Andrews or Charlton did not host the meeting. The answer is that this was a public meeting; no one but the owner of a public house would have wanted such a throng of people milling about their property. Additionally, their households would not have been prepared to provide the necessary food and drink. This was an event for a seasoned business. Walter Williams had held his ordinary license for no less than seven years. He had hosted many a public event, some perhaps larger than this.

While the local court commissioners would not have wanted the public milling about their homes, they each probably vied to host a guest from James City. Andrews and Charlton would likely have been the successful contenders, as they lived on the same neck where the court meeting was held at the ordinary. However, in good weather, Yardley, Whittington, and Jones were each a swift boat ride away.

On the second day of this historic joint court, some of the signers to the Hack's old fields paper explained themselves in a petition to the governor and the council members who were present. The petitioners noted that it had been said they were "revolted from the right honorable parliament" and that a "great sum of money is to be paid to satisfy for a ship taken here by Capt. Rich Husbands and restored by a court unto Mr. Walter Chiles." They had been afraid, they said, and to escape the danger, they wrote and signed a paper (the Hack's old fields paper). Their intent, they said, had not been to offend anyone or to cause any trouble in the county. Their motive was purely for self-preservation. They assured their fidelity and asked to be protected from payment for the ship.[12]

After hearing this petition, the court reviewed Littleton, Yardley, Andrews, and Charlton's petition, and they heard Harmanson's and Severne's depositions. After discussion, the court made its determinations. Many of the offenders, it said, had indeed displayed mutinous and scandalous behavior;

therefore, all the signers of the "writing called protest" (the Hack's old fields paper) would not be allowed to hold any public office until the governor and council reversed that decision.[13] Additionally, the court selected Thomas Johnson to receive the harshest monetary penalty in the amount of 500 pounds of tobacco. Stephen Horsey, William Johnson Taylor, and John Dolling were each fined 300 pounds of tobacco and were to put up security for their good behavior.[14] Also, Horsey, Taylor, and Dolling were to be imprisoned for as long as the governor said. All other signers of the paper were each to pay a fine of 100 pounds of tobacco.[15] In the next year, Edward Harrington, a currier, died still owing 100 pounds of tobacco for signing the paper "called a Protest."[16]

In addition to "the settlement of the peace," the "punishment of delinquents," and the Scarburgh issues, the Grand Assembly had instructed this special court to address the appointment of officers and the division of the county.

The division issue was a concern that no doubt stemmed from the northward push of settlement. At that time, the county stretched from today's Kiptopeke to Belle Haven, a span of thirty miles. Court meetings had been alternating between Old Plantation Creek and Hungars Creek. To address this concern, the court changed the southern court venue and added a third meeting place in the northern region. The court directed that from now on the Northampton court would meet on the 28th of each month, alternating between Cherrystone Creek, Hungars Creek, and Occohannock Creek. This new decree accommodated northern inhabitants by establishing a meeting at Occohannock. The precise location of this court has not been found, but it probably was near the area of today's Shields Bridge, outside of Belle Haven.[17]

In the map (Figure 18), the star represents the Occohannock court site. The oval represents the Hungars court site. The square represents the Cherrystone court site. The northern border of English habitation at this time was just above the star.

Also at this three-day joint court in the summer of 1653, the governor and council appointed five new Northampton court commissioners: Thomas Hunt, Samuel Goldsmith, Francis Pott, John Nuthall, and Thomas Sprigg. This broadening of county representation may have been in response to the people's concerns as had been expressed in the Hack's old fields paper. Horsey had implied that the county would be "ruinated" by the present Northampton County court commissioners. These new appointments would certainly infuse new blood into the local court. And the addition of a third meeting place would make the court more accessible to all county inhabitants.

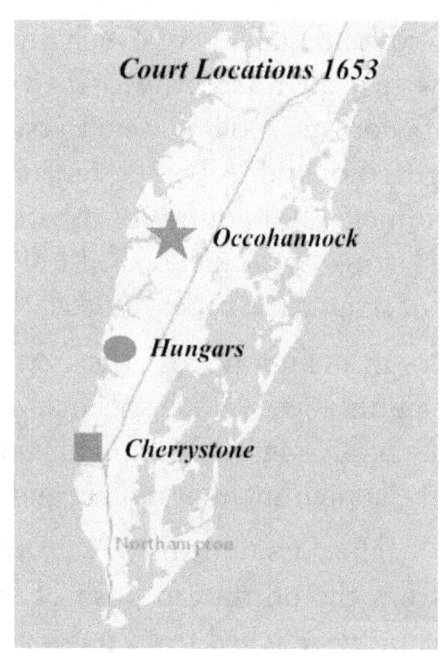

Figure 18

The joint court also addressed another issue that the Hack's old fields paper may have brought to their attention. This issue involved the collection of taxes from seventy people who had been missed in a previous collection, resulting in a shortfall to the widow and orphans of the former sheriff. The court ordered Commander Littleton to release the names for collection.

And finally, the joint court addressed its concerns involving Edmund Scarburgh, but these concerns do not relate to the Hack's old fields event. His problems at this time had more to do with debts and castle duties.[18]

Whatever happened about Walter Chiles's ship, *The Fame of Virginia*? Did Chiles sue Northampton as the residents had feared? It seems that the issue surrounding the Husbands/Chiles debacle was solved in a backroom deal during the first days of that same Grand Assembly session. This event is well known in Virginia history because the deal caused Chiles to give up his position as the newly elected Speaker.

When the Grand Assembly opened its session on July 5, 1653, Chiles was elected Speaker. In response, the governor sent a note to the burgesses, telling them that this was not a good time to elect Chiles as Speaker. The reason, the note said, was because some business would come before the burgesses that presented a conflict of interest for Chiles. In response to the note, the burgesses sent a four-man committee to the governor, asking for an explanation. The next day, Chiles explained to the burgesses that an extraordinary opportunity was at hand for him. He then resigned as Speaker, and the House allowed it. Several days later, Chiles paid a mere £400 for a captured ship, the *Leopoldus of Dunkirk*.[19] While it cannot be said for certain that the deal had anything to do with redress for his great loss in Northampton, Chiles never pursued any suits to recover that loss.

The people had not been privy to the behind-the-scenes wheeling and dealing. Throughout all that year, they had lived in fear that their tithes would soar. Even up to the day that the governor and council came to Northampton to quell the unrest, the people were still fearful that they were going to be made to pay for a ship that was lost due to no actions of their own. It was enough to make a person want to use words like "ruinated!" Surely the Northampton people had great hopes that the newly appointed court commissioners would loosen the oppressive grip of the old guard and bring more light to the inner workings of their local government.

The joint court had stripped Thomas Johnson of his offices, but that would have no effect on his popularity with the people. By November of the next year, 1654, he would again be elected as a burgess. In the following December, Governor Bennett would restore him to all his former positions and titles.

The sleepy fields off Warehouse Creek had been a hotbed of protest in June of 1653. Thinking back on that day, Johnson may have felt embarrassed by his momentary loss of composure. He may have winced as he remembered Horsey's reactionary insults. However, the irony would not have been lost on him that he, a mild-mannered fellow, through his unwitting behavior, had set the fire that led to necessary changes in how his beloved county was governed. The changes were relevant: five new court commissioners, accessible court meetings, and fair practice in tax collection. Johnson would also have seen the irony that Littleton, Yardley, Andrews, and Charlton's indignation at being called "asses and villians" was as much the spark of change as anything that happened that day. Had they not been so offended as to write a petition for redress and vindication, events may not have escalated to bring the governor to their door. Indeed, Thomas Johnson may have chided himself for his loss of composure, but by summer's end, it was clear that the event in Hack's old fields had fractured the old order and opened local government to the people.

Author's note: See Appendix III, **Edmund Mathews: Odd Notations in the Record**, for a brief look at Clerk Mathews's annotations pertaining to papers that were submitted to him about the Husbands/Chiles event.

NOTES, Chapter 18:

1. Pory, John, *Letter of John Pory, 1619*, Wisconsin Historical Society, American Journeys Collection, (www.americanjourneys.org), 2003, p. 283; also found in Tyler, Lyon Gardiner, ed., *Narratives of Early Virginia 1606 - 1625*, Scribner's Sons, 1907, pp. 283 - 284.
2. Leonard W. Johnson, in *Ebb and Flow* (McClure Printing, Verona, Va., 1982, p. 31) erroneously identified Thomas Johnson of Hack's old fields fame as the son of Thomas Johnson, the county commissioner. The son of Commissioner Thomas Johnson was only three years old at the time of the event in Hack's old fields. Commissioner Thomas Johnson was indeed the man of this story.
3. Northampton County, Virginia, Court Records, *Orders, Deeds, Wills &c, Book No. 4, 1651-1654*, f. 188–p. 189.
4. Walczyk, Book IV, pp. 105 - 107.
5. Kukla, Jon, *Speakers and Clerks of the Virginia House of Burgesses 1643 - 1776*, Virginia State Library, Richmond, 1981, p. 51. For those who enjoy imagining where events took place, I suggest that—because Husbands sailed out of Hungars—he had been detained in the area of Walter Williams's ordinary, where the court met at Nuswattocks (now called Church Neck).
6. Northampton, No. 4, page 144–folio 144.
7. Northampton, No. 4, folio 162.
8. Northampton, No. 4, page 171; Walczyk, Book IV, p. 146.
9. Northampton County, Virginia, Book 4, folio 183. (The spelling has been modernized.)
10. Ibid.

11 H. R. McIlwaine, editor. *Journals of the House of Burgesses of Virginia, 1619-1658/59*, (Richmond, VA, Library of Virginia, 1915), 90. The name "Accomack" continued to be used almost ten years after the county was renamed "Northampton." It may be that Northampton's then major waterway (now called Cherrystone Inlet) was still called Accomack and that this road was what people referenced.

12 Some readers may question what the danger was that the petitioners had feared. A thorough reading of the records and the sequence of events point to the fear that they would have to pay for the lost ship (Chiles's ship).

13 Note that the joint court called this paper a "writing called protest." This is part of the reason why some writers have confused this paper with "The Northampton Protest." In the case of the Hack's old fields paper, the use of the word "protest" was probably descriptive, as the purpose of the paper was to lay out the citizens' complaints and grievances. However, the actual paper (which is lost) may have been titled "Protest" or "A Protest." Unless the lost paper is discovered, we can only guess.

14 The record is not clear here as to whether the name was William Johnson Taylor or William Johnson, tailor.

15 Northampton County, Virginia, Court Records, Orders, Deeds, Wills &c, Book No. 4, 1651-1654, page 179–folio 183.

16 Howard Mackey and Marlene Almas Hinkley Groves, Editors, *Northampton County, Virginia, Record Book, Orders, Deeds, Wills &c, Volume 5, 1654-1655* (Rockport, ME, Picton Press, 2000), 118 (hereinafter: Mackey, Vol. 5).

17 This appears to be the time when the court officially discontinued southern meetings at the Fishing Point. Meetings at Cherrystone Creek at this time may have been in Obedience Robins's ordinary which had been built on the south shore of Cherrystone Inlet.

18 Northampton County, Book 4, page 180–folio 181. Castle duties were taxes on cargo going in and out of the harbors. These taxes were used to support the creation and maintenance of forts, thus the name "castle duties."

19 Kukla, Jon, *Speakers and Clerks of the Virginia House of Burgesses 1643 - 1776*, Virginia State Library, Richmond, 1981, pp. 49 - 52.

Chapter 19

The Northampton Protest

In Chapter 18, brief mention was made of a paper that has been dubbed "The Northampton Protest." Writers most often describe this paper as the nation's first protest against "taxation without representation." The paper did indeed protest the fact that Northampton was being taxed for the years between 1647 and 1651. In those years, the county had not been summoned to the Grand Assembly and thus did not have a voice in formulating laws for those years. Therefore, a part of the paper certainly qualifies as a protest against taxation without representation; however, the paper itself was not a protest, certainly not in the sense of the bombastic paper that came out of the event at Hack's old fields the next year (1653).

To understand this paper of March 30, 1652, it is necessary to know that just five days before, Northampton County submitted a document to the colony leadership with the signatures of seventy-three Northampton men. This represented nearly one hundred percent of the county's freemen. The document was called "The Engagement," and it was being signed in all the counties of Virginia. With this document, the counties promised "to be true and faithful to the commonwealth of England as it is now established without king or house of lords."

It had all come about because the new Oliver Cromwell government in England—Parliament—had sent commissioners to Virginia to effect a transition from royal rule to parliamentary rule. Governor Berkeley peacefully stepped away from the governorship. The parliamentary commissioners sent instructions to all the counties, directing that they elect burgesses, appoint sheriffs and military officers, and send their choice of governor to the upcoming Grand Assembly. Apparently, the instructions to Northampton specified that forty-six pounds of tobacco per head were to be collected by the sheriff as taxes that were due to the colony.

The Northampton court promptly attended to the commissioners' instructions on March 30, 1652. William Waters was elected as the new sheriff. Obedience Robins, Anthony Hodgskins, Edmund Scarburgh, Ralph Barlowe, Thomas Johnson, and William Jones were elected as burgesses to attend the upcoming Grand Assembly.[1] The court renewed Edmund Mathews's clerkship. Military officers were appointed. Walter Williams's house at "Nuswattoxe" was approved as an ordinary (or victualing house) where the court would meet.

In addition to the elections of burgesses and sheriff, the county inhabitants chose a committee "to give information and instructions to the gentlemen elected burgesses for the present grand assembly." Apparently, the county had received instructions to form such a committee to ensure that the local burgesses would represent their community regarding matters favorable to the "peace and safety" of county inhabitants, as well as to remedy any wrongs occurring in the county. This committee procedure was followed for many years, including the next year at Hack's old fields.

All the court business on this day no doubt took place at Walter Williams's ordinary, which was on the north shore of Hungars Creek on today's Church Neck. The first Hungars Parish church was close by on the same neck. People would have arrived via boats at landings on Hungars Creek, as well as on landings at Little Nuswattoxe Creek (today's Church Creek). Ferries would have taken some folks who walked up from the necks south of Hungars. Those walking in from the north squeezed into the neck just above today's crossing at Bridgetown. Walter Williams and his neighbors, many who helped to prepare food and drink, had probably never seen a crowd as large as what gathered in the community on that day.

It was a remarkable event in Northampton's history. The local leadership—including Argoll Yardley, Obedience Robins, William Andrews, Edmund Scarburgh, Stephen Charlton, and Thomas Johnson—piloted the county through the demands of the new government. Thankfully, the demands were few as the parliamentary commission hoped to keep the colony on an even keel. Still, the concept of parliamentary rule was alien. This was a reset in leadership, a renewal of promises for ensuring that people felt safe in what they had accomplished and what they could hope to accomplish. With Parliament coming to power, people had feared that their land would be taken from them, but the parliamentary commission had promised this would not happen. On March 30, 1652, Northampton's leadership, powered by blind faith, carried out its duty with ordered skill.

We have one report that suggests this "blind faith" was not spontaneous nor stable and perhaps had to be nurtured in some people. The one report came in the form of a deposition from the sheriff's deputy, who had been at the home of Thomas Johnson in February to discuss the court docket for that month. In their conversation, Johnson said, "Who has power to keep court, for we have given the power out of our own hands; it is nullified and abrogated by declaring for the parliament."

These words reveal that Northampton had consented to join Parliament's government prior to February 19th. The actual date was no doubt February 16th, as this was the day the court had ordered all "masters and freemen" to meet at Walter Williams' ordinary.[2] The court wanted to ensure "a fair correspondency and right understanding" in the matter. The deposition about Johnson's concern reveals that the county court "declared for parliament."

It is not known why the deposition was recorded. Even if someone thought Johnson was anti-Parliament, the terms of surrender had indemnified anyone who spoke, acted, or wrote against Parliament from the beginning of the world to the day Virginia accepted the terms on March 12th.[3] Perhaps the deposition merely reflects a debate among the court members regarding whether or not the parliamentary commissioners would be true to their words. Just over a month later, the committee paper (now called "the Northampton Protest") would state that concern.

On March 30th, the inhabitants selected the committee to instruct the burgesses who would be traveling to James City to participate in the first Grand Assembly since Parliament took over. The committee included Stephen Charlton, William Whittington, Levyn Denwood, John Ellis, John Nuthall, and Stephen Horsey. This committee drew up a paper that addressed several concerns for the burgesses to address. The first concern was about taxes being levied on Northampton during that time when it did not have representation in the Grand Assembly. Additionally, the committee asked that magistrates be chosen annually. It asked that all suits, causes, and trials be heard and determined within the county.[4] The committee reported that Northampton inhabitants unanimously voted for Richard Bennett to be governor, if a free and general vote was to be taken.[5] And finally—in reference to the local court's decision to have the new sheriff collect the taxes and hold them in custody—the committee asked that the forty-six pounds of tobacco per head not be collected by the sheriff until after the Grand Assembly answered their question about taxation without representation.

The Grand Assembly met in April (1652). Nothing in the record indicates that Northampton's concerns were specifically addressed. More than likely, they were addressed collectively with reports from the other counties.[6] Bennett was elected as governor with William Claiborne to be the colony's secretary and second to the governor. Among the listed names for the new Virginia Council were Nathaniel Littleton and Argoll Yardley.

At this first meeting, the Assembly addressed its own structure for conducting business, but it did make a provision that somewhat spoke to the Northampton concerns about magistrates. The new provision was that all county court commissioners would be chosen by the House of Burgesses and if any just complaint was proven against a commissioner, that commissioner would be suspended at the next Assembly session.[7]

If the tax question was ever answered, the resolution does not show in the Assembly records. Surrey County paid twenty-two pounds per tithable in 1652.[8] Surrey's assessment was not necessarily the same as Northampton's, but if it were, Northampton's inhabitants may have felt a little less burdened.

The Husbands/Chiles conflict in Northampton followed closely on the concerns about being taxed without representation. If the Grand Assembly did not fully resolve Northampton's tax concerns before rumors began to swirl about lawsuits, imagine the discontent of the average Northampton inhabitant. Surely tempers flared. Additionally, their own leadership withheld information for a full year about the Husbands/Chiles debacle. It was a recipe for a protest paper to scorch some eyebrows and burn some bridges, but that would be the next paper, the one written at Hack's old fields.

Author's note: The intent of presenting the two writings—The Northampton Protest and The Hack's Old Fields Paper—out of chronological sequence was to clarify the distinct issues addressed by each.[9] Being that two of the Eastern Shore's most frequently referenced historians, Jennings Cropper Wise and Ralph Whitelaw, missed the presence and importance of the second paper, it seemed necessary to provide a means to illustrate each paper's distinction.

Northampton County had grown to thirty miles in length, and it was essentially operating with two sets of court commissioners. By March 31, 1655, the Grand Assembly would decree two courts in Northampton, the upper court and the lower court, each to be held on the same day. The dividing line between the upper court and the lower court would be the headwaters of Hungars Creek.[10]

As reflected in the last two chapters, disharmony had reared its head in Northampton. The seed of division had been planted. Over the next two decades, disharmony would intertwine with continued physical expansion into the northern territory, and the county would finally be divided in two.

NOTES, Chapter 19:

1 Barlowe did not attend the assembly; the other five did.
2 Northampton County, Virginia, Court Records, Orders, Deeds, Wills &c, Book No. 4, 1651-1654, folio 79. The court of February 11, 1651/52, ordered that all masters and freemen meet at Walter Williams on February 16th for the purpose of discussing the surrender to Parliament.
3 Hening, *Statutes I*, 366-368.
4 This seems to be the issue that concerned Thomas Johnson. The fear was that—if county government was discontinued—all suits, causes, and trials would take place elsewhere, perhaps somewhere over the bay.
5 The parliamentary commissioners had sent instructions to all the counties, directing that they elect burgesses, appoint sheriffs and military officers, and send their choice of governor to the upcoming Grand Assembly. No doubt, Northampton took care of all this business on that one day, March 30th.
6 The records do not show any repercussions against the men who wrote the paper called "The Northampton Protest." Many authors have suggested that they were punished. Dr. Ames said they "were deprived of their right to hold public office or do any public work" (Susie M. Ames, *Studies of the Eastern Shore in the Seventeenth Century* (Richmond, VA: Dietz Press, 1940), 55). However, Dr. Ames confused this group of men with the ones

who wrote the next paper in preparation for the Assembly. That group was the one at Hack's old fields; they were the ones who were stripped of offices and fined.

7 Seven months later, the Assembly would revise this provision to include a recommendation from the county commissioners before appointment by the governor and council. Of note in that Assembly seven months later (November 1652), a new parish was created in Northampton County. The new parish, Ocquhanocke, was defined as from "the south side of Ocquhanocke [Occohannock] Creeke in the county of Northampton and so upwards" (Hening, *Statutes I*, 369-376). The creation of a third parish was certainly a nod to the growth in Northampton and to the changing need for adequate representation.

8 Warren M. Billings. "Some Acts Not in Hening's 'Statutes': The Acts of Assembly, April 1652, November 1652, And July 1653." *The Virginia Magazine of History and Biography* 83, no. 1 (1975): 74. http://www.jstor.org/stable/4247925.

9 The Hack's Old Fields Paper is capitalized here, finally, to draw attention to it being an important paper, as important as what has come to be called The Northampton Protest.

10 Hening, *Statutes I*, 409. At the time of this decision, Northampton had two men serving on the colony's council, Argoll Yardley and Obedience Robins. The three burgesses at this time were Peter Walker, William Waters, and Thomas Johnson. The decree specified "that the commissioners of the respective divisions shall attend the courts held therein.." A brief look at the records shows that two courts were meeting, one at Occohannock and the other at an unspecified location; it appears a meeting at Hungars occurred from time to time. Lieutenant Colonel William Andrews often presided at each court in these first months after the splitting of the court.

Chapter 20

Elizabeth Charlton, and Edmund Scarburgh's Finest Speech

While Elizabeth Charlton's story has been told many times, the story's intriguing layers compel a retelling. In *Virginia's Eastern Shore*, Whitelaw provided a thorough account of the story when he discussed the history of The Glebe, the land on Church Neck that provided a home and financial support to the Upper Parish minister. Whitelaw noted that the story "includes the best of the preserved writings of Colonel Edmund Scarburgh which is definitely to be considered on the credit side of the ledger in any evaluation of his complex personality."[1] In my opinion, that statement is spot on, but it tends to render Scarburgh as the central figure.

In this chapter, we will peel back a few of the story's layers, to gain a clearer picture of Elizabeth Charlton. She is usually portrayed as a sideline in order to reveal her father's generosity, Edmund Scarburgh's brilliance, or her husband's knavery. In this retelling, you will see how easy it is to sideline Elizabeth, but—be assured— this story's central character is Elizabeth.

To tell Elizabeth's story, it is helpful to know something of the world into which she was born. The year was 1649.[2] The day was about the first of February. Winter was peaking in Northampton on the colony's eastern shore. Although no one in the colony yet knew it, the new Oliver Cromwell government in England had just executed the king, Charles I. This event would have a profound effect on Elizabeth's father, Stephen Charlton, a local court commissioner and a wealthy merchant. All manner of government and politics were of importance to him.

Elizabeth's mother, Bridgett, née Pott, had earned a reputation in the colony as a resourceful, formidable woman. She had accompanied her uncle Francis Pott to the colony in the late 1630s, along with her brother, John.[3] Her older uncle, Dr. John Pott, now deceased, had been the colony's physician and had served a stint as a substitute governor. Bridgett's reputation for assertion and energy was earned during the time of her marriage to John Severne, a chirurgeon.[4] (That story is told in Chapter 15, "A Petticoat War.")

It is feasible that John and Bridgett Severne lived somewhere over the bay—perhaps Elizabeth City or James City—before coming to the Eastern Shore where they leased 150 acres at Old Plantation Creek. Their first appearance in the records was in 1638 when John Severne attended to two financial accounts and Bridgett endured the barbs of Alice Traveller. Alice had been telling people that Bridgett was known as a thief before she came to Accomack. The court ordered Alice to ask Bridgett's forgiveness in court and also in front of the congregation at the next church service.

John and Bridgett Severne had three children together. John was born around 1634; Mary may have been born either a year before or after John. Peter was born around 1636. Mary died sometime before her father died in 1644.

By the time John Severne, Sr., died, the family had moved to the northwest side of Hungars Creek at the property known today as Winona. John Sr. had certified for 300 acres in 1640 but had not yet exchanged the certificate for a patent when he died. Soon after her husband's death, Bridgett had the land certificate reissued to her in right of her son John. In the next month, the local clerk assigned 500 acres to Bridgett to be held until John came of age. The following July, in 1645, John claimed the patent as his own even though he was only about eleven years old; this early transfer was probably a precaution prior to his mother's upcoming marriage.[5]

By September of 1645, Bridgett had married her neighbor, the widower Stephen Charlton. He was about forty-three years old; she was about thirty. Stephen and his former wife, Elizabeth, had built a house and mill just three years before. Stephen had no children, but with his marriage to Bridgett, he gained two stepsons; John was about eleven and Peter was about nine. In the next year, 1646, Bridgett gave birth to a daughter, Stephen's first child. They named her after Bridgett who was also, it is believed, named after her own mother.[6]

The Charltons' circle of friends was broad. Stephen's sister, Grace, made her home nearby with her seven-year-old son John Waltham and her second husband, Captain Richard Vaughan. Bridgett and her old foe, Alice, must have made amends because Alice was godmother to Bridgett's son Peter. (Peter was likely named after Alice's third husband, Peter Walker.) Stephen's position on the county court brought the family into contact with other court commissioners such as Nathaniel Littleton, William Andrews, Thomas Johnson, Edmund Scarburgh, Obedience Robins, William Jones, and Argoll Yardley. In fact, Bridgett was godmother to Yardley's son, Argoll. The Andrews family lived merely three miles away (as the crow flies). The Hungars/Nuswattocks church was about a forty-minute walk, and the ordinary was just a bit further.

Bridgett seems to have remained close to her brother, John Pott. John had worked for Bridgett's first husband, and he now worked for their uncle Francis Pott, helping to manage business and property. John had continued his residence in the lower shore area, probably at his uncle's plantation, Golden Quarter.

In 1649, Elizabeth Charlton was no doubt born at home (on the property now called The Glebe). Her mother lived through the birth, so Elizabeth's family consisted of both parents, a three-year-old sister, a thirteen-year-old half-brother, and a fifteen-year-old half-brother. Sister Bridget's constant companion at that time was a six- or seven-year-old enslaved girl named Sisley. Other servants were present in the household; in particular, an African woman named Susanna, who had been given to Bridgett and her older son in 1642.[7]

Elizabeth was about three years old when her mother died, sometime between May 1652 and February 1653.[8] The circumstances of Bridgett's death are not known.

Perhaps his wife's death and the four children overwhelmed Stephen. In February after Bridgett's death, he complained to the court about his stepson John's disrespect toward him. Severne was now nineteen years old and apparently wanted to manage his own money. The court told Stephen to continue guardianship until Severne was twenty-one, but that Severne could rent out his own cows and keep the benefit. Stephen was to maintain twenty cows to turn over to Severne when he reached twenty-one years, and at that time, Severne could have his property. With some leeway for income, Severne likely bunked elsewhere, giving wide berth to his stepfather.

Three months later, in late May of 1653, Stephen made arrangements to place his stepson Peter into the care of William Westerhouse, who lived in the John Major house about a mile south of Stephen. Westerhouse, a chirurgeon, apparently had training or experience in treating "convulsive fits," a condition with which Peter suffered. Stephen noted that Peter had "found great help and ease of his infirmity" under Westerhouse's treatment.[9]

With the boys out from underfoot and only the girls (four years and seven years) at home, Stephen courted another widow. In November of 1653, he married Ann West, widow of Anthony West.

Ann Charlton may have had her charms, but they are scarce in the records. One of the first glimpses shows her rushing out to intercept a neighbor in her field. With a big stick in hand, she shouts, "What is your business here?" She proceeds to strike the man half a dozen times as she calls him "knave" and "rogue," two of the most offensive insults of the day. Further into the future, she would be sued for improper treatment of a servant. In that case, a witness reported that Mrs. Charlton had found a dead turkey in the hen house and, not knowing how long it had been dead, told her cook to make broth from it for a servant who was ill. The cook asked if it should be roasted, and Mrs. Charlton replied, "No, I do not intend to eat any of it." When the ill servant took a spoonful of the broth, he set it down. "It's fitter for dogs than Christians," he said. Later, when a friend propped the servant up as the bed was being changed, Mrs. Charlton came in and proceeded to call the servant a "hypocrite" and "dissembling rogue." When the man's friend challenged her to be kind, Mrs. Charlton charged across the room, plucked him by the hair, and said, "What do you have to do with it?" It was said that she made the ill servant sleep outside in the husks. He died soon thereafter, and his friend sued Mrs. Charlton for neglect. True to form, she countersued, claiming to be the victim. The court determined that the servant probably died of natural causes, but it did not let her off the hook. The court required her to pay court costs and to put up bond, ensuring that she would never again behave so carelessly.

When Stephen Charlton died in late 1654, the court immediately made arrangements for Peter Severne's welfare. He was taken into the custody of William Andrews, John Stringer, and William Jones. Mrs. Charlton was told to deliver Peter's bed, his clothes, and other "necessaries" to Mr. Andrews's home. Stephen's provisions to Peter were separated from the estate. The court had no need to concern itself with provisions for John Severne, as Stephen left him nothing.

When their father died, Elizabeth was six years old, and Bridget was nine. According to the orphans' accounts, trustees oversaw the girls' estates. It appears that Elizabeth lived with Mrs. Cornelius near today's Sparrow Point, and Bridget lived with Captain Whittington on today's Wilsonia neck.

Sometime within the next six years, Bridget met Isaac Foxcroft, a young man about six years older than she was. When he was about twenty-one and she was about fifteen, Bridget and Isaac married. Twelve-year-old Elizabeth returned to schooling at William Jones's home after the wedding. Jones served as a court commissioner and lived in the area of today's property near Machipongo called Sylvan Scene.

We have arrived at the crossroads where the story could have continued down a familiar path. That path would have seen Elizabeth finishing a few years of education and then marrying a suitable man of the community. Elizabeth did not take that path. She took a turn no one expected.

In late August or early September 1661, just four months after her sister's wedding, Elizabeth Charlton left William Jones's house in the company of her half-brother John Severne. Some writers have suggested that Elizabeth was kidnapped, implying that what happened was against her will. (In today's world, her age would certainly make that true, regardless of whether or not she left willingly.) Jones reported to his court colleagues that Severne had "delusively carried away and detained Elizabeth." Word was sent to Severne to appear before the court on September 4th to answer for his behavior. The court date arrived, yet Severne did not appear. The court found Severne in contempt and ordered that he return Elizabeth to Mr. Jones and appear at the next court.[10]

Severne was now twenty-seven years old. His first wife, Elizabeth Chapman, had died. Her death had been the subject of a court inquiry that revealed Severne's "harsh treatment" of her and the despair she expressed to neighbor Susanna Eyre.[11] The court inquiry was inconclusive as to the cause of Elizabeth's death. Severne's second wife was Damaris Gething; their baby girl, Jane, had been born in the month after Bridget and Isaac's wedding.

Damaris's parents, Mathew and Elinor Gething, had been implicated in the frightening discord of Severne's marriage to

Elizabeth Chapman. Elizabeth had said the Gethings were the chief cause of her marriage problems. Now they—including Damaris's brother, John Gething—were Severne's in-laws. After leaving William Jones's house with his half-sister, it is likely that Severne took Elizabeth to the Gethings' house, seventeen miles south of where Jones lived. The Gethings' house was just east of the Devil's Ditch.

John Severne did finally arrive at court before the end of the day that September 4th. It happened to be a special court, with Northampton hosting members of the colony's council. Thomas Swann, Nathaniel Bacon, Manwaring Hamond, Miles Cary, Edward Griffith, John Stringer, William Jones, John Tilney, William Waters, William Andrews, Randall Revell, and William Spencer were seated at the court that day. Severne stood before this daunting group and proposed that his sister Elizabeth be allowed to marry his brother-in-law, John Gething. Perhaps Severne thought his role as older brother would hold sway, but the court said no. It told Severne to return Elizabeth to her guardian, forthwith.

Nearly two months passed, and Elizabeth still had not been returned to Jones's house. On October 29, 1661, John Gething came to court to ask that he be given the estate "belonging to him" by the will of his wife's deceased father, Stephen Charlton. That the court was taken aback by this information might be an understatement.

It would later be revealed that the marriage took place over the bay. Big brother John no doubt provided permission and security. After hearing the petition, the court essentially sanctioned the union in its notation that Gething had "intermarried with Elizabeth ye Daughter of Capt Stephen Charlton."

In their world, marriage at the age of twelve was not unknown. In fact, just three years before Bridget's marriage, Sarah Douglas, daughter of court commissioner Edward Douglas, married at the age of twelve. Her eighteen-year-old husband, Edward Littleton, hailed from the Eastern Shore's most prominent family, that of Nathaniel and Ann Southey Littleton. Sarah died in childbirth a year after her marriage. Her death shook the community, but for a starry-eyed girl whose sister had just married, Sarah's death may have mutated into a convoluted tapestry of martyred romance. It would have heightened the danger, and thus the attraction. I believe Elizabeth Charlton was fully involved in these steps of her life; however, I believe also that her immaturity and vulnerability were fully exploited by adults who were thinking only of themselves.

This was a dramatic turn of events. As it happened, earlier in the day, the court had granted Isaac Foxcroft's petition for Bridget's inheritance. Now they were faced with the same request by Gething for Elizabeth's inheritance, the difference being that Elizabeth was two years younger than the age of inheritance specified by her father. Yet, she was now married. Given the circumstances, these men of law applied the law to the best of their ability, but with a cautious, self-serving caveat. To hold themselves harmless, they ordered Gething to put up a sufficient bond of security until Elizabeth attained lawful age.[12]

It will be helpful to look briefly at the provisions Stephen Charlton made for his two girls. First, before his last will and testament, while he was still living, Charlton gave deeds of gifts to his girls. To Bridget, he gave a mare colt and increase, three cows and their increase, and the enslaved girl named Sisley. To

Elizabeth, he gave a mare, three milk cows, six breeding cows, and all their increase. Then when he died, Charlton's will gave each girl one-third of his estate that remained after debts and legacies were paid, to be received when each girl reached the age of fourteen years. His wife, Ann, would receive the other third. Ann had life rights to the dwelling and mill, and the land and appurtenances supporting them. Bridget could live in the dwelling at the age of fourteen and she would then pick up the maintenance for repairs. When Ann died, the dwelling, mill, etc., would go to Bridget.

When Gethings asked the court for Elizabeth's estate, she was not yet fourteen, so she was entitled only to the deed of gift at that time. She could not qualify for the rest until she was fourteen years old. Bridget was beyond her fourteen years, and she was married; therefore, she could qualify for both the deed of gift and her willed legacy.

An accounting of the girls' estates for the past three years was written into the court record on October 29, 1661, and later in the day, John Gething's security was certified by five people other than himself. The five men supporting him were John Severne, Mathew Gething, Christopher Dixon, Robert Warner, and Lieutenant Colonel William Kendall. Once the bond was in place, Elizabeth's guardian would have had two days to deliver the estate to John Gething.

As we watch this story unfold, we never hear the voice of Elizabeth. We will never know if she found happiness in her new life. Did she miss her sister? Did she and Bridget ever see one another again? Was her mother-in-law kind to her? Did Damaris act "the big sister"? Was baby Jane a source of joy? Was John an attentive husband?

Hope is a word for the future, but in some cases, we hope into the past. We hope with all our might that Elizabeth found happiness.

On December 17, 1661, the bond was entered in the amount of 100,000 pounds of tobacco and cask. The six men signed. The bond was to be in effect until Elizabeth attained the lawful age of fourteen years when she would inherit in her own right.

Why would William Kendall, a court commissioner and rising star in colony politics, support Gething's claim to Elizabeth's property? The answer to that question is probably related to the fact that Kendall had married Susanna (Baker Eyre Pott) about two years before this event. Susanna had been a neighbor of the Gethings and may have held some sympathy for the situation.[13] Also, Kendall may have looked at the situation purely through legal, not moral, eyes. Gething had ignored the court's order, but no remedy existed for this transgression, particularly since Elizabeth was not protesting. She now had a husband, and she had an inheritance. The court followed inheritance laws, accounting for the difference in Elizabeth's age and the age specified in her father's will. The court, it appears, was attempting to normalize the situation.

Another possible factor is that young Elizabeth was with child. Such information would have been conveyed discreetly, perhaps by her mother-in-law, Elinor Gething, who was a known midwife. Such information would likely have engendered some sympathy and a desire to help the girl make the best of things. That is speculative but reasonable, based on how the story will unfold.

A full year after the court gave Elizabeth's inheritance to her husband, Gething came back to petition further regarding his wife's property. This time he asked for a letter of administration upon the personal estate of "his late deceased wife." Elizabeth had died after about nine months of marriage. No jury of inquest is on the books, so nothing is known of her death. Nine months is our most conspicuous clue.

On December 4, 1662, John Gething put up security for the letter of administration. Later in the court session, four women—Ann Dolby, Mary Paramore, Barberry Winbery, and Eliza Ratlife—testified that Elizabeth Gething was not yet fourteen years old when she died.[14] No explanation was given for the women's testimonies; however, their presence in the record reveals someone's effort to prove that Gething had no right to Elizabeth's estate. If Elizabeth had not yet reached lawful age when she died, this would mean, perhaps, that her estate was still within the realm of her father's intentions. The court that day included Captain William Jones, Mr. John Custis, Lieutenant Colonel William Kendall, Captain William Andrews, and Mr. William Spencer. The concept of lawful age apparently did not apply; the letter of administration was drawn up by William Jones the next day.

At the next court, December 28, 1662, Gething did not show. At court on December 30th, as the last item of business, the court ordered John Gething "to bring in an inventory of the estate of what he had or has in his custody belonging to his wife Elizabeth deceased." He was to bring the inventory to the next court. The Northampton court next met on January 28, 1662/63, and by the end of the meeting, Gething had not shown nor sent any word to the court. Three times he missed his deadline. This gave Colonel Edmund Scarburgh ample opportunity to prepare for what came next.

EDMUND SCARBURGH'S FINEST SPEECH

At the time of this event, Edmund Scarburgh was about forty-five years old and had been a member of court for seventeen years. He held the highest seat of seniority on this Northampton Court as his only superior to this position, Obedience Robins, had just died. Scarburgh had not been present for all of Gething's appearances, but he obviously stayed abreast of what was happening. As the meeting of January 28th drew toward adjournment, Scarburgh left his seat at the table and addressed his colleagues. Unusual for him, he read his speech from papers he held in hand. It is from this speech that we learn many particulars of the story. (Some spelling has been modernized. Punctuation and capitalization have been followed as closely as I was able to discern it. Spacing between paragraphs has been enhanced.)

> *Gentlemen: This case between Isaac Foxcroft on behalfe of Bridgitt Charlton & John Gething hath informed me to an unusuall intendment of writing what I speak that this may stand for affidavit to posterity who are most concerned and for whose sake I count myself chiefly obliged to vindicate truth & Justice, which must prevail or the world perish.*

In his first paragraph, Scarburgh relates that there is opposition to John Gething's petition to possess Elizabeth's property. From this, we can surmise that it was the Foxcrofts who contacted and arranged for the four women to testify about their remembrances of Elizabeth's birth and age. Scarburgh no doubt anticipated that this issue would be sent to the governor and council and thus committed his comments to paper so that they could be accurately recorded into the official record. (This also gave notice to his court colleagues that every word they were about to hear would be heard in James City.)

> *The Case in Question I take thus, Whether John Gethinge shall have the Estate he claimeth in right of Elizabeth Charlton, 2d Daughter to Stephen Charlton deceased or not, Or Whether Isaac Foxcroft in Right of Bridgitt Charlton oldest Daughter of the said Stephen Charlton hath any Right thereunto or not.*

Scarburgh identifies the issue as whether John Gething should have the estate or whether Isaac Foxcroft should have it. (Bridget was merely the conduit of wealth; she had none of her own as a married woman.)

> *The better to resolve this Question we are to consider by what pretended right the plaintiff in either case doth lay his claim which Requires of Review of Old Charlton & his disposures of that Estate for which he laboured long, to enjoy little and to complete that folly the wise man condemns in getting goods and cannot tell for whom: we see him now in his Care for his Children, contriving devising & securing estates for his 2 daughters.*

Because neither man has brought an action against the other, Scarburgh looks at the question as if either may one day sue. To begin, one must understand Stephen Charlton and how he settled his estate to take care of his two daughters.

> *That which concerns my present occasion is a Deed of gift to his Daughter Elizabeth dated the 27: October –54 In which I have noted careful Charlton gave his second Daughter Elizabeth land & chattels personal, The land*

in case of the said Elizabeth's decease in her Minority he wills to his eldest Daughter: The personal chattels he determined not, but is therein Mute. And the better to secure what was intended he appoints two Feoffees in trust until his said Daughter Elizabeth attained to fourteen years of age, who are to take care of and improve the Estate until the time designed by the Donor: Here we leave this Article until occasion reassumes the farther inquiry.

Now the more clearly to demonstrate this case we must track the progress of Charltons affairs, Charlton soon after this deed aforesaid dieth and made a will: The Contents and Issues whereof is so well known to this Court as needs not to be recited, only is to be noted he deviseth something more to his said Daughter Elizabeth.

Scarburgh narrows the focus to Charlton's deed of gift to his daughter, which included land and personal property. If Elizabeth died before she attained fourteen years, the land would go to her sister. Charlton appointed two trustees to maintain and improve Elizabeth's estate until she was fourteen. In his will, Charlton provided more for Elizabeth.

Scarburgh then leaves the issue of the deed of gift and the will to outline the pertinent events leading up to the question. He begins with the day Elizabeth was taken away from Jones's house.

Anno 1661

About the month of August John Severne by Clandestine means procures Elizabeth to go from Captain Jones house where she was in care for Education: and carries her to John Gethings, where a Marriage was endeavored with the said Elizabeth Charlton being a child about twelve years of age

September 4th

Upon complaint made, a special court condemns the said John Severne for stealing the said Elizabeth from School and engageth him to Return her thither and answer the abuse next Court; About the same time several endeavors were used to procure a License from the Honorable Governors substitute, that John Gething might be married with Elizabeth Charlton, which failing The said John Severn and John Gethings went out of the County & illegally procured a license by misinforming Colonel Yeo and so were married.[15]

November 29

John Gethings supplicates the Court of Northampton County to be possessed of the estate that he claimed in Right of Elizabeth his wife, wherein the Court proceeds with order for Security to save the Court harmless for delivering the Estate before the said Elizabeth was at age according to the will of her father Charlton

Anno 1662

About midsummer, Elizabeth Charlton dieth and soon after John Gethings obtaineth Letter of Administration upon the Estate of Elizabeth Charlton,

And now we are come to this present time where Foxcroft complains that he hath petitioned this Court for Justice and cannot be heard nor have his petition read, of which imputation to acquit myself and the Worshipful Commissioners and the due Administration of Justice we both hear recite the plea & proceed

Ah! So Foxcroft tried to be heard on the matter, but the court had shut him out. Based on my knowledge of what Scarburgh will say in the next few quotes, I deduce that the court saw Foxcroft as having no standing in this matter. The law allowed for a husband to claim his deceased wife's property, not her sister or brother-in-law. Scarburgh remedied the omission by reciting Foxcroft's plea so that it could be heard and considered.

> *Isaac Foxcroft in right of Bridgett Charlton his wife lays claim to all that Elizabeth had a possibility unto for that she died before she attained to fourteen years of age & does challenge Law for Just claim*

And though Foxcroft's petition tries to stay within the realm of law, what comes next reveals Scarburgh's analysis that the issue is much broader than the science of law.

> *And herein I am much to seek being a science I may not pretend unto, indeed it is a great study & much knowledge required, which I could never read any age determine without Contradiction: sometimes the Questions of right & wrong calls in for their support statute law: precedents: equity and when those lie not in a direct line to serve the occasion Analogy must come in, and where a Case is Cloudy or mysterious (and sometimes where it is most obvious) wit & interest are not vainly additional: But to shun Scylla & Pass by Charybdis I shall call all your aides for Conduct & desire you improve Reason the basis of all Law by which scale I shall measure the case & propose this Question*
>
> *If you would not think yourselves much injured that your own estates should not be at your own dispose: Doubtless the Question is resolved as soon as heard*

Scarburgh notes that he was not trained in law, and what law he had read was often inconsistent and unable to answer the question unless it fell in direct line with the law and precedents. To navigate between this rock and a hard place, Scarburgh asks his colleagues "to improve Reason the basis of all Law." He begins this task with a question that can have only one answer: If your own estates were not delivered as you had directed, would you not think it wrong?

> *Then why should not Charlton dispose his own according to his own will, If Charlton put an estate for his Daughter Elizabeth into the hands of Feoffees in trust, To be improved & delivered at fourteen years of age to the said Elizabeth will it seem reasonable to take this estate out of the hands of those entrusted by Charlton & deliver to John Gethings a person scarce thought on by old Charlton*
>
> *I am sure it is Reason the estate should proceed according to the will of the Donor what law there is against it I cannot tell*
>
> *Neither shall I presume to question the Judgment of this Worshipful Court but speak my own mind*
>
> *That I should not have altered any part of Charltons Will or deed of gift nor delivered Elizabeth Charlton much less John Gething that Estate which was laid up with Feoffees until Elizabeth attain 14 years of age, and I should have fortified this Resolve, from the Reason of the order Court of the 4th of September 1662 which condemned & questioned John Severn for suggesting the Match with John Gething, whereby I judge five of the Council and Burgesses together with the whole Court censured the intention of marriage as unfit, and how*

that fact which was in September condemned should in November following be approved by ordering the Estate to be delivered John Gething seems to me most preposterous: But Gentlemen your (by me) unquestionable Judgments have thought it fit, and that discretion which guided will undoubtedly guard the action

Scarburgh states that he would never have released Elizabeth's estate to anyone until Elizabeth was fourteen. That the court had refused the marriage as unfit in September of 1662 and then approved the marriage two months later by giving Elizabeth's property to Gething was absurd!

Nor did it seem necessary to me to grant J: Gething administration on his wives Estate for I take it to be A kindness giving him what he had before, By Reason what estate was his wives he was invested with in marriage, and what she had a possibility unto, and had not attained the end could not be his by Administration

They already had given what was his wife's estate to Gething, so it was unnecessary to grant him administration. However, what she had not yet received (because she had not attained fourteen years) could not be given to him.

Gentlemen give me leave farther to presume on your patience put the case Elizabeth Charlton had continued unmarried and died before she attained 14 years of age, who should then have had the Estate when the Donor is mute: I suppose none will say John Gething: I have said before I pretend not to the Law & Knowledge thereof, but I think it Reason it should return to the Donor or his heirs, which I take to be Charltons widow & oldest daughter not John Gething

It is interesting that Scarburgh injected Charlton's widow into this speech. Charlton's will had provided his wife, Ann, with a life interest in the home plantation, including the mill, the gardens, and the orchard. After Ann's death, it would all pass to Bridget. Had someone voiced the idea that Elizabeth's inheritance should return to the estate if she died underage, and that Ann should thus be the recipient? If so, it was not an idea that was further pursued. Perhaps Scarburgh had felt an obligation to mention this, as Ann was his own daughter's mother-in-law. (Matilda Scarburgh was married to Ann's son, John West.)

> *And now here comes another Material point into my thoughts: That the Marriage of John Gething with Elizabeth Charlton was after an Unlawful Manner: for these Reasons*
>
> *First, That the said Elizabeth Charlton was a child of about twelve years of age*
>
> *2ly, That she was stolen from Captain Jones' house where she was at School*
>
> *3ly, For that she was detained after five of the Council & burgesses and the whole Court of Accomack had ordered her return*
>
> *4ly, For that they were denied a license in the County where they dwelt*
>
> *5ly, For that they went over the bay & misinformed Colonel Yeo to procure A license*
>
> *6ly, For that the license was not procured according to Act of Assembly*

7ly, For that neither the Court entrusted by her father: nor her feoffees in trust nor the Keeper & interests of the child knew of or gave consent to the marriage

And it seems reasonable to me that no unlawful means can attain a Lawful end

Consider what I have said & take the consequence with you, wherein I appeal to physicians: knowing men & motherly women whether this early match with a Child of about twelve years of age might not Reasonably be supposed the occasion of her untimely death: let us look back to Sarah Douglas a Child of the same years who expired in haste because she was matched to soon

(Sarah Douglas: the twelve-year-old girl who had married Edward Littleton.)

There is none of you Gentlemen but have children your toil & care is for their future Support were learned Clerks & Council is wanting to devise your estates expressly to your nearest concerns would you not have the best construction made for the advantage of yours, would any of you think John Gething nearer to you (perhaps for accidentally killing your Child) then your surviving Child or Children, Do you think old Charlton intended that deed of gift to John Gething rather then his Daughter Bridget or widow: The Golden Rule prompts me to do as I would be done unto, and I doubt not but the same spirit is amongst you all

Consider you have Children and a wise man may be wanting to devise your last Wills, would you that a Stranger should enjoy your estates rather than your

> *Child, Before your eyes this day is the miscarriage of Elizabeth Charlton do you know whose turn is next*

[If this were a modern television serial, ominous music would be playing.]

> *Gentlemen you are zealous to do Justice do it in the Name of God think now your wives your Children & posterity Supplicate your tender care of this case, That he which labors may work in hope for him or his to reap the Harvest of all his toils*

He drives hard the question: Is this what you would want for yourself? If it could happen to old Charlton, it could happen to you.

> *Reason has dictated this discourse and many arguments to tedious to recite confirm me though express words are wanting that the best construction of the Donors intent is to be Received and thereby Bridgett the Daughter of Stephen Charlton and widow, not John Gething, ought to have the estate Elizabeth Charlton had possibility to enjoy had she lived to fourteen years of age*

> *That this is my judgment but still submitting to better reason, I fix my hand in open court this 28th January 1662. Edm: Scarburgh*[16]

Scarburgh had spoken for no less than fifteen minutes, probably twenty if he were prone to the dramatic pause. His fellow court commissioners had no doubt listened with ears tuned to how the governor and council would weigh these words. Scarburgh's obsequious deference to their judgment or better reasoning served only to make them look foolish. Faces had surely reddened and scowls had deepened throughout the monologue. As Scarburgh took quill in hand to sign his paper before handing it to Clerk Robert Hutchinson, one man's voice broke the silence. Which man among them had the strength of character and conviction to challenge the formidable words and manner of Edmund Scarburgh? Was that man William Waters? John Custis? William Kendall? William Jones? William Andrews (Jr.)? William Spencer? My guess is that William Jones spoke first, as he was the one who had written the letter of administration for Gething. Or maybe it was Kendall who had joined Gething to secure the original bond. Whoever spoke, his words prompted discussion. Afterward, Scarburgh added a notation to the record:

> *Upon debating the case above stated– The Court were pleased to declare their construction of former Orders concerning the Estate of Elizabeth Charlton alt Gething, And did resolve they never intended nor did at all dispose of any part of the Estate granted by deed of gift from Stephen Charlton to his Daughter Elizabeth, but are so farr from averring the same that have ordered the Feofee Sampson Robins to be brought by Summons to the next Court & their to give an account of the Estate & proceeds which was given to the said Elizabeth which for the County vindication & Repute of Justice is put on Record with the former*
>
> *by Edm: Scarburgh*

According to this paragraph, Scarburgh's colleagues defended their orders but said they never meant to transfer, and had not transferred, any part of what Charlton had given to Elizabeth in that deed of gift. However, it seems that no one was certain, so the court ordered Sampson Robins, the trustee, to attend the next court and give an account of Elizabeth's estate.

Scarburgh was not employed as an attorney when he made that speech, although he certainly supported the Foxcrofts' position. His authority came from his position on the court. His motive for speaking probably stemmed from his sense of justice and his incredulity regarding the actions of his fellow justices. Scarburgh seems never to have neglected an opportunity to castigate and embarrass colleagues whom he perceived as unwise.

If the court had allowed Foxcroft to address his grievance on behalf of Elizabeth's sister, Scarburgh may never have written this speech. However, it was one injustice too many. In all probability, Waters, Jones, Custis, Andrews, Kendall, and Spencer left court that afternoon of January 28, 1662/63, feeling a mix of astonishment, dismay, shame, anger, and indignation. Thoughts would have been racing to find words of justification for their decisions and words to diminish Scarburgh's damning speech.

Did anyone go home that night and think of Elizabeth and the life she might have had if the adults in her life had offered better judgment and care? Could this have been prevented? Did anyone resolve never to let this happen again?

No court meeting was recorded for February, but soon thereafter, the court met on March 3rd, 1662/63. Perhaps John Gething's supporters spurred him to answer the court's order because on this day, he submitted a listing of twenty cattle by type and age, two ewes, four mares, and an unnamed African man. That was it. Nothing more. Not even a mention of Elizabeth's name. Later that day, Bridget Foxcroft registered her own mark for sheep, cattle, and horses.[17]

On March 28, 1663, the General Court at James City condemned John Gething to make satisfaction to Isaac Foxcroft for the estate belonging to Elizabeth Charlton.[18] The court did not call her Elizabeth Gething, the implication being that the court did not recognize the marriage.

Twelve days later, on April 9th, 1663, Isaac Foxcroft of Nuswattocks declared that John Gething of Maggotty Bay had made full satisfaction for the estate belonging to Elizabeth Charlton. Foxcroft released Gething of any obligation "from the beginning of the world until the day of the date hereof."[19]

That next fall, Governor Berkeley appointed Isaac Foxcroft to the Northampton court, but the local court did not swear him in. The following January, Berkeley wrote to William Waters, commanding that Foxcroft be sworn in forthwith. The court's dithering on this appointment suggests a wariness regarding Foxcroft; or perhaps it was a blatant message.[20] Nine months later, on October 28, 1664, a full year after Berkeley's appointment, the local court finally swore Foxcroft in as a court commissioner. He took his seat that day among John Stringer, William Waters, John Custis II, William Andrews (son of William), William Kendall, and John Michael.

Something else on the docket that day leaves one wondering if some maneuvering behind the scenes took place. Before he was sworn in, Foxcroft failed to enter a bill of complaint against John Gething on an account. John Severne, representing Gething, was granted a nonsuit with Foxcroft paying the charges. Three months later, Foxcroft had entered an action against Gething but asked for a stay because Gething was not able to appear.[21] After that, John Gething was never heard of again.

Those are the facts as I know them. Elizabeth Charlton lived but thirteen years. At her death, she was at least a half year short of the age of majority as defined by her father's will.

After hearing this story, people often ask if Bridget received her sister's legacy. The question is revealing because it shows how muddled the material wealth of women could be in those early years. Bridget was the avenue through which her father's wealth was passed into the future, but as long as she was married, she never had control of anything that belonged to her.[22] When the General Court had ruled that John Gething was to release Elizabeth's estate that he held, it directed him to give the property to Bridget's husband. From that time forward, what had belonged to Elizabeth and what she was to inherit upon the age of fourteen became the property of her sister, or rather, her sister's husband. For all intents and purposes, Isaac Foxcroft owned the Charlton girls' legacies for the rest of his life.

Isaac Foxcroft died in 1702. He and Bridget had been married forty years and they had no children. Isaac's last will and testament left everything to his wife. As a fifty-seven-year-old widow, Bridget was now her own woman, and as such, she had a score to settle.

NOTES, Chapter 20:

1   Whitelaw, 425–430.
2   The year was 1648/49. I have used the new style year for clarity.
3   The assumption that Bridgett and John came with their uncle to Virginia is based on Francis Pott's headrights which included Bridgett Pott and John Pott Junior. That John was called a junior may mean that their other uncle, Dr. John Pott, was still living upon their arrival. It should be

noted that Bridgett's husband John Severne also used Bridgett and John as headrights, as did Thomas Savage the carpenter.

4 Chirurgeons were what today might be called "mid-level surgical providers." Severne has often been referenced as a doctor, but the early records show that his field was chirurgery. See Glossary for further information.

5 Nugent, *II*, 30-31.

6 While everyone else spelled the daughter's name with two ts, the daughter herself would spell her name without the extra *t*, as evidenced by her signature on her will. For this reason, I have spelled the daughter's name as "Bridget."

7 Six years into the future, John Severne would use the court to force his stepfather's next wife to release Susanna to him. After four years, Severne would sell Susanna to his Uncle Francis Pott. On Pott's death and his wife's remarriage, Susanna would become the property of William Kendall.

8 On May 12, 1652, Bridgett signed a deed with Stephen, giving Bridgett's godson, Argoll Yardley, a heifer. By the next February, Stephen was in court, attempting to give up guardianship of John Severne.

9 Northampton County, Virginia, Court Records, Orders, Deeds, Wills &c, Book No. 4, 1651-1654, folio 130–page 131. Reference to Westerhouse as a chirurgeon can be found in Book No. 5, in the April 1655 court minutes. His primary occupation was that of a shipowner/merchant. He came to Virginia from Holland.

10 Howard Mackey, *Northampton County Virginia Record Book: Orders, Deeds, Wills &c, Vol. 8, Court Cases, 1657–1664* (Rockport, ME, Picton Press, 2002), 181–182 (hereinafter: Mackey, Vol. 8).

11 Mackey, *Vol. 6, 7 & 8*, 161-162. The court inquiry took place in the summer of 1657.

12 Northampton County, Virginia, *Court Records, Orders, Book No. 7, 1657–1664*, p. 111. The bond was the court's insurance against anyone who might sue them for allowing Gething to have Elizabeth's estate prior to the legal age her father specified in his will. Bonds are often called "security" in the old records.

13 Susanna may not have held sympathy for the half-brother John Severne; she had been the one to report his former wife's pleas about his abuse toward her (Mackey, Vol. 6 and 7 - 8, 161–162; Mackey, Vol. 8, 10). The Gething family and Susanna must have maintained contact, as years later Damaris and John Severne's daughter (who was reared by her grandparents) would

marry one of Susanna's sons.

14 One of the women, Barberry Winbery (also spelled as Barbara Winbrow and Barbary Wingbrough), apparently was blessed with a flamboyant personality, one that landed her before the governor and council in 1657, accused of being a witch (McIlwaine, *Minutes*, 506). She was acquitted. However, five months later, the local minister, Francis Doughty, petitioned the Northampton court, saying that Barbara was "one of ill life and conversations and supposed guilty of Wichery" (Northampton County, Virginia, Court Records, *Orders, Book No. 7, 1657–1664*, 100). It seems Doughty was then new to the county, attempting perhaps to demonstrate his piousness through witch-recognition skills. The county did not buy it.

15 Probably Colonel Leonard Yeo of Back River, Elizabeth City (now Hampton).

16 Northampton County, Virginia, Court Records, *Orders, Book No. 7, 1657-1664*, fol. 156–p. 159.

17 Mackey, *Vol. 8*, 285. That Bridget registered her mark reveals her presence and her involvement in what was happening. Perhaps it was part of a strategy that she did this at this time to remind the court that she was an aggrieved party. Also, the mark would ensure that her stock would not be mistaken for her sister's stock.

18 Howard Mackey and Candy McMahan Perry, *Northampton County Virginia, Record Book: Deeds, Wills, &c: Volume 7: 1657–1666* (Rockport, ME: Picton Press, 2002), 290 (hereinafter: Mackey, *Vol. 7*). Note that no part of Elizabeth's estate went to her stepmother.

19 Mackey, *Vol. 8*, 233, 290-291.

20 Foxcroft's debts at this time would be an interesting study. It is known that he owed Colonel Richard Lee of the Northern Neck 38,446 pounds of tobacco and had to submit a payment schedule to Lee around the time of this trial. Whether or not his financial situation had any bearing on the court's reluctance to bring him in as a member is not known.

21 Mackey, *Vol. 8*, 359, 371. Northampton County, Virginia, Court Records, *Orders, Book No. 8, 1657-1664*, p. 199, p. 205.

22 The concept of "coverture" was still in practice; this concept essentially meant that women and their property were owned by their husbands. An unmarried woman did have control of her wealth unless the terms of her inheritance had specified a trustee or overseer.

Chapter 21

Bridget Charlton Foxcroft's Victory

While it has been the subject of several scholarly articles, the entire scope of Stephen Charlton's last will and testament (1654) has not been revealed.[1] The articles trace the sequence of events showing how Charlton's land, which contained his dwelling house, mill, outhouses, orchard, and gardens, became The Glebe of Hungars Parish or, in other words, church property. When fully told, the story includes Bridget's own last will and testament that appears to thwart her father's intentions. Her motive for doing this has been seen as perplexing; however, when the story is viewed from Bridget's perspective, her motive becomes clear.

To understand what happened, it will be helpful to review the salient point of Stephen Charlton's will. He had left the grounds of his house, mill, outhouses, orchard, and gardens for the use of Ann, his wife, for her lifetime.

After Ann's death, this property would revert to Bridget. If Bridget died having no heirs of her own, the house, mill, and all the land and appurtenances that went with them would go to the minister who preached to the inhabitants of "this parish."[2] When he wrote his will, Stephen's parish was the original Hungars Parish, sometimes called the Upper Parish, sometimes Nuswattocks Parish.

Our first glimpse of a conflict regarding this part of Charlton's will came on April 21, 1691. On this day, a vestry representative from the Lower Parish, John Robins, and a vestry representative from the Upper Parish, Thomas Harmanson, met with Virginia's governor and council. At this time, Bridget and Isaac Foxcroft had been married for thirty years. Isaac was about fifty-one years old and Bridget was about forty-six. Twenty-eight years had passed since the General Court at James City determined that Elizabeth Charlton's inheritance belonged to her sister, Bridget. Nothing suggests that the Foxcrofts were anything but a well-respected couple. Isaac, in particular, had served as a court commissioner, a churchwarden, sheriff, and as a military captain. Additionally, he had twice been popularly elected to represent Northampton as a burgess.

Robins and Harmanson met with the governor and council to ask that Northampton's two parishes be combined into one. The county, they said, was small and did not have enough tithables to support two parishes. The inhabitants had been unsuccessful in maintaining a minister in each parish, the representative said, and had not been able to build a decent church in the Upper Parish. Robins and Harmanson requested that this proposed, one parish be named "Hungars," as they wished to comply with any gift given to Hungars parish, "and more especially one by the last will of Stephen Charlton."

It is interesting that Robins and Harmanson would make this qualification at this time about naming the parish. What prudent mind had foreseen a problem with Charlton's will if the parish was dissolved? Or, was the qualification the result of heated debate that had taken place within Charlton's parish? I suggest that the topic had been discussed within the county for some time and that strong disagreement had ensued. Further, I suggest that Bridget was the lead voice in the disagreeing faction. As such, she would have championed the idea that combining the parishes would nullify her father's legacy to "this parish," because "this parish" would no longer exist. Probably, as far as she was concerned at the time, such a change would render her cousin, John Waltham, as the rightful heir to the property in question, if she died with no heirs of her own.

After hearing the request, the governor and council ordered that Northampton "be from hence-forth one parish and goe by the name of Hungars Parish, and that the same shall be noe prejudice to the gift of the aforesaid Charlton to the said parish of Hungars." They also ordered that the Northampton inhabitants meet to choose a vestry for this new parish.[3]

If the discussions within the community prior to this time had been hypothetical, they now became personal. For all intents and purposes, the highest-ranking men of the colony had nullified Bridget Foxcroft's beliefs about her own father's will, and perhaps, from her point of view, they had nullified Bridget Foxcroft.

On June 11, 1691, the Northampton court met for the purpose of electing a new vestry, but the inhabitants present complained that full notice had not been given "the county over." The date was reset, and on June 22nd, the attending county inhabitants elected the Hungars Parish Vestry. Isaac Foxcroft was one of the new parish's vestrymen, along with John Robins, John Stockely, Benjamin Nottingham, Thomas Eyre, Jacob Johnson, Pierce Davis, John Custis (III), Benjamin Stratton, John Powell, John Shepheard, and Michael Dickson.[4]

We have no knowledge of Bridget's experience with motherhood. Had she suffered miscarriages? Had she given birth only to see a child die before anyone had time to record a deed of gift? Did a longing for motherhood lace her emotions? How had it felt to think that this new vestry, including her husband, was just waiting for her to die so that they could move the minister in? It is easily imaginable that Bridget, at some point, turned to her husband and, through hot tears, said, "I'm not dead yet!"

Seven years later, Bridget's cousin, John Waltham, died. His death may have renewed her concerns about the property, as he was her father's named legatee if the church defaulted on their obligations. She may have longed for someone who could represent her interests as Scarburgh had done thirty-six years before when her sister's estate was about to be given away according to how the local court had interpreted the law. To Bridget, the issue then and now was the same: her father's will was being corrupted.

If indeed she wished for a Scarburgh-esque champion, her wish came true. A man named Andrew Hamilton became a close associate of the Foxcrofts by the year 1700. On October 20th of this year, Hamilton witnessed an indenture between Frances Drighouse and Isaac Foxcroft.[5] Foster C. Nix, in a fascinating article, *Andrew Hamilton's Early Years in the American Colonies,* gave justification for the idea that Hamilton may have lived with the Foxcrofts when he first came to Northampton County.[6]

Andrew Hamilton was about twenty-four years old in 1700. He hailed from Scotland, having come to Virginia with an avid interest and natural ability in the science of law. According to biographer Burton Alva Konkle, Hamilton had lived with Reverend Francis Mackemie in Accomack for several years prior to going to Northampton to teach the classics.[7] Many details about his life during this time are missing, but we can guess that he at least knew the Foxcrofts after 1700, based on his presence as a witness for the indenture. Within three years of his signature on that indenture, Hamilton had a very busy practice as an attorney.

When Isaac Foxcroft died in 1702 at the age of sixty-two, he left everything to his wife. Not only that, but he also named her as the sole executrix with no overseers. This means that Bridget was responsible for all the property and had the final say about everything. It is significant that Isaac did this; it demonstrates that he believed in her intellect. He wrote his will four years before he died, so this was not a deathbed decision.

Bridget lived in the house that had belonged to her father. Perhaps she and Isaac had lived there since the time of her stepmother's death, thought to have been in the late 1670s. Bridget lived just sixteen months longer than Isaac. In her will, written on January 13, 1703/04, Bridget left many things to many people. Most surprisingly, she left what she called "my divident of Land whereon I now live situate upon Nusswattox Creek" to her "beloved friend Andrew Hamilton.["]8]

Historian Ralph Whitelaw commented about Bridget's legacy to Hamilton, saying that it was not understandable how she could have attempted this disposition, as she surely knew the terms of her father's will.[9] That was probably the sentiment of the vestry when they heard the details of her will. That point of view was predictable, a factor that probably figured in to Bridget's reason for doing what she did.

Andrew Hamilton, in his lifetime, would prove to be a brilliant lawyer. After practicing in Northampton and Accomack, his career took him to Maryland and then to Philadelphia where he served in many public offices, including attorney general for Pennsylvania and judge for the vice-admiralty court. He is best known for winning an important 1735 case that defended freedom of the press.[10] In 1741, Benjamin Franklin wrote Hamilton's obituary in The Pennsylvania Gazette. In this eulogy, we find a character description that may apply to his part in Bridget's clash with the vestry.

> *He lived not without Enemies: For, as he was himself open and honest, he took pains to unmask the Hypocrite, and boldly censured the Knave, without regard to Station and Profession.... He was no Friend to Power, as he had observed an ill use had been frequently made of it in the Colonies; and therefore was seldom upon good Terms with Governors. This Prejudice, however, did not always determine his Conduct towards them; for where he saw they meant well, he was for supporting them honourably, and was indefatigable in endeavoring to remove the Prejudices of others....* [11]

If Bridget had wished for a champion, she received one in Andrew Hamilton. Not only did she leave her property to him, but she also made him the sole executor of her last will and testament. It is highly likely that this man—who would later warrant such an epitaph—had been an ally of the Foxcrofts. He had heard Bridget's point of view in the matter of her father's will and he had agreed. I believe he also knew and advised Bridget that little could be done to change the course of events; upon her death, the parish would receive the land to support the minister.

While Hamilton had not been present for the initial hubbub in the community a dozen or so years before, he had perhaps been acquainted with the Foxcrofts at the time of John Waltham's death in 1698. John Waltham was Bridget's cousin who had been named in her father's will to inherit the property upon the church's failure to meet the will's conditions. This cousin's death may have profoundly touched Bridget and renewed her wrath toward the vestry for their actions. When Andrew Hamilton signed as a witness to Frances Drighouse's indenture in 1700, Peter Waltham signed with him. Peter was a son of John Waltham.

Seven years earlier, in 1693, the Foxcrofts had given 1,300 acres of land in Accomack County to Peter upon certain conditions. The conditions were that he could not have the land until Isaac died or until Peter reached the age of twenty-one years. Also, he was to "continue and remain with my now wife Bridget Foxcroft or at her disposing until he accomplishes the said age," unless Bridget were to die before Peter attained twenty-one years. Four years later, in 1697, Isaac voided the deed, because Peter was not living up to his end. It was said that Peter was disobedient, obstinate, and willful. He would not obey Bridget.

The Foxcrofts' legal filing to void the gift must have had its desired effect. Four years later, Peter sold the land for £85 with the endorsement of Isaac and Bridget. Almost a year and a half later, Isaac died.

The story of Bridget's motive obviously has more layers than a Smith Island cake.[12] Bridget left personal property to twenty-two people. Andrew Hamilton was the only person to whom she left land. Had she done this in protest, knowing that it would stymie and gall the men of the vestry? Upon Bridget's death, Hamilton likely worked out of the house to settle her estate. The vestry would have been hobbled by this turn of events. All it could do, really, was wait to see what Hamilton would do.

On August 20, 1704, Andrew Hamilton bought 550 acres from John Andrews. He paid £300 sterling. The land was located on Hungars Creek where the Upshur family would later build the house called Vaucluse. A year and a half later, Hamilton married the widow Anne Preeson, daughter of Thomas and Susanna (Denwood) Browne.

Hamilton's presence as a man of law must have been imposing and formidable. At Northampton's court on March 1, 1705/06, Hamilton was able to accomplish a change in procedure that had been a long time coming. He complained in court about the neglect of the records. He blamed the clerk, but in the ensuing discussion the blame must have landed squarely on the senior court commissioners, specifically Colonel John Custis (III). The record books, it seems, had traditionally been kept by a court commissioner. On this day, Custis (who lived at today's Wilsonia Neck) declared that he would no longer keep the records. The court ordered the clerk to provide a convenient place to keep the records safe and to give them "due attendance." He was to have this done by the next court and to give people notice of where the office was kept.[13] It is believed that this is when the records became truly accessible for public use.

Bridget had chosen well. Leaving the land issue in the hands of a brilliant, tenacious lawyer may have given her great satisfaction to imagine that she might prevail in her belief that the vestry did not meet the terms of her father's will. Although victory would have to come from beyond the grave, she was content to know that Hamilton could make it happen.

Unsurprisingly, Hamilton gained a local reputation as "a man of bad character;" however, as Whitelaw said, that was merely an "unfounded local prejudice against him." Such prejudice was likely rooted in men such as John Custis, III, who had proved no match for Hamilton in the records debate.[14]

It appears that Hamilton never addressed the Charlton land issue. He later moved to Maryland and then to Philadelphia. It was not until about four years after his death in 1741 that the House of Burgesses made decisions about Charlton's land. At that time, an "incumbent" was noted to be on the 1,600 acres. The burgesses approved to sell the old glebe at Old Plantation Neck in order to support the new glebe and build a new glebe house.[15] By that time, forty-one years had passed since Bridget's death. It is difficult to be certain, but her actions truly may have foiled the vestry, at least for a few years. Perhaps that was not the coup she had hoped for, but it would have been a victory nonetheless.

NOTES, Chapter 21:

1   Susan Stitt. "The Will of Stephen Charlton and Hungars Parish Glebe." *The Virginia Magazine of History and Biography* 77, no. 3

(1969): 259–76. http://www.jstor.org/stable/4247484; Mason, George Carrington. "The Colonial Churches of the Eastern Shore of Virginia." *The William and Mary Quarterly* 20, no. 4 (1940): 449–74. https://doi.org/10.2307/1919927; Thos B. Robertson. "Hungars Church, Northampton County, Va." *The Virginia Magazine of History and Biography* 13, no. 3 (1906): 315–17. http://www.jstor.org/stable/4242750.

2   Northampton County, Virginia, Court Records, *Orders, Deeds, and Wills, Book No. 5, 1654-1655*, folio 56. Bridget was the older child, so she was the one designated to receive the dwelling, etc. If Elizabeth had lived, she would have been next in line, if Bridget died with no children.

3   This was likely a key point in the "opposition's" argument. If the two, old vestries were nullified by this decree, then were not the two, old parishes also nullified? And, would not nullification of the parish nullify Charlton's bequest to that nullified parish?

4   Northampton County, Virginia, Court Records, *Orders and Wills, Book No. 13, 1689-1698*, 117. The court's instructions to reset the date also included instructions about how to give "full notice." The notice was to be given "to the two lowermost Constables in the said county the one on the seaboard side and the other on the bay side forthwith to give notice to the inhabitants in their precincts of the said meeting and so to be delivered to the next Constables upwards to give notice accordingly unto the extent of this county." The June 22nd election took place at the courthouse, newly built by Joseph Godwin. This courthouse was near present-day Grove Court on Cherrydale Drive, outside of Eastville.

5   Northampton County, Virginia, Court Records, *Deeds & Wills, Book No. 12, 1692-1707*, 348.

6   Nix, Foster C. "Andrew Hamilton's Early Years in the American Colonies." *The William and Mary Quarterly* 21, no. 3 (1964): 393. https://doi.org/10.2307/1918453.

7   Konkle, Burton Alva, 1861-1944. *The Life of Andrew Hamilton, 1676-1741*. Philadelphia: National Publishing Company, 1941, 6.

8   Northampton County, Virginia, Order Book 14, (1698-1710), 188-189. Bridget's will was probated on March 28, 1704.

9   Whitelaw, 431.

10 Britannica, The Editors of Encyclopaedia. "Andrew Hamilton." Encyclopedia Britannica, 31 Jul. 2022, https://www.britannica.com/biography/Andrew-Hamilton. Accessed 18 February 2023. The famous case is known as the Zenger Trial, 1735.

11 Franklin, Benjamin, "Obituary of Andrew Hamilton, *The Pennsylvania Gazette*, August 6, 1741, https://founders.archives.gov/documents/Franklin/01-02-02-0079.

12 A Smith Island (Maryland) cake has eight layers.

13 Northampton County, Virginia, Court Records, *Order & Wills, Book No. 14, 1698-1710*, 279.

14 Whitelaw, 415. The quotation, "a man of bad character," comes from the diary of William Byrd of Westover, who visited John Custis III in 1709. At that time, Byrd met Hamilton and found him to be "very courteous."

15 Hening, *Statutes V*, 390.

Johann-Baptist Pflug (German, 1785–1866), Tavern Scene (cropped), 1827, courtesy of Wikimedia Commons, public domain.

This photo of the painting has been cropped to render the image more reminiscent of a small establishment, like the one where Nuswattocks community members may have gathered to discuss their plan. The only woman who signed the petition is, perhaps, a clue that meetings took place near Sparrow Point, on the north shore of Hungars Creek. Mary Cornelius was known to provide refreshment here at her house. Because the court met at nearby Walter Williams's ordinary, Mary's would have been a more practical meeting house for those planning to challenge the court. Mary may have been particularly upset with the court and vestry. Her husband, John, a popular, local merchant, had recently died. With the minister suspended, Mary would have had to bury him without a proper service. It was indeed a galling situation.

Chapter 22

The Nuswattocks Community of 1656

Six years before Edmund Scarburgh gave that well-reasoned speech about the disposition of Elizabeth Charlton's estate, he embroiled himself in a debacle with the parish minister. Scarburgh's behavior in this event was so odd and extreme that it has engendered doubts about his mental health during this time. If he had not followed with that marvelous speech six years later, one might think that his ability to reason had withered away.[1] Examining the mind of Edmund Scarburgh is always compelling; however, the focus here is not Scarburgh. The focus here is the "Nuswattocks" community of 1656.

The community and parish were often called by the name Hungars and also by the name Nuswattocks. This dual naming came about because the area's main road was Hungars Creek and the main neck was then known as Nuswattocks. (Today it is called Church Neck.) The Upper Parish church stood on this neck; its doors had been opened to worship for nine years at the time of this event.

Thomas Teackle held the position of parish minister in 1656. This twenty-seven-year-old, unmarried man had been ministering to the Upper Parish for no less than four years when thirty-eight-year-old Colonel Edmund Scarburgh began "passing speeches" (gossiping) about him. It was either late in 1655 or early in 1656 when Scarburgh told others that Teackle had engaged in fornication with Mrs. Scarburgh and that Teackle had attempted to poison him. This was not just private gossip; Scarburgh publicly made these claims. Apparently, the accusations prompted the vestry to dismiss Teackle from his official duties as minister. After several months in limbo, Teackle—sufficiently exasperated with the situation—petitioned the local court, asking that it "take the matter into serious Examination and give such reparations" as it found necessary.

On May 28, 1656, the court—consisting of Obedience Robins, Thomas Johnson, Samuel Goldsmythe, William Andrews, William Kendall, George Parker, and John Tilney—referred the case to the governor and council at James City; however, the court noted that Scarburgh had dropped the charge of fornication for reasons that had persuaded him (Scarburgh) "to alter and better his opinion concerning his wife."[2] He held to the accusation against Teackle, though, for attempted poisoning.

No record has survived to assure us that the James City officials took a look at this case, but after another month of waiting, the Nuswattocks community took matters into its own hands. Thirty-four men and one woman signed a petition supporting Mr. Teackle. They asked the local court to consider their cause: if Teackle has not "appeared guilty" of those crimes charged against him, return him to minister to the people. The petitioners noted that Teackle's behavior and conversation had been unblemished before Scarburgh's reproach. Teackle was under contract to minister to the people, and he was being kept from his work. If the court would do its work, then "God's public worship" could be continued, as the minister would no longer be "undeservedly suspended." With the minister returned to his place, the community would no longer be deprived of holy communion "to the great discord of god and to the most manifest discomfort and detriment of your petitioners."[3]

This was a distressed, aggrieved community. In their view, Scarburgh had spoken unsubstantiated words, and the vestry had acted on those words to suspend their minister. The minister, though, had essentially begged the court to charge him if he had committed a crime. The court passed the problem to the colony's General Court. Essentially, the community felt that a month was more than enough time to wait for the General Court to act. They wanted something done now.[4]

The community, in its petition, took a novel approach. Instead of complaining about Scarburgh or about Teackle, it shifted the blame directly to the local court commissioners. The court's inaction was depriving people of their God and of the sacrament. What transgression can be more serious than keeping God from his people?

It was brilliant. The words hit their mark, and the local court acquiesced. Citing Teackle's history of "civil and honest behavior," the court returned him to his ministry.[5]

Thirty-six Northampton, Upper Parish inhabitants had displayed considerable courage to oppose Edmund Scarburgh and to challenge the court commissioners. These thirty-six people deserve to be known. Their names are: *William Jones, John Custis, William Smart, Sampson Robins, Elias Hartree, Christopher Major, Thomas Selby, Michael Ricketts, John Greene, Walter Price, Henry Vause, John Willyams, Robert Burrell, Thomas Budd, Nathaniel Bradford, Thomas Marshall, John Pannell, John Hinman, Mary Cornelius, Thomas Harmanson, William Ward, William Gaskins, Phillip Mathews, Symon Foskue, Allexander Maddocks, John Johnson, William Westerhouse, James Barnaby, William Roberts, Thomas Benthall, Nicholas Granger, Richard Hudson, John Edwards, George Bourer, Cornelius Corneliuson, and John Smyth.*[6]

These men and one woman no doubt attended divine services at the church on Nuswattocks Neck. Some are easily identified as having lived in the neck, such as Smart (who married the widow of William Andrews), Sampson Robins, Elias Hartree, Mary Cornelius, William Ward, Thomas Selby, and William Westerhouse.[7] No contemporary court official signed this petition, because—the truth is—to do so would have been contrary to the oath of office. All officials were charged with the responsibility to treat each person equally. This is why no court commissioner could act as counsel to anyone within their jurisdiction. Maintaining a stance of neutrality was essential in the role of court commissioner. Justice was to be dispensed without prejudice.

While the local court officials may have tried to keep clear of any prejudice in the matter, it appears that they did not handle this situation very well. In the end, they dealt with the problem, which means it could have been resolved earlier, when Teackle insisted that they consider the matter. It is interesting that Scarburgh backed off the fornication charge when the issue became a court matter (rather than just a matter before the vestry). It reads as if his bluff was called—perhaps a thing that rarely happened—but rather than drop it all and lose face, he dropped what would have been most damaging to himself and his family.

William Jones's name was first in the list of signers to this petition, so it seems likely that he instigated the idea. Perhaps the one or several who signed behind him helped to craft the document. It was an inspired course of action, exemplifying how the collective wisdom of neighbors can solve the thorniest of problems, even one such as ol' Scarburgh at his worst.

NOTES, Chapter 22:

1. For those who may wonder where this story fits in with Scarburgh's relationship with Ann Toft, Toft first appeared in the records four years later, in 1660, at the age of seventeen. For those who do not know anything about Ann Toft, suffice it to say that she was a business partner of Scarburgh's for the rest of his life. Also, she is thought to have had three daughters with him, although he was still married to his wife, Mary. Ann Toft married Daniel Jenifer after Scarburgh's death in 1671.
2. Northampton County, Virginia, Court Records, *Orders, Book No. 5, 1654-1655*, 94.
3. Northampton County, Virginia, Court Records, *Orders, Book No. 5, 1654-1655*, 105.
4. In this year, the Parliamentary governor was Edward Digges, a one-year governor. It is possible that he and the council did not view this as a high priority, or that they were not organized well enough to act with expediency.
5. Mackey, *Vol. 5*, 198–199.
6. Mackey, *Vol. 5*, 198–199.
7. The John Custis who signed is the one who eventually built Arlington

Plantation on Virginia's Eastern Shore. In the year of this petition, he was a widower with a two-year-old son. Perhaps Custis resided with or near his sister, Ann Yardley, who married again in this year. She married John Wilcox, and they eventually lived on Nuswattocks Neck.

Chapter 23

Edmund Scarborough, the Father of Edmund Scarburgh

If anyone has written about the local family's change of spelling from Scarborough to Scarburgh, I have not read it. However, it is fairly apparent in the old records that the elder man of that name—the father—used the Scarborough spelling, and the younger man—the son—used the Scarburgh spelling. The change does not matter when speaking of the two men, as both spellings are pronounced the same. In this chapter, I will use the different spellings. The father is Scarborough. The son is Scarburgh.

In late February 1633/34, Captain Edmund Scarborough and Phillip Taylor made a deal while at John Major's house on Old Plantation Neck. In this deal, Scarborough sold half an ox and an old wild bull to Taylor. The price was 200 pounds of tobacco "in comodities this shippe" and 200 more pounds of tobacco at the next crop.[1] Sometime after the bargain was made, Scarborough changed his mind about the old bull and asked to be released from that part of the sale. Taylor objected and held Scarborough to the bargain. Further, Taylor instructed Scarborough to "cause the said bull to be put in to any boat with his chattels bound over the bay, that then the said Phillip Taylor would accept of him for his own and take him upon his own account so soon as the bull was shipped or put in to any boat." Based on what happened next, Taylor probably regretted his decision, or at least his choice of words.

On March 10th, with a fair easterly wind, Scarborough hired William Andrews's boat with John Wadlow at the helm. The old bull was led onto the boat with Scarborough's "cattell bound over the Bay." Not long after setting sail, a southwest wind came up and forced Wadlow and Scarborough to land the cattle, "otherwise they would have perrished." Before landing the bull, Scarborough and Wadlow went to Taylor's house to ask what to do with the bull. Taylor was not home, so Scarborough discussed the issue with Mrs. Taylor. After "long conferences," she sent two of her servants to unload the bull and brand it with her husband's earmark.[2]

Several weeks later, the court, with Scarborough presiding, heard Major and Wadlow's depositions, each being "an eye and an eare witness" to the bull event.[3] According to the testimonies, the facts were simple: Taylor bargained for the bull, the bull was put in a boat bound for over the bay, and Mrs. Taylor received and marked the bull.

The court record does not state why the depositions were heard. Had Taylor brought suit because the bull was not delivered over the bay? Had Scarborough sued for payment? Nothing more was heard on the matter.

All of these men lived at the Accomack Plantation.[4] Scarborough is believed to have lived on Old Plantation Neck;

his cattle pen would have been nearby on Kings Creek. Taylor lived on Accomack River (today's Cherrystone Inlet) at a part of the land today called Eyre Hall.

Captain Scarborough was a popular man; he had been elected as a burgess three times, and he was among the first court commissioners appointed for Accomack. His son, Edmund, was now about sixteen years old and had been working with his father for at least a year.[5]

When Phillip Taylor made that deal with Captain Scarborough, he was a planter, perhaps a trader, and certainly a young family man. A decade later, Taylor would be elected as a burgess and appointed to the court. He would also serve a term as sheriff, a most demanding position.

Some people hear this story as a depiction of an early business deal. Others hear it as insight into the personality of the father who reared the infamous Edmund Scarburgh. We will explore this second point of view with a theory.

In the stories about the false raid (Chapter 16) and Scarburgh's famous speech (Chapter 20), we saw how Edmund Scarburgh (the son) could turn a situation to his own advantage, often leaving his opponent dumbstruck, if not destroyed. It seems that Scarburgh had a knack for finding a weakness and weaving it into a scheme of retribution

In this story about the bull, Captain Scarborough asked Phillip Taylor to make a change in their deal; Scarborough wanted to keep the old bull. Taylor refused the request; he held Scarborough to the agreement. I suspect [remember: this is a theory] that Scarborough was offended that this young whippersnapper would be so bold as to refuse his request, as well as to instruct him how to make the delivery before payment. In his umbrage, Scarborough decided to show young

Taylor the meaning of holding to an agreement. Subsequently, Scarborough choreographed the delivery exactly to the terms of the deal. The bull was put on a boat with Scarborough's cattle bound over the bay; that fulfilled the contract. Nothing had been said about actually delivering the bull to a destination over the bay. When the weather turned—and whose call was that?—Scarborough went to Taylor's, probably fully aware that Taylor was not home. In "long conversations" with Mrs. Taylor, Scarborough no doubt steered her toward taking the bull and having its ear marked with Taylor's brand. It would be an understatement to say that Taylor was livid upon learning what happened. He had intended for that bull to be delivered over the bay. Now it was in his own pen and branded with his own mark.

We would not know about this event except that one of the two parties complained, or perhaps both complained. On the two days in April of 1634, when depositions were heard on the matter, Scarborough sat as the senior Accomack County court commissioner. Scarborough's employee, John Major, gave one deposition and the helmsman John Wadlow gave the other. After these two days, Scarborough never again joined his colleagues in court. It appears that he died soon after, and thus, the situation was not pursued further.

Was this deal with Phillip Taylor an example of business that young Scarburgh never forgot? As it happened, this was his father's last case. We will never know if it unfolded as laid out in this theory, but those who have studied Edmund Scarburgh will likely agree that perhaps this apple did not fall far from the tree.

HARSH, EARLY LESSONS

Writings that mention Edmund Scarburgh often portray him as a son of privilege who inherited land and position; however, the old records tell a different story. He did not at all have the standing of someone like Argoll Yardley who was listed for the Council of State when he was twenty-one. Edmund first earned his place as a burgess at the age of twenty-six. He would put in his time on juries—demonstrating his leadership as a foreman—before the governor appointed him to the local court at the age of twenty-eight, eleven years after his daddy died.

At the time of his father's death, Edmund did not inherit land, but he did inherit eight headrights, including his own. With these headrights, he acquired two two-hundred-acre tracts at the age of eighteen. Two-years later, young Edmund lost his prized Magatty Bay plantation to a London merchant for a debt he could not pay. It would take him seven years to finally get it back. In the meantime, it was reported that he said, essentially, "No man whatsoever shall live in quiet upon that plantation if I can by any means help it."

We pass through that plantation every time we travel the road just above the Chesapeake Bay Bridge-Tunnel's north toll booth. Scarburgh had owned that tract, including about 1,500 feet of virgin shoreline. It would have been a perfect port for shipping across to the mainland or for landing trade from anyone coming or going on the Chesapeake Bay.

Definitive provenance of Scarburgh's mercurial, enigmatic personality will always elude us. However, the records do certainly demonstrate that privilege and entitlement were not a part of his early life.

NOTES, Chapter 23:

1. "Commodities this ship" meant goods from a ship in port or about to be in port.
2. Earmark in this case is the mark put on the ear of a domesticated animal to signify its ownership.
3. Ames, *1632*, 12, 14.
4. Accomack was still a plantation at the time of the bargain and the delivery of the bull. Just four days after Scarborough delivered that bull, the Grand Assembly would name Accomack as one of Virginia's original counties (Hening, *Statutes I*, 224; Ames, *1632*, 17–18; McIlwaine, *Minutes*, 481). Scarborough is believed to have been a burgess in that session; if so, he made it "over the bay" (from the Eastern Shore to the mainland) after all.
5. Ames, *1632*, 12.

Chapter 24

The First Chesapeake Bay Retriever?

Peter Stafferton, an Elizabeth City resident, sued Henry Bagwell of Accomack for a debt greater than Bagwell had money to pay. The colony's court ruling in James City was against Bagwell, and the governor wrote a warrant allowing Bagwell's property to be seized and appraised for the debt in the amount of 2,357 pounds of tobacco. Under the eye of Obedience Robins, Accomack's acting commander, twelve men appraised Bagwell's property in the spring of 1634 and seized what equaled the value of the judgment. Bagwell essentially lost everything that day: twenty-three barrels of corn (valued at forty pounds of tobacco per barrel), two breeding sows (sixty pounds of tobacco each), three shoats and a pig (100 pounds of tobacco), the houses and grounds (valued at 400 pounds of tobacco), John Clay's indenture (700 pounds of tobacco), a water dog (100 pounds of tobacco), and a pestle and an axe (seventeen pounds of tobacco). Robins turned the property over to Stafferton, who then returned to his home over the bay.

Stafferton's servant, Andrew Bashawe, had just finished his indenture and decided to stay behind on the Eastern Shore. Before leaving, Stafferton promised to send Bashawe's clothes on the first boat back. Robins signed the surety on behalf of Stafferton for a suit of clothes, a pair of shoes, a pair of stockings, and a shirt; this represented Bashawe's "freedom dues."

The first boat came and left. Then another boat. And another. No clothes arrived. After two months, Bashawe sued Robins as the surety for Stafferton. That summer, the Accomack court ordered Robins to pay for the clothes within two weeks. Because no further complaints were heard on this issue, we know that Robins paid.[1] Peter Stafferton never again appeared in the local records.

Henry Bagwell, first Clerk of Court at Accomack, may have lost the houses and ground he had at the time, but five years later he would patent a neck on the east side of Old Plantation Creek. Shrewdly, he would claim Bashawe as one of his headrights.[2]

The fate of Bagwell's water dog is unknown. It is possible that a water dog in this instance was a type of fire dog. Fire dogs were andirons. A mulling fire dog, for example, was fashioned with a basket-shaped receptacle to hold cups or bowls. A water dog may have been an andiron made to hold a water receptacle. However, the value of this item in Bagwell's household equaled a quarter of the worth of his house and grounds. This high value is more in line with the worth of a prized, domestic animal. A trained dog would have been quite valuable. It is a satisfying thought that this water dog may have been a retriever, one of the first on the Chesapeake Bay.

Bernhard Schreuder, printmaker (1767-1780), after a drawing by Aert Schouman (1710-1792), Zittende hond, courtesy of Rijksmuseum, Amsterdam, public domain.

NOTES, Chapter 24:

1 Ames, *1632*, 16, 18. The order was given in July 1634. Robins's signature on the surety was like co-signing a loan. On Stafferton's default, Robins was responsible.
2 Nugent, *I*, 112.

Edwin Austin Abbey (American, 1852–1911), *Anne Hutchinson on Trial*, 1901, courtesy of Wikimedia Commons, public domain.

Anne Hutchinson's trial took place in Massachusetts in 1637, three years after Joane Windley addressed her local court in Virginia. Surely the setting was similar in that each was a lone woman addressing what seemed a passel of men. (By the way, men were not allowed to wear hats in Northampton's court.)

Chapter 25

Joane Windley, the Eastern Shore's First Attorney of Record

It might surprise a modern reader to learn that the first lawsuit in America's oldest surviving, continuous court records was initiated by a woman. Colonial women had few rights in comparison to colonial men, but as this case reveals, they had the right to hold someone to a contract. In 1632/33, on what was probably a cold January morning, Joane Windley addressed Accomack's court. She accused James Knott of "the misse usage" of her son, Pharoah, who was apprenticed to James for an unspecified vocation.

Joane was not trained in the law—she was not a lawyer—but as a representative of her son for a legal matter, she was an attorney. It is a distinction often missed in the old records; many people served as attorneys, but few had any training in the law.

The records are silent about the nature of the apprenticeship James had promised to Pharoah, but Joane was adamant that he had been mistreating her son. The court agreed and ordered James to correct the problem and pay the court charges. If this happened again, the court said, Pharaoh's indenture would be annulled and the boy would be returned to his mother.[1]

Pharaoh's parents were Joane and Richard Young. After Richard's death, Joane married David Windley. Although four years would pass before the Windleys applied for a patent, it appears that they were working a 100-acre farm off the south side of the branch that separated their land from that of John Howe. Edward Drew was their neighbor to the west.[2] Today this neighborhood is in the general area of Eyre Hall Neck.

Two months later, Accomack's James Knott leased a house with fifty acres in Elizabeth City. The house, "commonly called the great howse," was located at the lower side of the mouth of Southampton River (today's Hampton River in the area of Hampton VA Medical Center). Knott's plans were "to keepe a howse of entertainment," providing accommodations for strangers and others.[3] Such businesses were highly encouraged in the colony because new arrivals often had no place to live when they came ashore. Also, as the governor and council occasionally met in Elizabeth City, accommodations were at a premium on court days. It is not known if this was the business Pharoah was learning as an apprentice. The records do not say.

Six years later, in 1639, somewhere in Accomack, a man named Thomas Lee died and left his silversmithing tools to Joane. On his deathbed, Thomas dictated his will and signed with a mark. He left a blue blanket and a sow shoat to his godchild, Grace Shed. Everything else, including his crop, he left to Joane, wife of "Davy Winlye." Thomas's "grave makeing" cost twenty pounds of tobacco, and his shroud and coffin cost 100 pounds of tobacco each.

Thomas's inventory showed that he owned a box of tools, a silver forge, and "ode ends twenty eight shillinge starlinge," all worth twenty-eight shillings. His other silver items included a spoon, a bodkin, a tooth picker, and horns set in silver.[4]

Perhaps Thomas's hope had been that Joane would pass his tools and forge on to her son. Or, maybe Joane knew the art of how to make repairs using those odd ends of sterling silver shillings.

In 1642, Pharoah Young returned home, having survived his indentured childhood. Ten years had passed since his mother stood before the court to demand fair treatment for him. Upon his return, Pharoah found that his widowed mother, through her hard-scrabble life in a remote settlement, had kept his legacy safe. David Windley had died, but five years before, he had patented 100 acres at "Cherry Stones" in right of Joane. Upon Pharoah's return, Joane petitioned the local court to have this land certified in her son's name. In the next year, Pharoah would renew that patent for himself, bringing Joane's efforts full circle.[5]

Joane's story reflects those of countless women whose diligent work, care, and support were instrumental to the colonists' survival. The recorded details about early colonial women's lives are sparse, but those we find give us a glimpse of extraordinary strength and endurance.

NOTES, Chapter 25:

1 Ames, *1632*, 1. McCartney, *Immigrants*, 449.
2 Nugent, *I*, 77, 147.
3 Nugent, *I*, 18.

4   Ames, *1632*, 123–125, 134–135, 138, 143. Ames, *1640*, 184–185. Lee's will was dated September 11, 1638.

5   Ames, *1640*, 184–185. Nugent, *I*, 77, 147. Pharoah renewed the patent on August 31, 1643. In 1648, "Pharoh Younge of Hungars" would sell 100 acres in "Chirryston Creecke" to Christopher Jarvis. At that time, the bounds were noted to be Edward Drew's land to the south, Howes Branch to the north, Cherrystone Creek to the west, and Edward Drew to the east (Mackey, *Vol. 3*, 310). This would be on the northern point of Eyre Hall neck. (Joane was still living in 1648.)

Chapter 26

An English Trick

In February 1641/42, John Pannuell, a Northampton freeman, received a payment in tobacco from someone who owed him. The law required that all such exchanges take place in an official storehouse, under the supervision of the storehouse keeper. In the transaction, Pannuell received 800 pounds of tobacco in the form of a certificate representing tobacco that was actually stored in the storehouse. The storekeeper would have kept a ledger of who owned what.

"I wish I had six pence per pound clear for this tobacco," Pannuell mused. "Then I should think I had money enough."

A man standing nearby overheard Pannuell's comment. "How much will you take for your tobacco?" the man asked him.

"Seven pence," Pannuell replied.

The man reached into his pocket and pulled out some coins. "Let me see your hand," he said.

Pannuell hesitated, but then tentatively put out his hand.

"I'll have it at seven pence per pound," the man said. "Weigh and pay in London." He put twelve pence into Pannuell's hand.

(The buyer was Richard Lemon. This was his first appearance in the records. Later, he would marry Thomas Johnson's sister-in-law, Jane, but that was before Johnson became a burgess or a court commissioner.)

Did Pannuell immediately balk at the deal, or did it take him a while to figure out that Lemon had duped him? Pannuell's wish had surely been for the seven pence per pound right then and there. Now, as Lemon had framed the deal, Pannuell would have to ship the tobacco to London, be responsible for any damage, and receive only seven pence per pound for what tobacco was left as merchantable. Lemon would receive it at seven pence and resell it at twelve, having suffered no risk at all.

Pannuell did indeed balk. By the end of the next month, he was standing before the local court. Two men told what they had witnessed at the storehouse on the day of the exchange. The court, consisting of Nathaniel Littleton, Obedience Robins, William Stone, William Burdett, William Roper, John Neale, and Stephen Charlton, told Pannuell to honor the bargain. Not only that, but they told him to put up security for the deal if Lemon asked for it.[1]

The court's decision would have been based on the facts of the transaction, not on the emotion that spilled out. Still, each justice would have felt some of that emotion. Had Lemon been seen as shrewd, or as a swindler? Two months later, a case surfaced that may shed a bit of light on whether or not the court had been troubled by Lemon's behavior. It was a case that began in early May of 1642, in the home of John Stringer, the chirurgeon.

Stringer was hosting a small gathering of men, and he was preparing to tell a story about another man named John Stringer. The other John Stringer was a carpenter, and the story was about a "trick" the carpenter "had like to have served" Luke Stubbins, the merchant. Just as Stringer began to tell the story, Stubbins and William Roper arrived.

"We were but now talking of you," Stringer said to Stubbins.

"Of whom were you talking? Of your cousin cheat?" Stubbins asked.

"I was just about to tell that story to Richard Lemon," Stringer said, "because he has not heard it."

Stringer then told the men about how the carpenter tricked Stubbins. (Unfortunately, the records do not give the details.) What happened next is interesting because it seems to be a choreographed moment.

Roper turned to Lemon. "What would you advise in this matter?" Roper asked.

Roper was a court commissioner who had been present to hear Pannuell's lawsuit against Lemon. Had Roper seen a similarity in the carpenter's trick on Stubbins and Lemon's trick on Pannuell? Was he pointedly cornering Lemon to see the true mettle of the man? Would Lemon applaud the carpenter's trick, or would he see it as objectionable?

"The business was very foul in my opinion," Lemon replied.

Regardless of whether anyone was trying to make a point with Lemon, Stubbins was further irritated by all this talk. "He is an idle, cheating fellow," Stubbins said, speaking of the carpenter, "and he came on purpose to cheat me of my goods!" Stubbins ended his tirade with an adage: "Where there is but one rascal in a county, he will have many others take his part."

By the end of the month, Stringer (the carpenter) had heard about the words against him, and he sued Stubbins for defamation. The court (including Roper) heard from three witnesses. Lemon was one of two who seemed to remember everything; Stringer recalled that they were all at his house, but he had no memory of "any vilifying speeches." The court found for Stringer (the carpenter) and ordered Stubbins to pay him 300 pounds of tobacco at the next crop.[2] We can only imagine how maddened Stubbins was at this verdict, but he had learned his lesson. He said no more.

Two years later, the Dutch captain David Pietersz De Vries would note in his log that he did not like trading with the English. They had a penchant, he said, for trying to deceive and then patting themselves on the back if they were successful. De Vries warned that in trading with them, they would attempt to play one "an English trick."[3]

Of course, not all Englishmen were out to trick another person in a deal, but—then as now—everyone liked to feel that a deal was balanced. In the old records, most infractions that came before the court were those of money, physical harm, or moral turpitude. Every now and then, something odd came along that surely must have had people shaking their heads in disbelief. For example, on May 31, 1642, an unusual case was brought to the local court by Thomas Hunt. Hunt told the court that he had given Henry Weede a cow calf for which he expected only thanks, but Weede had failed to thank him. The court ordered Weede to return the cow calf to Hunt if he was not going to thank him for it. The records do not say if Weede ever muttered a thanks to Hunt. Either way, thanks or not, Weede's lapse of gratitude cost him the court fees.[4]

NOTES, Chapter 26:

1 Ames, *1640*, 139-140. While it seems that the court could have corrected what seems unfair, the court—in most instances—tried to apply law to the cases before them. In this case, Pannuel probably shook on the deal, only later realizing his error. A deal was a deal.

2 Ames, *1640*, 172-173. Northampton County, Virginia, *Orders, Book 2, 1640-1645*, 85. The two business deals, Lemon's and the carpenter's, seem to reflect increasing common knowledge about the law, and thus, a greater understanding about how it could be engineered to one's favor.

3 David Pietersz De Vries, Henry C. Murphy, translator, *Voyages From Holland to America, A.D. 1632 to 1644* (New York, 1857), 186-187.

4 Ames, *1640*, 171-172.

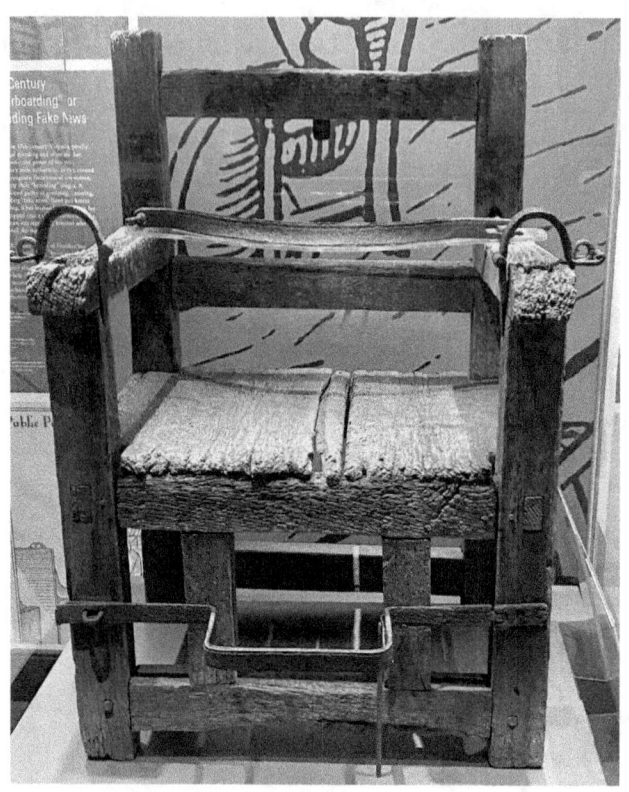

"Your chair awaits you, Madam."

This seventeenth century, English ducking chair is on display behind plexiglass at Jamestown Settlement, Williamsburg, Virginia. Notice the metal straps for arms and legs. Also, note the metal strap across the chest; this would be tightened with screws at the back.

(*Jamestown Settlement* is administered by the Jamestown-Yorktown Foundation, an agency of the Commonwealth of Virginia accredited by the American Alliance of Museums.) Author's photographs.

Chapter 27

Dunking Was Not Always About Doughnuts

The title of this chapter may give the impression that this is a lightweight essay. No mystery iron furnaces will be found here, nor any fake raids, nor kidnappings. What will be found here is an account of the Eastern Shore's compliance with an early form of prescribed punishment for women whose gossiping created havoc on men's reputations. This method of punishment was to dunk the women into water. The actual term for this was "ducking."

Ducking required a specially made apparatus that consisted of a chair on the end of a lever. A woman would be tied in the chair and lowered into the creek (or other body of water). She then would be held under the water for perhaps thirty seconds each dunk. The purpose was to break the woman, to have her beg for mercy and promise to sin no more.

We know this was a punishment designed especially for women because the Grand Assembly wrote a law in 1662 that leaves no room for doubt:

> *Whereas oftentimes many brabling* [squabbling, bickering] *women often slander and scandalize their neighbors for which theire poore husbands are often brought into chargeable and vexatious suites, and cast in greate damages; Bee it therefore enacted by the authority aforesaid that in actions of slander occasioned by the wife aforesaid after judgment passed for the damages the women shalbe punished by ducking; and if the slander be soe enormous as to be adjudged at a greater damage then five hundred pounds of tobacco, then the woman to suffer a ducking for each five hundred pounds of tobacco adjudged against the husband if he refuse to pay the tobacco.*[1]

That the law was written in 1662 does not mean that duckings were nonexistent before then or that they had been used in any other way than this law described. It means only that the Assembly picked up the issue at that time, along with other punishment laws. The first reported ducking on Virginia's Eastern Shore was as early as the fall of 1637. This did not mean that the settlers refrained from malicious gossip up to this time; in fact, the records are replete with scandalmongering from both men and women. In all probability, what this meant is that the behavior was viewed as especially egregious, and that it was directed at a man who had the means to sue. Before we look at this first ducking, it will be useful to see what types of punishments for women preceded it.

Corporal punishments were rare in the records until late 1634. Ellen Muce is on record as the first Eastern Shore woman to be publicly whipped. Joane Butler is the first woman sentenced to be towed or pulled through water behind a boat.

Ellen Muce was Phillip Taylor's servant. Someone told Taylor that a local laborer, John Little, while out working in the field, was boasting to the other men, saying "the Cooke was up, and the steale downe, reddy to give fyre."[2] When confronted, Little confessed and said that he had been drunk at the time. Taylor made a complaint to the local court "against John Little for abusing his house in going to bed to the mayd of the syd Taylors." For this transgression, the court sentenced Little to "lay neck and Hyels close for 3 howres."[3] For having been drunk, he was fined five shillings.

Then the court turned its attention to Ellen Muce. She accused Little of having "to doe with her in the act of fornication," but, she said, she did not approve. The record reflects no debate on this information; the court sentenced Ellen to be whipped.

On that same day in September 1634, Edward Drew petitioned the court against Joane Butler for calling his wife, Marie, "a common Carted hoare." Two witnesses, John Holloway and John Baseley, testified that Joane had indeed said those words. The court sentenced Joane Butler to be towed. It said that she was to "be drawen over" Kings Creek at the stern of a boat or canoe, from one cow pen to the other. However, she had a choice. Instead of being towed, she could present herself to the minister at the next Sunday service, between the first and second lesson. At that time, she could say the following words after the minister: "I Joane Butler doe acknowledge to have called Marie Drew hoare and thereby I confesse I have done her manefest wronge, wherfor I desire befor this congregation, that ye syd Marie Drew will forgive me, and alsoe that this congregation, will joyne, and praye with me, that God may forgive me."

Joane Butler's husband then came forward with his own petition against Marie Drew. Thomas Butler accused Marie of reporting him for having to do with Bridgett, the wife of John Wilkins, in an act of adultery. Apparently, Thomas had failed to think this through, not realizing that he was reporting himself for a crime rather than reporting Marie for gossip. A female witness came forward to say that Joane, Thomas's wife, had shown her where in the woods Thomas himself had said the adulterous act with Bridgett had taken place. Bridgett's husband, court commissioner John Wilkins, was not—perhaps thankfully—present in court that day. The court did not officially address Thomas's petition against Marie or the unexpected information about Thomas's infidelity. It went on to other business.

A week later, the court met again. Perhaps someone informed John Wilkins of the accusations involving his wife, as he was present in court on this day. However, Thomas Butler had learned his lesson; he said nothing about Bridgett Wilkins or his own misbehaviors. Instead, he lashed out at Marie Drew for calling his wife "carted hoare" and for saying she had seen Joane "carted in England."[4] Two witnesses, William Cozier and William Ward, confirmed that they heard Marie say those words. The court then ordered that Marie "shall aske the syd Thomas Butlers wife forgiveness in the Church on the next saboth day." The court specified the same conditions for Marie as they had for Joane, including the script for what to say. And then it said something very revealing about the character and personality of Joane Butler: "or else suffer the like punishment as the syd Joane Butler hath done."

Those words make plain that Joane, after being given a choice, had chosen to be towed rather than to ask Marie's forgiveness. The record gives us no hint about what choice Marie made, but it seems highly likely that she did whatever she thought would be most galling to the Butlers.

Three years later, the court heard another case of a cow pen ruckus. This is the one that would result in the Eastern Shore's first ducking—a double ducking at that.

It was again a fall meeting of the court, September 25th, 1637. John Wilkins's wife Bridgett had died, and he had remarried. His new wife, Anne, reported to the court what she knew about an event involving Anne Williamson, wife of Roger Williamson, and Anne Stephens, wife of Christopher Stephens. Mrs. Williamson and Mrs. Stephens had come to the cow pen where Anne Wilkins and Grace Waltham were already engaged in milking (or whatever other duties awaited women at the cow pen). According to Mrs. Wilkins, the other two Annes "did in a jeering manner abuse Grace Waltham saying that John Waltham husband of the said Grace hade his Mounthly Courses as Women have." Additionally, Mrs. Wilkins reported that Mrs. Stephens said that "John Waltham was not able to gett a child."

This was cruel business. The court called the women's behavior vile and scandalous, and ordered them to be "duckt." Additionally, they were to ask the Walthams' forgiveness "in the publique Congregation." No choices here.[5]

This was the first official ducking on record. Unfortunately, the court left no information about how the double ducking was choreographed. The court was then holding its meetings at

Town, not far from the church. Therefore, the duckings likely took place in Kings Creek. Perhaps the officials announced that the duckings would be after church on the day when the two women asked for forgiveness. No doubt, such an event guaranteed good attendance. Both sides of the creek would have been lined with witnesses.

Years later, a letter would surface, describing a ducking in Hungars Parish in 1634, three years before the first, official ducking. However, the date is probably wrong. Hungars Parish was not formed until 1643; therefore, the year is in doubt, but the description certainly reads as accurate. In the letter, Thomas Hartley, a traveler through the area, said the ducking took place at two o'clock in the afternoon. Minister Cotton was present, as well as a magistrate and a large number of people. Hartley described the parish ducking machine as a lever between two posts on a rolling platform. A stool, he said, was tied to the end of the lever. (The "stool" was more of an armed chair with or without legs.) The woman was tied into the stool, "her gown tied fast around her feet." (See Figure 27.) The contraption was rolled to the water's edge where the depth was deep enough to cover the woman when she

Figure 27 (from a Pearson Scott Foresman textbook. Public domain.)

was lowered into the water. Each duck lasted a half minute. Hartley indicated that the woman had remarkable stamina, as it took five ducks before she cried, "Let me go, Let me go, by God's help I'll sin no more." According to Hartley, she had been a vicious gossip.[6] [7]

While the Grand Assembly did not address ducking stools until 1662, Eastern Shore records show a long use of the apparatus. In 1656, a ducking stool was made to be placed at Occahannocke. In 1658, one was made to be placed at Ward's Point.[8]

Not long after the Grand Assembly's instructions in 1662, the new county of Accomack was formed from Northampton, and apparently, each of the counties needed new punishment devices. The Northampton court ordered Sheriff William Waters to employ workmen to build a pillory, a pair of stocks, a whipping post, and a ducking stool.[9] On July 16, 1663, the Accomack court consented to George Crump's offer to provide a ducking stool to the court if it would acquit his servant, Isabella Wall, from a court-ordered whipping. Later that same day, the court authorized Anthony Hodgkins—who owned the house where the court met—to employ workmen to build a pillory, stocks, and a whipping post.[10] With these orders, both counties would have their full array of choices for legal, corporal discipline. A month later, on August 17th, the Accomack court ordered its first ducking. Actually, it ordered three.

On a Sabbath day earlier that summer, Robert Brace, his servant Elizabeth Leveret, and a free woman named Alice Boutcher, all "lawlessly scolded, fought, and misdemeaned themselves on the Sabbath day." The court sentenced Elizabeth and Alice to be ducked. And, in a most unusual move, it sentenced Brace to be ducked along with Elizabeth and Alice. The court's reasoning for this unusual order was that Brace had "degenerated so much from a man" in being unable to control his house. Later that day, Brace begged the court to allow him to pay a fine instead of being ducked. The court agreed to the amount of 100 pounds of tobacco and court costs.[11]

Perhaps the appearance of that brand-new ducking stool had intrigued the court commissioners, or maybe it was that they were new, a little too inexperienced to understand the correct application of ducking. Ducking was supposed to be for gossip that was scandalizing, the kind of gossip that hurt a man's reputation. In the case of Brace, Leveret, and Boutcher, the court applied ducking for general, noisy misbehavior on the Sabbath.

Three months later, Alice Boutcher ranted and raved to Jane Brookes, saying that the ducking had caused her to miscarry a child "as big as her fist." Alice blamed the court commissioner, George Parker, and said she would take revenge on him within a year. Brookes reported Alice's words to the court and Alice confessed to what she had said. She promised to behave better. This time, the court ordered only that Alice pay the court costs.[12]

Perhaps someone instructed the court about its misapplication of ducking, because a year passed with no further use of the ducking stool. The next mention of the ducking stool at the Accomack court was on October 17, 1664, and this was to arrange for the stool's repair. It could be that Elizabeth's and Alice's duckings had been more rigorous than the builder anticipated. More likely, the stool was damaged in storage. Whether stationary or on rollers, it would have been an attractive nuisance, perhaps appearing as a seesaw. Five more years passed with no mention at all of the ducking stool in the Accomack Court. Either all of the county gossips learned their lesson after that double ducking, or the court commissioners just did not have the stomach to repeat such a spectacle in the name of justice.

NOTES, Chapter 27:

1 Hening, *Statutes II*, 166–167.
2 Apparently, this was an analogy for sex, using firearm terminology, specifically *cock, steel*, and *fire*.
3 Ames, 1632, 20. According to William Dwight Whitney (Editor, *The Century Dictionary and Cyclopedia: Dictionary*, The Century Co., New York, 1996, 2771), the phrase "to lay by the heels" meant to shackle or tie a person's hands or feet. "to lay neck and heels" meant to immobilize a person completely by tying them up.
4 The Whipping Act of 1530 authorized several forms of whipping. One involved being tied by the arms to the end of a cart and then whipped across the back.
5 Ames, *1632*, 88. Grace Waltham was Stephen Charlton's sister. She and John Waltham had a baby boy about three years after this event. This baby, John Waltham, was the nephew whom Stephen Charlton named in his will. He would have been about fifteen or sixteen years old when Charlton died.
6 Susie M. Ames, *Studies of the Eastern Shore in the Seventeenth Century* (Richmond, VA: Dietz Press, 1940), 190. Benson John Lossing, ed., *The American Historical Record, Repertory of Notes and Queries Concerning the History an Antiquities of America and Biography of Americans, Vol I* (Philadelphia: Chase & Town, 1872), 204–206. Hartley's letter has several problems: 1) It is dated 1634, but Hungars Parish was not formed until 1643; 2) No court record corroborates a Betsey Tucker's ducking; 3) Hartley spelled the county as "Ackowmake," which is similar to the spelling Clerk Thomas Cooke used between May 1641 and April 1642. The Lossing letter was taken from a copied letter, so transcription errors may be present. The letter rings true in its description, but I suspect the actual year was 1643, not 1634.
7 Hartley's next to last paragraph reveals his purpose for writing this letter: "Methought such a reformer of great scolds might be of use in some parts

of Massachusetts Bay, for I've been troubled many times by the clatter of ye scolding tongues of women yt like ye clack of ye Mill seldom cease from Morning till Night." Humph.

8 Mackey, *Vol. 6, 7-8*, 93; Mackey, *Vol. 8*, 62. The Occahannocke court location was near Richard Smyth's house, probably near today's Shield's bridge. Ward's Point in 1658 may have been at Benoni Ward's house on Nathaniel Littleton's land, south of the site of today's Custis Tomb. At that time, the Lower Parish church was still in Town on Kings Creek. The governor had ordered court meetings to alternate between Cherrystone, Hungars, and Occohannock. If Ward's Point was at Benoni's house, it was a fair distance from the church and the court, but it was accessible to the Magothy Bay community. Perhaps this point was near Pigot's Hole (see Whitelaw, 86–88), a common landing for the community (see William Byrd's diary, 1709). The 1662 Grand Assembly ordered that the pillory, stock, and whipping post were to be near the court, but that the ducking stool was to be in a place as the court "shall think convenient" (Hening, *Statutes II*, 75).

9 Mackey, Vol. 8, 304.

10 Accomack County, Virginia, *Deeds & Wills, 1663-1666*, fol. 18.

11 JoAnn Riley McKey, *Accomack County, Virginia, Court Order Abstracts, 1663-1666*, Vol. 1, (Bowie, Md., Heritage Books, Inc., 1996) 27, 28–29. That the court said Brace had "degenerated so much from a man" and therefore sentenced him to a punishment reserved for women certainly reveals the court's attitude toward the sexes.

12 Accomack County, *Deeds & Wills, 1663-1666*, 38. Alice's husband was William Boutcher.

Chapter 28

Northampton

When the English colonists began recording county court meetings on Virginia's Eastern Shore, they called their settlement "Acchawmacke." That name was used in various spellings until 1642, when Governor Berkeley used the name "Northampton," and the county (and Assembly) followed his example thereafter. Throughout the next twenty years, the county would grow large enough to be divided into two counties. When it was divided in 1663 (New Style), the southern portion of the Eastern Shore peninsula retained the name *Northampton*, while the northern portion revived the name *Accomack*.

It was a noteworthy event that a new county was created, yet no record exists to memorialize the event. The date historians use for the formation of Accomack County is based on events. For example, the election of Northampton and Accomack sheriffs on March 23rd, 1662/63 (William Waters for Northampton and Edmund Scarburgh for Accomack), is the first indicator in the old records that Accomack had become a new county. A month later, on April 21st, 1663, the Accomack court met for the first time. The following September, two burgesses from Accomack (Devoreaux Browne and Hugh Yeo) attended the Grand Assembly. These events solidify the fact that Accomack had become a new county, separate from Northampton. The earliest dividing line between the two counties was not where it is today; it was about seven miles further south, near today's crossroad at Weirwood.

This peculiar history of names has resulted in some confusion over the years. To be called Accomack and then Northampton, and then to divide, becoming Northampton and Accomack, is odd, but it does show that the old, original name was highly regarded.

Also odd in this history of names and counties, Accomack's name and status as a county was taken away seven years after it was first formed. The Virginia Grand Assembly adopted the following resolution on October 3, 1670:

> *Whereas the late disturbance in the Counties of Accomack and Northampton can by noe better means bee composed or settled then by reducing the said Two Counties into one, Itt is ordered that both the said Counties bee united & soe remaine one County untill there shall appeare good cause to again divide them.[1]*

On October 16, 1670, the former Accomack court met and was called "The Court of Upper Northampton." It was continued with this name for three years before finally, again, being named Accomack. Since that time, the two counties have been Northampton (to the south) and Accomack (to the north).

The disturbance that caused the temporary reunification of the two counties was never reported in the records; however, just four days after the Assembly made that decision, Edmund Scarburgh was arrested to appear before the governor. Two and a half weeks later, Scarburgh was suspended from all his offices and military titles for misdemeanors brought against him by the colony's attorney general.[2] Most speculation about the reunification of the two counties places Edmund Scarburgh directly in the center of what the Assembly called "the late disturbance," although the records never shed adequate light on the topic.

FOR WHOM WAS NORTHAMPTON NAMED?

Governor Sir Francis Wyatt, in his second term (1639-1641), had initiated a new plan for Virginia's counties, and the governor who followed him, Sir William Berkeley, continued this work. In the hope of bringing order to the colony, the plan called for the number of governmental units (counties) to be reduced. During Governor Wyatt's last Assembly meeting, these units were reduced from about fifteen to ten. They were James City, Henrico, Charles City, Charles River, Warwick River, Isle of Wight, Upper Norfolk, Lower Norfolk, Elizabeth City, and Accomack. Governor Berkeley made further changes to the list: Charles River County's name was changed to the County of York (and the river's name was changed to York); Warwick River County was changed to County of Warwick; and Accomack (the original county) was changed to Northampton. Beginning in July 1642, the Eastern Shore county court recorded that its meeting was held "att Northampton." With this name change, all Virginia counties now had English names. (Warrosquyaoke had been changed to Isle of Wight several years before.)

A persistent Eastern Shore legend weaves a fascinating story, revealing Obedience Robins as the author of the new name, Northampton. The legend was first published by writer and illustrator Howard Pyle, who visited the county in 1879. Historian Thomas T. Upshur repeated the legend in his 1900 address to a crowd gathered for a courthouse dedication. Ten years later, Jennings Cropper Wise wrote that Robins "took advantage of the general shake up and secured passage" of the Grand Assembly act that changed the name to Northampton.[3]

It seems a small matter to dispute, but no record was left to tell how or why the name Northampton was chosen. After attributing the footwork to Robins, Jennings Cropper Wise then noted the most likely source of the name was from the king's longtime friend, Spencer Compton, the 2nd Earl of Northampton. King Charles had probably encouraged Berkeley to name a county after this loyal friend. The depth of Compton's loyalty was made plain nine months later when the Earl of Northampton died leading a Royalist force in battle at Hopton Heath.[4]

The thread of the Robins legend seems to be based on Robins having hailed from Long Buckby, a village in Northamptonshire in England. Later in his lifetime, Robins was surely worthy of the honor to name the county. However, by 1642, he had not yet gained the authority to maneuver such power and influence, even if it had been his desire to do so. Robins had served as a substitute settlement commander and three times as a burgess. He had the highest seniority among the commissioners. Still, for all that, he had no military rank at this time, and his authority within the county was third behind Council members Nathaniel Littleton and Argoll Yardley.

In summary, the name Northampton has been used in Virginia since 1642. It may be surprising to learn that Northampton, on Virginia's Eastern Shore, predates other places of that name in the United States. It is a name you will find on the east coast of the country—in Massachusetts, Pennsylvania, New York, North Carolina, and Maryland—but not likely anywhere else. However, no matter where you find Northampton in the country, Virginia's is the oldest. Or, as some of us like to say: the first.

NOTES, Chapter 28:

1   Northampton County, Virginia, *Order Book No. 9, 1664-1674*, fol.91.
2   McIlwaine, *Minutes*, 238. The misdemeanors are never explained other than that they involved "complaint of the Indians and other matters." Scarburgh died before May 23, 1671, the date when his wife, Mary, relinquished the estate and the General Court granted administration of the estate to their son, Charles Scarburgh, and their sons-in-law, John West and Devorax Browne.
3   Howard Pyle, "Peninsular Canaan," *Harper's New Monthly Magazine*, 58, no. 348 (May, 1879): 804. Thomas T. Upshur, "Eastern-Shore History," *The Virginia Magazine of History and Biography* 9, no. 1 (1901): 94; http://www.jstor.org/stable/4242409. Jennings Cropper Wise, *Ye Kingdome*, 95–97.
4   David Plant, "Spencer Compton, 2nd Earl of Northampton, 1601-43," http://bcw-project.org/biography/spencer-compton-earl-of-northampton; accessed 2019-4-6.

Jean Francois Millet (French, 1814–1875), *Woman and Child (Silence)*, 1855, courtesy of The Art Institute of Chicago, public domain.

Chapter 29

Merchant

This is the last chapter of this book. In the previous twenty-eight chapters, we have heard stories of some of the men and women who lived and worked on Virginia's Eastern Shore during its first half century as an English colony. Through these stories, we have been able to see familiar characters more clearly. Personalities, such as those of Sir George Yeardley, Thomas Johnson, and Edmund Scarburgh, nudge at the page; we can almost perceive them gazing upon the Shore's creeks and marshes, feeling that same stir of home that we feel today. And through these stories, we met others who called this place home. Frances Burdett was slightly known to local history, but now we see her with a little more clarity, and it is not all ribbons and bows. Elizabeth Charlton and her sister, Bridget, can hereafter be remembered as individuals, each having her own mark on the history of Hungars Parish. And Joan Windley: we can almost imagine her fascination as she watches a bit of silver melt in Thomas Lee's crucible. More importantly, though, we feel Joan's anguish as she hugs her son before he leaves, bound to James Knight. And thankfully, we can imagine her joy on Pharoah's return ten years later.

The records brim with stories of everyday men and women doing everyday things; however, what we rarely see are the stories of children. Elizabeth Charlton would be considered a child today, but in her day, she was on the brink of womanhood. Pharoah is really only a name that we know through his mother's strivings. The early records rarely mention children in any detail unless they were being mistreated.

For example, in 1640, Thomas Wood was a boy, bound in service to Peter Walker. Walker had been a London merchant before coming to Virginia where he had acquired land from another London merchant, William Holmes. The land was an area just north of today's Chesapeake Bay Bridge-Tunnel. The story is tangled with other matters, but enough material is present to see Thomas through his words and actions.

Thomas must have been a small boy, because he had been put to work "beating at the mortar," but he could not do it. In Chapter 11, when Frances Burdett confronted her servants in the quarter house, it was noted that mortars could be large and made of metal. This one, apparently, was too big for Thomas. It was hard work to pound corn or grain into meal, especially in the summer heat. Every time Thomas would stop, the overseer hit him with a rope that was about as big around as a finger. "I can't do it!" Thomas said. "I'd rather go into the woods and die!"

Perhaps in the cover of night, Thomas ran away. He hid in a neighbor's calf house, where he could milk a cow for sustenance. Probably just a day or two later, Thomas was found, and the overseer took him back to Walker. Upon questioning, Thomas could give no reason for running. Walker almost let him go, but then remembered that this was not the first time Thomas had run. Walker made a whip (of what, we are not told), and the overseer whipped him. Then Walker whipped him. Several witnesses said that the whipping was not extreme, but Thomas soon fell ill. Chirurgeon John Severne was called in about a week after the whipping. Severne decided that cupping would do him good.[1] He noticed no marks on the boy. Thomas died and an inquest was held with a jury of ten men, all neighbors apparently. They all put their signatures or marks to a document, saying that Thomas had died "of scurvy being much swelled and not to have received any wrong by his master's usage of him."[2]

It is no wonder that Joan Windley kept a close eye out for how Pharoah was treated in his indenture. Thomas had no women looking out for him. Would it have made a difference for him if he had?

Two years after Thomas's death, the Grand Assembly addressed indentures that were made in Virginia. For a person twenty years of age or more, the indenture was to be no more than four years. For a person between the ages of twelve years and twenty, the limit was five years. For a child below twelve, the indenture could be no more than seven years.[3]

The court records do not lend themselves to finding positive stories about people, much less about children. However, powerful stories can be found there, showing that children—hopefully most of them—were deeply loved, sometimes by kinsfolk, sometimes by friends.

For example, when Henry Weed was dying in 1643, his wife, Elizabeth, asked if he still wanted to give a yearling heifer to a friend's child.

"I shall leave you a very poor woman yet I would happily give the child something," Weed said.

"Give him what you please," Elizabeth said.

"Then let him have the calf which came of the cow called Moll," Weed replied.

Here we know that Henry and Elizabeth cared for the child, but we see nothing of the personality of the child. The same is true in contracts; you can tell a child is loved, but you cannot see the child. Note the following indenture (spelling has been modernized):

> *This indenture witnesses that I Roger Farbrasse of the County of Northampton, Planter, do bind my son Roger Farbrasse unto Toby Selbye (or his Assigns) to serve him until he comes to be 21 years of age from this ensuing year 1647 being seven years of age. And the said Tobias is to find him meat and drink, apparel and clothing; and the said Roger nor his wife is not to make nor meddle not with the child; nor make any disturbance concerning the child (except you can show a lawful cause of abuse or misusing of him). And in consideration hereof the aforesaid Tobias is to learn him to be an English Scholar and when the child is 14 years of age and capable of understanding; then the aforesaid Tobias does hereby bind himself to do his endeavor to learn him my trade of coopering as well as I can do it, and not to hide nothing from him. And at the expiration of his time the aforesaid Tobias is to give him three barrels of corn and two suits of apparel.[4]*

Schooling was often a condition of childhood indenture, but "learn him to be an English Scholar" is unusual phrasing; it suggests that English was not the family's first language. Roger signed with a mark, an indication of illiteracy.

Parents often gave detailed instructions for their children's educations, especially that of sons. When John Waltham, Stephen Charlton's brother-in-law, wrote his will in 1640, he left instruction for his son, John, to begin schooling at the age of six years. He was to be "put to school unto "some good and godly schoolmaster" for the "space of five years and no longer until he shall accomplish the age of eleven years." Waltham prescribed that his son should be "grounded in the rudiment of scholarship and school learning."

Numerous record entries demonstrate that parents tried to ensure the care of their children in case of the parents' deaths. In 1650, Anne Ward, widow of Thomas, gave her two children three cattle each. She also gave her daughter, Ann, a feather bed, and she gave her son, Benoni, a gun and a Bible. George Smith, a neighbor, agreed to take care of the cattle and their increase along with a servant. Profits from half the increase would be used to keep and maintain the children and to provide for their education. When the children came of age, Smith promised to deliver the other half of the increase and a full-time servant.[5]

The following story, the last one in this book, is a poignant story about the love of children. Again, the records show nothing about the children's personalities, but the love surrounding them is almost palpable.

The year was 1646. Francis Pott, who then lived at his plantation, Golden Quarter (about five miles north of today's

Chesapeake Bay Bridge-Tunnel), was preparing to go to England. Before leaving, Francis sold "a Negro woman" called Merchant and "a Negro boy called William" to Stephen Charlton. Stephen had married Francis's niece, Bridgett, the year before. The plan may have been for Merchant to help care for the Charlton's new baby girl, Bridget.

While out of the colony, Francis left his property and business in the hands of his nephew, John Pott. Stephen soon came to Golden Quarter and took Merchant back to his home on Nuswattocks Neck, which was about a twenty-five-mile drive northward. A month or two later, Merchant ran away and returned to Golden Quarter. In the meantime, John sold two children to John Browne (who lived across the creek from Charlton). The children were three-year-old Will and five-year-old Prew.[6] Within a short time, Merchant ran away from John Pott to go back to the Charlton home.

John Pott traveled to Nuswattocks and asked Charlton for either Merchant or his uncle's bill of sale. Stephen said he did not care which. John then went to Merchant and asked her with whom she wanted to live. She said she did not want to go back, she wanted to stay at Charlton's. Apparently, Merchant did not run again.

Six years later, Charlton made a statement in open court, denying any claim to a boy now in John Browne's possession. This probably means that young Will had been allowed to live at Charlton's with Merchant, provided that when the time came, Charlton made it clear that the boy belonged to Browne. Prew was not mentioned, which may mean that she was not Merchant's child or that she had been old enough at five to act as a companion to Browne's youngest children.

At the time of Charlton's statement, Will was nine, probably about to be ten, an age considered old enough for work.

I wonder what route Merchant took to traverse those twenty-five miles to and from Nusswattocks Neck. Had she purposefully memorized the way on the ride up, or had the plan come to her later? How many hours did she walk? Had she been fearful of wild dogs known to lurk about?

My guess is that Merchant was Will and Prew's mother. Every footfall toward them must have felt like she was running backward, until she could actually see recognizable landmarks of Golden Quarter. At that point, joy would have hastened her steps. I cannot begin to imagine the depth of her despair when she could not find the children and heard that they had been sold away.[7] When she learned that the children had been sold to a neighbor of Charlton's, did she chide herself for leaving, or did she simply begin planning her journey back?

Merchant's story illustrates both the wealth and the poverty of the old records. Her story is substantial, yet her name appears but once.[8] Merchant's story is one of scant shadows, and the stories of her children are as penumbras, the lighter regions of those shadows. As meager as the facts are, Merchant's story rises to greatness, equal to those of the colonial men and women for whom we have scores of facts.

For those who feel the draw of history when gazing across a verdant or plowed field in places like Golden Quarter, thousands of stories await you. Take up your pen if you are so inclined. Always remember Merchant, whose abbreviated name was written once, but whose story speaks volumes and endures for all time.

NOTES, Chapter 29:

1. Cupping was a treatment in which a heated glass was placed on the skin. The heat created a partial vacuum which pulled on the skin. This technique was thought to stimulate muscles or blood flow, or some such.

2. Northampton County, Virginia, *Orders, Wills, & Deeds, 1640-1645*, folio 13-folio 14; Ames, *1640*, 22-26. Spelling and punctuation have been changed in the quotation. The jury consisted of John Neale, George Travellor, Luke Stubbins, Mathewe Gettings, William Fisher, Henry Chapman, Richard Hill, Thomas Gilbert, Davey Dale, and a man named Walter whose surname is unreadable due to page damage.

3. Hening, *Statutes I*, 257.

4. Mackey, *Vol. 3*, p. 184; Northampton County, Virginia, *Orders, Deeds, Wills, No. 3*, folio 96.

5. Mackey, *Vol. 3*, 421.

6. Mackey, *Vol. 3*, 105, 116.

7. Walczyk, Book IV, 64-65, 68. Northampton County, Virginia, *Orders, Deeds, & Wills, No. 4, 1651-1654*, folio 81. The records do not say anything further about the "boy called William" who was sold on the same bill with Merchant. It appears that this William may have gone to Charlton's separately. I had wondered if he might have been the father of Will (who was also called William in the records). Nothing more was found about Merchant.

8. Clerk Edmund Mathewes wrote Merchant with the er abbreviated in superscript. Otherwise, Merchant was referred to nine times in the paragraph as "the Negro woman" or "said Negro woman."

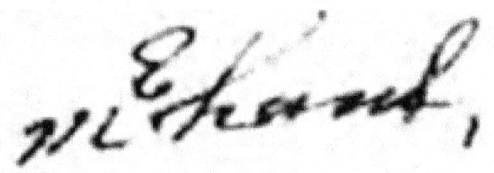

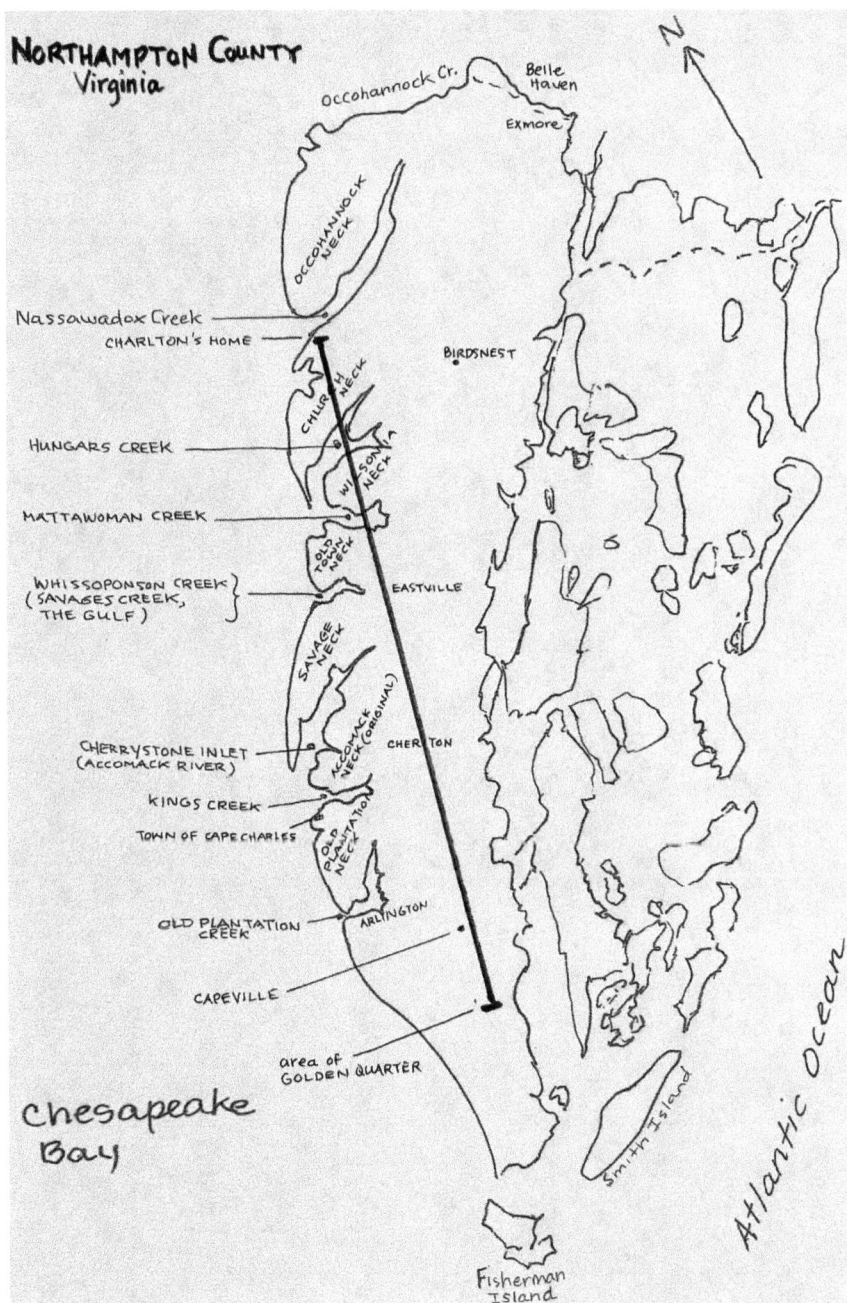

The distance that Merchant traveled between Stephen Charlton's house and Francis Pott's Golden Quarter was about twenty miles as the crow flies (see the map above) and about twenty-fives miles as one might walk. In Merchant's day, the land roads were mere paths, some wide enough for pulling a cart or rolling a hogshead.

Appendices

APPENDIX I   Yeardley's Eastern Shore Commission (with modified spelling of some words):

A Commission to Sir George Yeardley for the Easterne Shore &c

Whereas through the large extention of ground heretofore graunted, both to Comporations, Hundreds, particuler Plantations, and private Dividends, this Colony was so dispersed & people so straglingly seated, that we were not only bereft of the frendly comerce and mutuall societie one of another in religeous duties, the first fruits of Civility; but were also disabled any way to provide for the common safety either against forraine [foreign] or domesticke invasion, the carefullest charge of Christian charity, wittnes those vexed Soules and troubled Spirits of ours, when in this last outrage of these Infidells we were forced to stand and gaze at our distressed bretheren, fryinge in the furies of our enimies, and could not relieve them. And whereas throug these occasions, We have been forced to quitt most of our habitations, so that many of our people are not unsetled. These are therefore, both to provide for the good of the one, and prevent the danger of the other, (such places as we now hould in this River, being already filled with sufficient numbers) to desire, and require you Sir George Yeardley knight, and on[e] of his Majesties Counsell established for Virginia, to levy at your best conveniencie, such a number of the people of this Colony, as for this present intended imployment shall by you be thought sufficient; and that imbarking your self and said Company, in such Shipps Pinaces or Shallops, as you shall make choise of, you presently depart out of this River in discovery both of the West and Eastern Shores of this Bay, or any other of our Sea Coasts, which shall seeme best unto you within the limits of 33 and 40 degrees of Northerly latitude, there to search for and find out some convenient place, both for quantity and quality of ground apt safely to entertaine some three or foure hundred men, uppon which, or uppon any other place whatsoever, that in your discresion you shall think fitt for your present necessity and use, it shalbe lawfull for you presently to sett downe, and leave such and so many of our Colony as are now under your Command, to make a begining there for a Plantation, giving to every one of them fouer acres of land for his particular employment, placing your present buildings in such forme as may be by addition of numbers intended to be sent imediatly after the Cropp, capable of fortification;

for the better execution whereof. These are to give you full power and command over all our people that shall accompany you in this vioadge, or that you shall find inhabiting in any of those precincts aforesaid, and to punish them according to theire delinquencie, and the necessitie of the occasion. And because through the late revolt and failinge off, of our Neighbouringe Savages, we are uncertaine of frendshipp with any of those Natives, These are to give you leave, and absolute power, either to make peace or warr with any of them, as it shall seeme most behoofull and necessarie for the present estate of this our Common-Wealth, as also peaceably to trade for Furrs, Corne, or any other Comodities, with such as shalbe frends, and forceably to take such or the like from those that dare be our enemies. Itt is also thought expedient, and graunted to you Sir George Yeardley knight, that if in this your passage, you shalbe chased or encountred, by any man of Warr, or other Saile whatsoever, that shall go about to hinder these your proceedings, either by takeing away your provisions, or by offering any other such violence (except by his Majesties authoritie he be thereunto licensed) that you may with all your power & uttmost endevors repell, resist, and defend your self, and our honors against that force, or anyother of like nature and condition, either outward or homeward bound, in all Harbors, or Rivers, members of the teritory of this Plantation. And to prohibitt, forbid, and compell thereunto, any shipping of what Nation soever within the said limits (without speciall Comission from his Majestie, or from his Majesties Counsell and Company of Virginia) from trade, fishing, or other bussines, then such as the law of Nature and Nations allow to every distressed person. And for your better ease in the execution of these imployments, John Pountis Vice-Admirall, and Counsellor of State here resident is requested freely to accompany you in this vioage, whose Counsell & advise you are desired to use in case of importance. given at James Citty under my hand & the great Seale of the Colony this 20th of June 1622. Francis Wyatt.[1]

APPENDIX II: **Anthony Longee (Longo, (Longoe), release from Nathaniel Littleton**

[*To All to whome these presentes shall come greetinge in our Lord* [*god everlastinge*].] Know yee that whereas Antony Longee the Negro beinge [formerly] my servant and soly and propperly belongeing unto mee [Nathaniell Litt]leton of Accomack in the Colony ov Virginia Esquire And allsoe whereas I the said Nathaniell Littleton haveing Formerly viz. in the yeare of our Lord god one thousand six hundred thirty and Five and on the sixteenth day of March in the same yeare by a certen wrytinge under my hand dated as afforesaid really and Freely acquitted discharged released and sett Free him the said Anthony Longoe From all service and servitude whatsoever from the Beginning of the World untill that present day viz. the sixteenth day of March above specified Nowe Knowe yee that I the said Nathaniell Littleton in confirmation of my aforesaid deed in wrytinge expressed and for the certen considerations mee thereunto moveinge doe hereby as my acte and deede doe hereby for mee my heires and assignes, in like manner acquit and discharge release exonerate and Free him the said Antony Longo from all and all manner of service and services servitute and servitudes or anie manner of obligementes or dutyes thereupon depending or formerly due even from the beginninge of the World untill this present day without anie Fraud or mentall reservation provisoe contracdiction or anie other exception whatsoever thereof as my absolute act and deed at the humble request of him the said Antony Longoe I have hereunto put my hand this thirtyeth day of July Anno Domini 1640. And in the sixteenth yeare of the raigne of our Soveraigne Lord Charles by the grace of god of England Scotland France and Ireland Kinge defender of the Fayth etc.

Nathaniell Littleton

Signed in the presence of

George Dawe[2]

APPENDIX III: Edmund Mathews: Odd Notations in the Record

In Chapter 18, Clerk Edmund Mathews's annotations in the official record were noted to be unusual. It was rare for a clerk to make a personal note in the record. To do so would be considered extremely poor form; however, in this case, the circumstances seemed to call for it. Mathews saw that something was amiss.

The annotations in this case included three personal observations about the origin of the material Mathews copied into the record concerning the Husbands and Chiles conflict. These observations can be found on page 129 and folio 129 of Northampton County, Virginia, Deeds, Wills, Etc., Book 4, 1651-1654.

It appears that Mathews was copying the material into the book a full year after Captain Husbands captured Captain Chiles's ship, the *Fame of Virginia*. The material that

Mathews copied into the book in June of 1653 began on folio 126 of Book 4. Following is a list of what he copied, including (in italics) Mathews's unusual notes in the places they were written.

- A. June 17, 1652: Captain Walter Chiles's petition to Northampton court commissioners;
- B. June 17, 1652: the Northampton County magistrates command to Captain Husband's ship's crew to release Captain Chiles's ship and its goods;
- C. June 18, 1652: Nathanial Littleton and Argoll Yardley command to the Keepers of the Liberties of England to appear before the court;
- D. June 18, 1652: the Keepers of the Liberties of England response in writing with an acknowledgment of their fault and their promise that they would not repeat their mistake.
- E. June 18, 1652: the Northampton Court (Nathaniel Littleton, Argoll Yardley, William Andrews, William Jones, Stephen Charlton, and William Whittington) minutes, recording its determination that Chiles's ship and goods were not a "prize." The court noted that Husbands had ordered his company to surrender the ship. Husbands was to be kept in custody until the ship and goods were surrendered to Chiles.
- F. June 18, 1652: Captain Richard Husbands's response. He held his ground that this ship he seized had been approved for seizure by the Keepers of the Liberties of England and was, indeed, a legitimate prize. Having been imprisoned and the ship retaken, Husbands demanded "immediate satisfaction from you" for the

prize and for his time. He saw himself as operating under the Act of Parliament, in service to England. Husbands asked for a response or else, he implied, he'd have his answer in England.

G. June 18, 1652: Husbands, Littleton, and Yardley's acknowledgement that Husbands had disapproved of his ship's crew for detaining The Fame and its goods contrary to Husbands's order.

H. not dated: Husbands's letter to his men who were onboard The Fame, directing them to surrender the prize to Captain Henfield.

I. not dated: Reply of Husbands's men from his ship, stating that it was their intention to have their captain back onboard and then he could do as he liked. Regarding goods, they said they had none except for "a little drink" already "half drank."

J. not dated: An account, apparently from the Northampton magistrates, telling of Chiles's suit against Husbands for detaining the ship and goods. Both men were willing to put the issue before Littleton, Yardley, Charlton, and Andrews, Sr. for their determination. After the decision, Husbands agreed to surrender the ship (according to the judgement of the magistrates) provided that Chiles discharged Husbands from any liability. The account ended with the following sentence: "Wherefore I the said Walter Chiles accordingly do hereby discharge the said Capt Husbands of & from all manner of suits, actions, debts, dues, or demands whatsoever to this day."

This page was delivered to me by Col. Argoll Yardley (inter ceter) neither subscribed, dated, or attested. [inter ceter is a Latin term meaning "among the rest.]

K. June 19, 1652: A letter to Husbands from Northampton court commissioners, expressing their outrage that he had failed to keep his promise that his men would return the goods to Mr. Chiles. They proclaimed that if he does not return the goods or the men who took them, the Virginia government will charge him in England for the "piracyes Acted by your self and Company."

This proclamation delivered with those aforenamed but no subscription thereunto.

Teste Edm:Mathews [Clerk of Court]

L. not dated but following the above letter: A letter appearing to be from Northampton court commissioners to Governor Bennett ("as the representative power of the country"). The court informed the governor that it intends to sue Husbands and his company. It asks that the governor have papers prepared for such a purpose and it will second them. All papers will be provided to Mr. Edmund Scarburgh who will prosecute the suit in, it appears, England.

This page was neither under written, nor dated when it came to the hands of me

Edm: Mathews [Clerk of Court]

It seems apparent that Clerk Mathews, while handling these records, was sufficiently suspicious that he felt compelled to qualify the last three items with his comments. He noted that these items were not signed nor dated. (This implies that the pages he usually copied into the record were signed and dated.) The last entry is most interesting. This entry (marked as L. above) reveals that the county was preparing to sue Husbands and that Edmund Scarburgh was to be the prosecutor. Given Mathews's apparent suspicion of this document, I wonder if this item was planted in the record for the purpose of assuaging the county inhabitants who were riled up about this situation. The inhabitants in the northern section of the county seemed to be the ones who were more distrusting of the local government. If they thought Edmund Scarburgh was involved with the local court to sue Husbands, their anger might be assuaged. Thomas Johnson and Edmund Scarburgh were trusted in that northern region. Johnson would be reading these entries to the people at Hack's old fields. For the people to hear from him that Scarburgh would be handling the situation would be like pouring oil on troubled waters.

Such a plant into the records would be corrupt, illegal, immoral. It seems unthinkable, except that the purpose would have been to lessen the public's fear and anger. This motive might be seen as acceptable, especially if the perpetrators knew that a backroom deal was possible and that all would turn out okay in the end. Argoll Yardley would have known of such backroom deals; his is the only name given in Mathews's notations. [For any Yardley descendants who might take offense that I would suggest their ancestor might have been involved in such political wheeling and dealing, he is my direct ancestor, too. As is Nathaniel Littleton, who would also have been involved.]

Keep in mind that this is speculation. We are likely never to know the clerk's purpose in annotating the record. Despite not knowing his motive, the notes do furnish a glimpse of how the clerk's office operated in Mathews's day. From the notes, we learn that Argoll Yardley delivered the documents to the clerk. Because the one note was noted to be inter ceter ["among the rest"], we can guess that Mathews recognized it as different, out of place, odd. Does this mean that the court commissioners wrote the orders that Mathews copied into the record? Or, does this mean that Mathews wrote the orders as he heard them, and then, a court commissioner proofed his work? (Some years later, such review would be required and easily identified in the records.)

In Chapter 18, I judged Mathews's style of clerking as "to attend to it when he could." After looking closely at these odd notations, that assessment appears too harsh. It may have been the usual course that Clerk Mathews did not receive the papers in a timely fashion from the commissioner who provided them to him, or who reviewed them before official entry into the book. Either way, the efficiency of the Northampton clerk's office suffered greatly in those years. For whatever reason, the delay was real.

The story told in Chapter 18 shows that Northampton's inhabitants could not find official answers to their burning questions for one full year. And then, when they did receive the answers, something was not quite right. I envision Clerk Mathews as champing at the bit when he wrote those notes. It seems certain that he would not have written the notations if it had been the normal course. He seems to have been disturbed by the manner in which the pages came to him. He used the only means he knew to draw attention to the issue without compromising his employment.

Edmund Mathews continued as Northampton's Clerk of Court for five more years. His career in this position spanned twelve years.

NOTES, Appendix:

1　Kingsbury, *VCL-3*, 656, 657.
2　Ames, *1640*, 32.

Bibliography

Accomack County, Virginia, Circuit Court Clerk's Office, *Deeds & Wills, 1663-1666.*

Accomack County, Virginia, Circuit Court Clerk's Office, *Orders, 1666-1670.*

Ames, Susie M. *County Court Records of Accomack-Northampton, Virginia, 1632-1640.* Washington, D.C.: American Historical Association, 1954.

Ames, Susie M., editor. *County Court Records of Accomack-Northampton, Virginia 1640-1645.* Charlottesville: The University Press of Virginia, 1973.

Ames, Susie M. *Studies of the Eastern Shore in the Seventeenth Century.* Richmond, VA: Dietz Press, 1940.

Betham, William. *The Baronetage of England, Vol. 4.* Ipswich: Burrell and Bransby, 1804.

Beverley, Robert. *The History and Present State of Virginia In Four Parts.* London: R. Parker, 1705.

Billings, Warren M. "Some Acts Not in Hening's 'Statutes': The Acts of Assembly, April 1652, November 1652, And July 1653." *The Virginia Magazine of History and Biography* 83, no. 1 (1975): 22–76. http://www.jstor.org/stable/4247925.

Britannica, The Editors of Encyclopaedia. "Andrew Hamilton." Encyclopedia Britannica, July, 31, 2022. https://www.britannica.com/biography/Andrew-Hamilton.

Chance, Burton. "Charles Scarborough, An English Educator And Physician to Three Kings: A Medical Retrospect into the Times of the Stuarts." *Bulletin of the History of Medicine* 12, no. 2 (1942): 274–303. http://www.jstor.org/stable/44446270.

Cummings, Janet. "Marriage, Death, Taverns, A Royalist Plot, and an Expensive Face in 17th Century Virginia: Ann Custis Yeardley & sarah Thorowgood Yeardley Interwoven, Part II." Thorowgood World (blog). July 5, 2023. https://thorowgoodworld.wordpress.com/.

De Vries, David Pietersz, and Henry Cruse Murphy (translator). *Voyages From Holland to America,* A.D. 1632 to 1644. New York: Billin and Brothers, Printers, 1857.

Forman, Henry Chandlee. *The Virginia Eastern Shore and its British Origins: History, Gardens & Antiquities.* Easton, MD: Eastern Shore Publishers' Associates, 1973.

Forman, Henry Chandlee. *Virginia Architecture in the*

Seventeenth Century. Charlottesville: The University Press of Virginia, 1957.

Franklin, Benjamin. "Obituary of Andrew Hamilton." *The Pennsylvania Gazette,* August 6, 1741. https://founders.archives.gov/documents/Franklin/01-02-02-0079.

Glencross, Reginald M. "Virginia Gleanings in England." *The Virginia Magazine of History and Biography* 29, no. 1, January 1921.

Hall, Jenean, *An "Uncertaine Rumor" of Land.* Independently published, IngramSpark, and KWE Publishing, LLC, 2022.

Hampton Museum of History, "This Is Hampton, Virginia," *Bringing History to Life,* www.VisitHampton.com.

Hening, William Waller (editor). *Statutes at Large, Being a Collection of all the Laws of Virginia, Vol. I-XIII.* Richmond, VA: George Cochran, 1819-1823.

Hinman, Michael "Fierce Arrow," historian of the Accohannock Tribe, lecture, Eastern Shore Public Library, summer, 2014.

Holt, Eleanor Sayer. *The Second Church of Elizabeth City Parish, 1623/4–1698, An Historical-Archaeological Report.* Hampton, VA: 1985.

Hotten, John Camden (editor). *The Original Lists of Persons of Quality: Emigrants, Religious Exiles, Political Rebels, Serving Men Sold for a Term of Years, Apprentices, Children Stolen, Maidens Pressed, And Others, Who Went From Great Britain to the American Plantations, 1600–1700.* London: Empire State Book Co, 1874.

Kingsbury, Susan Myra (editor). *The Records of The Virginia Company of London. Vol. I-IV.* Washington, D.C.: Government Printing Office, 1906-1933.

Konkle, Burton Alva. *The Life of Andrew Hamilton, 1676-1741.* Philadelphia: National Publishing Company, 1941.

Kukla, Jon. *Speakers and Clerks of the Virginia House of Burgesses 1643 - 1776.* Richmond, VA: Virginia State Library, 1981.

Johnson, Leonard W. *Ebb and Flow.* Verona, VA, McClure Printing, 1982.

Library of Virginia. *Legislative Petitions.* https://www.lva.virginia.gov.

Library of Virginia, *Virginia Land Office Patents and Grants, Patent Book No. 1 (1623-1643, Vol. 1 & 2).* https://lva-virginia.libguides.com/land-grants

Library of Virginia, *Virginia Land Office Patents and Grants, Patent Book No. 2 (1643-1651). https://lva-virginia.libguides.com/land-grants*

Library of Virginia, *Virginia Land Office Patents and Grants, Patent Book No. 4 (1655-1664). https://lva-virginia.libguides.com/land-grants*

Library of Virginia, *Virginia Land Office Patents and Grants, Patent Book No. 7 (1679-1689, Vol. 1 & 2). https://lva-virginia.libguides.com/land-grants*

Lucketti, Nicholas M. "Archaeology at Arlington: Excavations at the Ancestral Custis Plantation, Northampton County, Virginia." Richmond, VA: The Association for the Preservation of Virginia Antiquities [Preservation Virginia], 1999.

Marshall, James Handley. *Abstracts of the Wills and Administrations of Northampton County, Virginia 1832–1802.* Camden, ME: Picton Press, 1994.

Mason, George Carrington. "Hungars Church, Northampton County, Virginia," in *Colonial Churches in the Original Colony of Virginia: A Series of Sketches by Especially Qualified Writers.* Richmond, VA: Southern Churchman Company, 1908.

Mason, George Carrington. "The Colonial Churches of the Eastern Shore of Virginia." *The William and Mary Quarterly,* 20, no. 4, 1940. https://doi.org/10.2307/1919927.

Mackey, Howard and Marlene A. Groves (editors). *Northampton County, Virginia, Record Book, Orders, Deeds, Wills &c, Volume 3, 1645-1651.* Rockport, ME: Picton Press, 2000.

Mackey, Howard and Marlene A. Groves (editors). *Northampton County, Virginia, Record Book, Orders, Deeds, Wills &c, Volume 5, 1654-1655.* Rockport, ME: Picton Press, 2000.

Mackey, Howard and Candy McMahan Perry (editors). *Northampton County Virginia, Record Book: Deeds, Wills, &c: Volume 7: 1657–1666.* Rockport, ME: Picton Press, 2002.

Mackey, Howard and Marlene A. Groves (editors). *Northampton County, Virginia Record Book: Deeds, Wills*

&c, *Volume 6 and 7-8, 1655-57*. Rockport, ME: Picton Press, 2002.

Mackey, Howard (editor). *Northampton County Virginia Record Book: Orders, Deeds, Wills &c, Vol. 8, Court Cases, 1657–1664*. Rockport, ME: Picton Press, 2002.

Mackey, Howard and Marlene A. Groves (editors). *Northampton County, Virginia, Record Book: Court Cases, Vol. 9, 1664–1674*. Rockport, ME: Picton Press, 2003.

Mariner, Kirk. *Slave and Free on Virginia's Eastern Shore*. Onancock, VA: Miona Publications, 2014.

McCartney, Martha W. *Virginia Immigrants and Adventurers: A Biographical Dictionary, 1607-1635*. Baltimore: Genealogical Publishing Co., 2007.

McIlwaine, H. R. (editor). *Journals of the House of Burgesses of Virginia, 1619-1658/59*. Richmond, VA: Virginia State Library [Library of Virginia], 1915.

McIlwaine, H. R. (editor). *Minutes of the Counsel and General Court, 1622–1630, 1670–1676*. Richmond, VA: Virginia State Library [Library of Virginia], 1924.

McKey, JoAnn Riley (editor). *Accomack County, Virginia, Court Order Abstracts, 1663-1666, Vol. 1*. Bowie, MD: Heritage Books, Inc., 1996.

McKey, JoAnn Riley (editor). *Accomack County, Virginia, Court Order Abstracts, 1666-1670, Vol. 2*, Bowie, MD: Heritage Books, Inc., 1996.

Middleton, Arthur Pierce. "Anglican Virginia: The Established Church of the Old Dominion 1607–1786."

Colonial Williamsburg Library Research Reports Series - 0006. Colonial Williamsburg Foundation Library: 1990. www.research.history.org.

Miles, Moody K., "MilesFiles 23.0." Parksley, VA, Eastern Shore Public Library, https://www.espl-genealogy.org/.

Mooney, James. "The Powhatan Confederacy, Past and Present." *American Anthropologist,* 9, no. 1, January-March, 1907.

Nerney, Sarah. "The Gingaskins of Virginia," November 18, 2011, (Library of Virginia, The Uncommonwealth: Voices from the Library of Virginia) https://uncommonwealth.virginiamemory.com.

Nix, Foster C. "Andrew Hamilton's Early Years in the American Colonies." *The William and Mary Quarterly* 21, no. 3 (1964) https://doi.org/10.2307/1918453.

Northampton Count, Virginia, Circuit Court Clerk's Office, *Orders, Book No. 1, 1632-1640.*

Northampton County, Virginia, Circuit Court Clerk's Office, *Orders, Deeds, Wills, &c, Book No. 2, 1640 - 1645.*

Northampton County, Virginia, Circuit Court Clerk's Office, *Orders, Book No. 3, 1645-1651.*

Northampton County, Virginia, Circuit Court Clerk's Office, *Orders, Deeds, Wills &c, Book No. 4, 1651-1654.*

Northampton County, Virginia, Circuit Court Clerk's Office, *Orders, Deeds, and Wills, Book No. 5, (1654-1655).*

Northampton County, Virginia, Circuit Court Clerk's Office, *Orders, Book No. 7, 1657–1664.*

Northampton County, Virginia, Circuit Court Clerk's Office, *Deeds, Wills, &c, Book No. 7–8, 1655-1668.*

Northampton County, Virginia, Circuit Court Clerk's Office, *Order Book No. 9, 1664-1674.*

Northampton County, Virginia, Circuit Court Clerk's Office, *Deeds &c, Book No. 11, 1668-1680.*

Northampton County, Virginia, Circuit Court Clerk's Office, *Deeds & Wills, Book No. 12, (1692-1707).*

Northampton County, Virginia, Circuit Court Clerk's Office, *Orders and Wills, Book No. 13 (1689-1698).*

Northampton County, Virginia, Circuit Court Clerk's Office, *Orders, Book 14, (1698-1710), 188-189.*

Northampton County, Virginia, Circuit Court Clerk's Office, *Orders, Book No. 15, 1710-1716.*

Northampton County, Virginia, Circuit Court Clerk's Office, *Orders, Book No. 35, 1808-1816.*

Nugent, Nell Marion (Abstractor and Indexer). *Cavaliers And Pioneers: Abstracts of Virginia Land Patents And Grants, Volume One, 1623–1666.* Richmond, VA: Library of Virginia, 2004 (originally published by Press of the Dietz Print Co., Richmond, 1934).

Perry, James R. *The Formation of a Society on Virginia's Eastern Shore, 1615-1655.* Chapel Hill: The University of North Carolina Press, published for the Institute of Early American History and Culture, 1990.

Plant, David. "Spencer Compton, 2nd Earl of Northampton,

1601-43." http://bcw-project.org/biography/spencer-compton-earl-of-northampton; accessed 2019-4-6.

Pory, John. *Letter of John Pory, 1619*, Wisconsin Historical Society, American Journeys Collection (www.americanjourneys.org) 2003; also found in Lyon Gardiner Tyler, editor, *Narratives of Early Virginia 1606 -1625*, New York: Charles Scribner's Sons, 1907.

Pyle, Howard. "Peninsular Canaan," *Harper's New Monthly Magazine*, 58, no. 348 (May, 1879).

Robertson, Thomas B. "Hungars Church, Northampton County, Va." *The Virginia Magazine of History and Biography* 13, no. 3 (1906): 315–17. http://www.jstor.org/stable/4242750.

Rolf[e], John. "A True Relation of the State of Virginia left by Sir Thomas Dale Knight in May last 1616." https://encyclopediavirginia.org/entries/a-true-relation-of-the-state-of-virginia-lefte-by-sir-thomas-dale-knight-in-may-last-1616-1617/.

Sainsbury, William Noel. *Calendar of State Papers, Colonial Series, [American and West Indies] 1574–1660*. London: Longman, Green, Longman, & Roberts, 1860.

Semmes, Raphael (editor). "Claiborne vs. Clobery Et Als. in the High Court of Admiralty," *Maryland Historical Magazine*, Vol. 26, Vol. 27, Vol. 28 (1931-1933).

Sheppard, Henrietta Dawson (Ayres). *Ayres–Dawson and Allied Families, Volume 1, Recording the ancestry of Richard Johnson Ayres Jr. of Accomack County, Virginia and of his wife Elizabeth Hack Dawson of Loudoun County,*

Virginia. New York, The American Historical Company, Inc., 1961.

Smith, John. *The Generall Historie of Virginia, New England, & The Summer Isles*. London: 1624; Reprint Bedford, MA: Applewood Books, 2006.

Stephen, Leslie and Sidney Lee, editors., *Dictionary of National Biography, Vol. XXIV*. New York: Macmillan and Co., 1890.

Stitt, Susan. "The Will of Stephen Charlton and Hungars Parish Glebe." *The Virginia Magazine of History and Biography* 77, no. 3 (1969): 259–76. http://www.jstor.org/stable/4247484.

Tourtellot, Arthur Bernon. *The Charles*. New York: Farrar & Rinehart, New York, 1941.

Turman, Nora Miller. *The Eastern Shore of Virginia 1603 - 1964*. Onancock, VA: The Eastern Shore News, 1964.

Turman, Nora Miller. *George Yeardley*. Richmond, VA: Garrett and Massie, Incorporated, 1959.

Tyler, Lyon Gardiner. *History of Hampton and Elizabeth City County, Virginia*. Hampton, VA, The Board of Supervisors of Elizabeth City County, 1922.

Upshur, Thomas T. "Eastern-Shore History," *The Virginia Magazine of History and Biography* 9, no. 1 (1901); http://www.jstor.org/stable/4242409.

Virginia Historical Society. "Early Episcopacy in Accomack." *The Virginia Magazine of History and Biography* 5, no. 2 (1897); http://www.jstor.org/stable/4242029.

Virginia Historical Society. "Acts, Orders and Resolutions of the General Assembly of Virginia." *The Virginia Magazine of History and Biography* 23, no. 3 (1915); http://www.jstor.org/stable/4243447.

Walczyk, Frank V., transcriptionist, *Northampton County VA, Orders, Deeds, & Wills, 1651 - 1654, Book IV.* Coram, NY: Peter's Row, 1998.

Walter, Alice Granbery. *Lower Norfolk County, Virginia, Court Records: Book "A" 1637-1646 and Book "B" 1646-1651/2.* Baltimore, MD: Genealogical Publishing Co., 2002.

Whitelaw, Ralph T. *Virginia's Eastern Shore: a History of Northampton And Accomack Counties.* Richmond, VA: Virginia Historical Society, 1951 (reprint, Gloucester, MA: Peter Smith, 1968).

Whitney, William Dwight, Editor. *The Century Dictionary and Cyclopedia: Dictionary.* New York: The Century Co., 1996.

Wise, Jennings Cropper. *Ye Kingdome of Accawmacke, Or, The Eastern shore of Virginia in the Seventeenth Century.* Richmond, VA: Bell Book, 1911.

Wright, Louis B. & Marion Tinling (editors), *The Secret Diary of William Byrd of Westover, 1709-1712.* Richmond, VA: The Dietz Press, 1941.

Index

A

Ackomack (Accomack, Acchawmacke) *xi*, 2, 13, 19, 31, 34, 35, 37, 38, 40, 45–48, 50–52, 54, 57–59, 63–73, 78, 79, 81, 83, 98, 101, 102, 105, 108–110, 119, 122, 123, 135–138, 142, 153, 160, 167, 176, 186, 187, 205, 219–221, 236–238, 240–242, 245, 246, 261–267, 282

Accohannock Tribe 20

Addams, Ann 45–46

Affryca (ship) 46, 49

Africa 48

African residents (first known) 49

    Alexander 49, 53

    Anthony 49, 53

    Cassanga 49, 53

    Jane 49, 53

    John 49, 53

    Palatia 49, 53

    Polonia 49, 53

    Sebastian 49, 53

Allen, John 99, 100
Ames, Susie M. 33, 34, 46, 183, 263
Andolo 101
Andrews (Andrewes), Garrett 50, 92
Andrews, John 222
Andrews, Susanna 104
Andrews, William 67, 79, 96, 104, 105, 108, 139, 140, 142, 144, 148, 150, 151, 152, 161, 165, 166, 168, 179, 184, 188, 190, 192, 196, 207, 210, 228, 230, 284
Angood, John 123
Angoods Creek 123
Argall, Samuel xv, 24
Arlington Plantation 48, 96, 232

B

Bacon, Nathaniel 192
Bagwell, Henry 72, 76, 241–242
Baily (Bailey), Richard 140, 147
Baker, Betsey 125
Baker, Daniel 138
Baker, Susanna (see Eyre, Pott, Kendall) 133, 192, 195, 211, 212
Baker, Thomas 125
Ball, Mr. and Mrs. 93
Barber-Surgeons' Hall 155
Barlow, Ralph 178
Barnaby, James 230
Baseley, John 257
Bashawe, Andrew 242
Beavans, Molly 125, 127
Beavans, Samuel 127

Beavans, Susan   125

Belle Haven   171

Bennett, Elizabeth   53

Bennett, Richard (Governor)   153, 168, 174, 181, 286

Bennett's Plantation (fn)   60

Benthall, Thomas   230

Berkeley, Lord John   156

Berkeley, Maurice   156

Berkeley, Sir William (Governor)   112, 115–118, 121, 122, 125, 142, 143, 153, 156, 178, 209, 210, 265, 267, 268

Bernard, William   142

Berriman (Berryman), William   67, 74–79, 81, 86, 159

Berry, Robert   141

Bingham, John   125

Bingham, Peggy   125

Blower (Blore), John   2, 15, 58, 63, 70, 71, 75–77, 82, 85, 86, 98

Blower (Blore), Frances   2, 56, 70, 71, 76, 77, 82, 85–87, 89, 92, 93, 95, 96, 98

Blower (Blore), William   73–77, 82, 85, 86, 90, 91, 92

Bolton, Francis   55, 56, 57, 58, 59, 60, 61

Bolton, Richard   60

Bourer, George   230

Boutcher, Alice   260, 262, 264

Boutcher, William   264

Bowman, Edmund   52

Brace, Robert   261, 262, 264

Bradford, Nathaniel   230

Brickhouse, Nathan   127

Brookes, Jane   262

Brown, R. K. (M.D.)   14, 21

Browne, Devorax 266, 269

Browne, John 276

Browne, Thomas 99, 222

Bruce (Bruse), James 92

Budd, Thomas 230

Burdett (Burditt), Frances (see Blower) 2, 56, 70, 71, 76, 77, 82, 85–87, 89, 90, 92, 93, 95–98, 100, 271, 272

Burdett (Burditt), Thomas 91, 92

Burdett (Burditt), William 20, 30, 67, 72, 76, 78, 79, 85, 86, 90, 91, 93, 96, 98, 105, 250

Burrell, Robert 226

Butler, Joane 251–253

Butler, Nathaniel 26

Butler, Thomas 252

Burton, William 70

Byrd, William 221

C

Cape Charles 24, 27, 68, 73

Cape Charles Natural Preserve 70

Capps, William 13

Carsly (Carsley), Henry 90

Carter, John 125

Carter, Nancy 125

Cary, Miles 190

Cedar Cottage 156

Chandler, Samuel 29

Chapel of Ease 80, 83–87

Chapman, Elizabeth 189, 190

Chapman, Henry 272

Charles I (King) 64, 184, 261

Charles II (King) 116, 153, 154

Charles City 6, 261

Charles City County 25

Charles Hundred 29

Charles River 261

Charlton, Ann (see West) 187, 188, 192, 211

Charlton, Bridgett (née Pott, see Severne) 185, 186, 199, 204, 208, 209, 270

Charlton, Bridget (see Foxcroft) 188, 189, 270

Charlton, Elizabeth 183-186, 189, 191-193, 196-202, 204, 205, 207, 208, 223, 265, 266

Charlton, Stephen 67, 70, 72, 116, 117, 136, 137, 142, 145, 146, 150, 156, 159, 163, 164, 167, 168, 172, 177, 179, 184-192, 196, 197, 200, 202-205, 211-213, 219, 244, 257, 269-271, 273, 280, 281

Chase, William 52

Cherrydale Drive 220

Cherrystone Inlet xi, 3, 4, 40, 174, 231

Chester, Mary 53

Chickahominy 26

Chiles, Walter 140, 158-163, 168, 171, 173, 180, 279-282

Chirurgery 209

Church Creek 177

Claiborne, William 43, 46, 49, 161, 166, 179

Cole, Thomas 53

College, The 6

Collins, Betsey (Junior) 125, 127

Collins, Betsey (Senior) 125

(Collins), "Mac" 127

Compton, Spencer, 2nd Earl of Northampton 262, 263

Cooke, Thomas 257

Cornelius, Mary 222, 226

Cornelius, Mrs. 188

Corneliuson, Cornelius 226

Cossongo 50

Costin Pond *xix*, 49

Cotton, William 64, 67, 72, 254

Courtney, James 53

Cowdrey, William 131

Cozier, William 252

Cradock, William 24

Cromwell, Oliver *xiv*, 157, 176, 184

Cropp, William 92, 276

Crump, George 255

Cugley, Daniel 40, 118

Cugley, Hannah (see Savage)

Culpeper, Lord Thomas (Governor) 123

Custis, John I 100

Custis, John II 96, 100, 135, 194, 205, 207

Custis, John III 100, 214, 218, 219, 221, 226, 227

Custis, John IV 100

Custis Tomb 258

D

Dale, Davey 272

Dale, Sir Thomas *xii, xv*, 3, 15, 23–25, 28–34,

Dale, Lady Elizabeth 5, 20, 23, 25–34, 48, 94, 96, 97

Dales Gift *xv*, 3, 19, 23–25, 32, 34

Daniel (Daniell), Edward 91, 92

Davis, Pierce 214

Davis, Thomas 53

Dawe, George 94, 104, 106, 107

Debedeavon 103

Denbigh 134

Denwood, Levyn 179

DeVries, David Pietersz 246, 247

Dew, Thomas 166

Dickson, Michael 214

Dixon, Ambrose 138

Dixon, Christopher 192

Dolby, Ann 194

Dollinge (Dolling), John 138, 169

Doughty, Francis 210

Douglas, Edward 30, 31, 32, 33, 34, 116, 117, 138, 146, 147, 150, 167, 191

Douglas, Sarah (née Littleton) 191, 203

Drew, Edward 67, 240, 242, 251

Drew, Marie 251, 252

Drighouse, Anne 125

Drighouse, Betty 125

Drighouse, Frances 214

Drighouse, William 125, 127

Dumpling Island Creek 101

Dunn, Anna 136

E

Eastern Shore Indians *xv*, 36–39, 118, 119, 125

Eaton, Mrs. 112

Eaton, Nathaniel   104, 112

Edwards, John   226

Elizabeth City   *xvii, xxiv*, 3, 5, 13, 55–60, 65, 66, 69, 93, 184, 210, 235, 240, 261

Elizabeth River   84, 85, 87

Elkington (surname)   44, 45

Ellis, John   156, 179

Epps, William   35–39, 44, 48, 57, 63, 70, 93, 111

Eyre, Susanna (née Baker)   189, 193

Eyre, Thomas   214

F

Fallassa   50

Falling Creek Ironworks   17

Fame of Virginia (The Fame) (ship)   158, 171, 279, 281

Farbrasse, Roger   268

Ferrar, John   7, 12

Fisher, William   272

Fishing Point   73–75, 78, 87, 96, 174

Fleet Prison   135

Fletcher, George   166

Fogel Grip (ship)   69

Forman, H. Chandlee   14, 21, 70

Foskue, Symon   226

Foster, Urmstrong (Armstrong)   132

Foxcroft, Bridgett (née Charlton)   189, 191, 192, 196, 202–220, 265

Foxcroft, Isaac   188, 195, 196, 198, 199, 206–208, 212–215, 217

Francis, Ebby   125

Francis, Tabby   125

Franklin, Benjamin   216, 221

Furnace, iron, near Indiantown Creek 14, 131

G

Gaskins, William 226

Gates, Sir Thomas 24

Gething (Gettings), Damaris 189, 190

Gething (Gettings), Elinor 189, 193

Gething (Gettings), Mathew 189, 192

Gilbert, Thomas 272

Gingasscount (Gangascoe, Gingaskoyne, Gingaskin, Gingas King, Chincoskin) 119–125, 130, 139

Glebe (lands) xvii, 63, 67–70, 183, 186, 211, 219,

Godwin, Joseph 220

Golden Quarter 186, 269–271, 273,

Goldsmith (Goldsmythe), Samuel 170, 224

Governor Hawleys Creek 21

Grand Assembly x, xiii, xv–xviii, 36, 48, 78, 79, 83, 87, 93, 103, 155, 156, 161, 165, 169, 171, 175–177, 179, 180, 181, 234, 250, 255, 258, 260, 262, 267

Granger, Nicholas 226

Graves, Mrs. 73

Graves, Thomas 67, 70

Graves, Verlinda (see Stone) 104

Greene, John 226

Griffith, Edward 190

H

Hack, Peter (Dr.) 156

Hamby, William 27

Hamilton, Andrew 214–221

Hamond, Manwaring 190
Hamor, Ralph 39, 45
Hampton River *xix*, 240
Hampton University 69
Hampton VA Medical Center 240
Hanby, Richard 29
Harmanson, John 131
Harmanson, Susanna (see Kendall) 131
Harmanson, Thomas 122, 123, 163, 164, 212, 213, 226
Harmar, Ann (née Southey) 50
Harmar (Harmoun), Charles 27, 28, 33, 35, 36, 48, 49, 50
Harmar, John (brother to Charles Harmar) 48
Harmar, John (uncle to Charles Harmar) 48
Harrington, Edward 169
Hartley, Thomas 254, 255, 257
Hartree, Elias 226
Harvard School 104, 112
Harvey, Sir John (Governor)
Hawley, Henry 130
Hawley, Jerome 130
Hawley, William 130–132
Henrico 6, 261
Hill, Edward 140
Hill, Richard 117, 138, 272
Hinman, John 226
Hogs Island (James River) 45
Holmes, William 266
Holloway, John 29, 251

Holwell, Richard 30

Horsey, Stephen 156, 157, 162–165, 169, 170, 179

Hoskins (Hodgskins), Anthony 78, 176

House, William 125

Howe, John 67, 240

Hudson, Richard 226

Hungars 60, 78–80, 102, 112, 158, 159, 167, 170, 173, 177, 182, 186, 211–214, 219, 220, 223, 254, 257, 258, 265

Hungars Creek 104, 112, 125, 167, 169, 177, 181, 185, 218, 222, 223

Hunt, Thomas 170, 246, 247

Husbands, Richard 158–160, 163, 164, 168, 173, 279–283

Hutchinson, Robert 205

I

Indiantown Creek 14, 21, 123, 130, 131

Iron Works 6

Isle of Wight 59, 60, 261, 262

J

Jacob, John 166

James I, (King) *xxv*

James City (Jamestown) *xvii, xix*, 2, 3, 27, 37, 42, 45, 50, 60, 67, 101, 104, 107, 116, 117, 123, 133, 134, 136–138, 140, 143-145, 148, 149, 151, 156, 158, 168, 179, 184, 196, 207, 212, 224, 235, 248, 261

James City Council of War 137, 140, 143, 144, 148, 149

Jarvis, Christopher 242

Jeffery, Littleton 125

Jeffery, Solomon 125

Jeffery, Sophia 125

Jeffery, Stephen 125

Jeffery, Thomas 125

Johnson, Jacob 214

Johnson, John 146, 226

Johnson, Thomas 116, 117, 137, 138, 140, 142, 144–150, 157, 161–164, 167, 169, 172, 173, 176–178, 181, 182, 186, 224, 244, 265, 283

Jones, Evan 53

Jones, John 94, 96, 97, 98, 100

Jones, William 20, 118, 167, 168, 176, 186, 188–190, 194, 197, 202, 205, 206, 226, 280

K

Kalmar Nyckel (ship) 69

Keepers of the Liberties of England 158, 280

Keltridge, Elizabeth 97, 98

Kendall, John 121, 122, 130, 131

Kendall, Susanna (née Baker; also Eyre, Pott) 131, 209

Kendall, William (I) 192, 193, 194, 205–207, 209

Kendall, William (II) 224

Kent Island 43, 46

Kicotan (Kecoughtan, Kiccowtan) xix, 62, 65, 66

King Tom 139, 150

Kiptopeke 169

Knight, Frances 101

Knott, James 239, 240

L

Lacke, Ellinor 90

Lacke, Margarett 90

Lake, Edward 90

Lake, Jane 90

Lake, Richard 90

Laughing King (Laughing Kings Indians) xx, xxvi, 4, 20, 36, 38, 40, 41, 44, 82, 102, 103, 111, 112, 115, 118–120, 124–126

Lawson, Thomas 99

League of Trade 137

Lee, Thomas 97, 98, 240

Lee, Richard 140, 210

Lemon, Jane 244

Lemon, Richard 244, 245, 246

Leopoldus of Dunkirk (ship) 171

Leveret, Elizabeth 255, 256

Little, John 251

Little Nuswattoxe Creek 177

Littleton, Ann (née Southey; also Harmar) 50, 104, 191

Littleton, Edward 30, 191, 203

Littleton, Nathaniel 29, 31, 50, 51, 96, 104, 106–109, 116, 118, 138, 145–148, 159, 163, 164, 166, 168, 171, 172, 179, 186, 191, 244, 263, 278–281, 283

Littleton, Sarah (née Douglas) 191, 203

Littleton, Southey 122

Lingaskin, Tribe of xix, 120, 124, 126

Long Buckby 262

Longo (Longoe, Longee), Anthony 51–54, 278, 279

Lower Norfolk County 84, 87

Lower Parish 212, 258

Lucas, Samuel 30

Ludlowe, George 140

M

Mackemie, Francis 215

Maddison, Isack 5

Maddocks, Allexander 226

Magatty Bay Pond *xix*, 49

Magothy Bay *xix*, 14, 75, 258

Major, Christopher 226, 230

Major, Edward 166

Major, John 187, 232

Manning, Lazarus 53

Maria 101

Marshall, Thomas 226

Martins Hundred 6

Maryland 130, 139, 216, 219, 263

Mason, George Carrington 74, 75, 81, 82, 220

Massachusetts 104, 112, 238, 263

Mathews, Domingo 139

Mathews, Edmund 142, 143, 151, 161, 173, 176, 279, 280, 282–285

Mathews, Henry 128, 131

Mathews, Phillip 226

Mathews, Samuel 133–136

Matomkin, King of 138

Mattawoman Creek *xix, xx*, 4, 102, 104, 112

Mattawombes town *xx*, 102, 115, 116

Melling, William 157

Merchant 94, 270-273

Michael, John 207

Mongum, Phill 139

Mooney, James 126

Morrison, Francis 140

Mountney, Alexander 67

Moye, Roger 99

Muce, Ellen 251

Mulberry Island 134

Munns, Jane 111

Munns, William 110, 111

Muster (1623/24) 27, 44

Muster (1624/25) 27, 45, 60, 63, 64, 66, 93

N

Nandua 103

Nansemond River 101

Nanticoke Indians 139

Neale, John 72, 134, 244, 272

Neale, Mrs. 133, 134, 136

Necotowance 138

Negro, John 50

Newport, Christopher 19, 46

Newport News 5, 134

Newton, Richard 53

North Carolina 114, 263

Northampton xi, 31, 47, 78, 88, 116–118, 120, 125, 128, 129, 131, 135, 138-140, 143–145, 148, 149, 155–161, 165–167, 169–172, 174–182, 184, 190, 194, 207, 212–216, 218, 226, 243, 255, 259–263, 268, 280–282, 284, 285

Northampton, Earl of (see Compton, Spencer) 262, 263

Northampton Council of War 144, 147

Northamptonshire 262

Norton, Toby 138

Nottingham, Benjamin 214

Nuce, Thomas 56, 58, 59, 68

Nuswattocks 145, 167, 173, 186, 207, 212, 222–224, 226, 228, 270

Nuthall, John (Jonathan) 156, 170, 179

O

Occohannock Creek 147, 169

Ocquhanocke (Occohannock) Parish 182

Old Plantation Creek *xix*, 5, 20, 27, 28, 32, 48, 69, 73, 75, 76, 78, 80–83, 87, 96, 99, 167, 169, 184, 236

Old Tony 50

Old Town Neck *xix*, 21, 104

Onnamus, James 139

Opechancanough 8, 19, 138

P

Palmers Island 149

Pannuell (Pannuel, Pannell), John 226, 243–245, 247

Parker, George 52, 224, 256

Parramore, John 31

Paramore (Parramore), Mary 194

Patrick "the Irishman" 99

Patrick, Richard 132

Pennsylvania 216, 263

Perreen, (Perrin) James 31, 136

Perry, James R. 141, 142, 151

Pigot's Hole 258

Pitt, Robert 166

Point Comfort Fort 135

Point House 78, 81, 167

Poplar Hill 122, 130

Pory, John 14, 15, 25, 34, 81, 118–120, 126, 173

Pott, Francis 135, 170, 184, 186, 208, 209, 269, 270, 273

Pott, John (Dr.) 135, 184, 208

Pott, John 186, 208, 270

Pott, Susanna (née Baker) 193, 209

Pountis, John 278

Powell, John 93, 214

Powhatan (Wahansnechav) *xxii*, 19, 46, 120

Powhatan Confederation 1, 19, 126

Press, Edmund 125

Press, Molly 125

Prew 270, 271

Price, Jenkin 138

Price, Walter 226

Prince George County 25

Pungoteague Creek 139

Q

Quarter Court *xiv, xvii, xxii*, 36–39, 108, 133, 134

Queen of Pocamoke (Pokomoke) 137, 138, 139

R

Ratclife, Elkington 45, 46

Rayman, Arthur 99

Revell, Randall 190

Ricketts, Michael 226

Roberts, Williams 226

Robins, Grace 93

Robins, John 212, 213, 214

Robins, Obedience 29, 30, 31, 67, 93, 105, 116–118, 137, 138, 141, 166, 176, 177, 182, 186, 195, 224, 235-237, 244, 262

Robins Sampson 205, 226

Robinson, John 138

Rolfe, John 24

Ronoke (Roanoke) *xxii*, 138, 144, 150

Roper, William 96, 108, 116, 136, 244, 245, 246

Ryding, Rose (née Yardley)

S

Salt works 2

Sanders, John 85, 86, 92, 93

Sanders (Saunders) Roger 70, 85, 86, 98

Sandys, Sir Edwin *xxv*, 7, 9

Sandys, George 9–13, 15, 18

Sandys, Samuel 10

Satchell, William 132

Savage, Hannah (also Cugley) 40, 43–46, 110–112, 119, 125

Savage, John 43, 44, 112, 113, 119, 121, 125, 130, 131

Savage (Salvage), Richard 20

Savage, Thomas (Carpenter) 209

Savage, Thomas (Ensign, interpreter) *xv, xxv*, 4, 17, 19, 20, 21, 35, 36, 38–40, 42, 43, 44, 46, 48, 82, 102, 103, 107, 110–113, 118, 121, 132

Savage, Thomas Lyttleton 121, 122, 123

Savages Choice 40

Savages Creek *xxvi*, 4, 21, 40, 79, 82, 108, 130

Scarborough, Charles (Dr.) 153, 154

Scarborough, Edmund 229-232, 234

Scarburgh, Edmund 52, 105–107, 113, 116–118, 130, 137, 140–151, 153, 154, 165–167, 169, 171, 176, 177, 183, 186, 194–197, 199, 200–202, 204–206, 214, 223–227, 229, 231–233, 260, 261, 263, 265, 282, 283

Scarburgh, Charles 227, 263

Scarburgh, Mary 227, 263

Scott, Apphia 93

Scott, Peirce (Pearice, Percis, Pervis) 91, 93

Scott, Samuel 93

Scott, Walter 93

Scovill, George 95

Sea Flower (ship) 45

Secretary's Land 2, 14, 66, 72

Selby, Toby (Tobias) 138, 150, 268

Selby, Thomas 226

Selby, Mrs. 138, 150

Severne, Bridgett (née Pott) 133–136, 184, 185, 209

Severne, Damaris (née Gething) 189, 190, 209

Severne, Jane 189, 209

Severne, John (chirurgeon) 135, 136, 163, 164, 168, 184, 185, 209

Severne, John (Jr.) 185–190, 192, 197, 198, 207, 209, 267

Severne, Mary 185

Severne, Peter 185, 187, 188

Sewell's Point 84

Shed, Grace 240

Shepheard, John 214

Sheppard, Henrietta Dawson (Ayres) 141, 142, 151

Sherlie Hundred 29

Shichams (Shichoms), Esmy or Lui   111, 119, 120, 126
Shields Bridge   169
Shrimpton, William   29-32, 34
Sisley   186, 191
Slaughter, Rebecca   53
Smart, William   226
Smith, George   269
Smith Island   2, 14, 25, 218, 221
Smith, John   xxiv, 12, 13, 15, 21
Smith, Thomas   xxv
Smyth, John   226
Smyth, Richard   258
Smyths Hundred   38
Smyth, Sir Thomas   29, 30, 34
Southampton River   xix, 5, 240
Southey, Ann (see Harmar, Littleton)   50, 104, 191
Southey, Henry   50
Spencer, William   190, 194, 205, 206
Sprigg, Thomas   170
Stafferton, Peter   235, 236
Stampe, Thomas   104
Stanley, Christopher
Stanton, Thomas   91, 92
Stephens, Anne   253
Stephens, Christopher   253
Stockely, John   214
Stockley, Joan   99
Stone, Verlinda Graves   104

Stone, William 29–31, 67, 72, 79, 96, 102, 104, 105, 108, 244

Stratton, Benjamin 214

Stribling, Christopher 75, 85

Stringer, John (carpenter) 245, 246

Stringer, John ("phillomedico") 29, 31, 116, 145, 147, 150, 167, 188, 190, 207, 245

Stubbins, Luke 245, 246, 272

Strong, William 90

Sugar Run 113, 132

Surrey (Surry) County 180

Susanna 186, 209

Swann, Thomas 190

Sylvan Scene 189

Symons, John 53

T

Taylor, Mrs. 230, 232

Taylor, Phillip 29, 31, 49, 108–110, 113, 133–136, 229–232, 251

Taylor, William 140

Taylor, William Johnson 169, 174

Taylor Creek 139

Teackle, Thomas 224, 225, 227

The Gulf xxv, 4, 21, 40, 42, 82, 108, 130

Third Anglo-Powhatan War 138

Thorpe, George 26

Throckmorton, Elizabeth 24

Tilney, John 190, 224

Toft, Ann 227

Tompkin, John 91, 92

Tomson, Richard 49

Travellor (Traveller), Alice 184, 185

Travellor (Traveller), George 93, 272

Tucker, Betsey 257

Tucker, William 5

Turman, Nora Miller 33, 34, 60, 81, 141, 142

Tyndalls Neck 102, 109

U

Upper Norfolk County 101

Upper Parish 78, 79, 80, 183, 212, 223, 224, 226

Upshur, Thomas T. 218, 262, 263

V

Vaughan, Grace (see Waltham) 185

Vaughan, Richard 138, 185

Vause, Henry 226

Vestry Act 67

Virgine (ship) 43, 46

Virginia Company of London xxv, 1, 19

Virginia House of Delegates 120, 121

W

Wachiowamp, King of the Occohannock Indians 103

Wadlow, John 230, 232

Wahansnechav (see Powhatan) 120

Walker, Peter 146, 182, 185, 266, 267

Waltham, Grace (see Vaughan) 185, 253, 257

Waltham, John 185, 213, 214, 217, 253, 257, 269

Ward, Ann 269

Ward, Benoni 258, 269

Ward, John 111

Ward, Thomas 269

Ward, William 226, 252

Ward's Point 255, 258

Warehouse Creek 156, 162, 172

Warner, Robert 192

Warrosquyaoke 262

Warwick River 133, 134, 261

Waters, William 176, 182, 190, 205, 206, 207, 255, 259

Watkins, Henry 26, 27

Weed (Weede), Elizabeth 268

Weede, Henry 246, 247, 268

Werowance *xxv*, 3, 4, 36, 103, 106, 118, 119, 120, 124, 144

West, Ann (see Charlton) 187, 202

West, Anthony 187

West, James 125

West, John 202, 263

West, Matilda (née Scarburgh) 202

West, Molly 125

West, Rachel 125

West, William 125

Westerhouse, William 187, 209, 226

Whissoponson Creek *xxv*, 4, 130

Whitby, William 31, 166

Whitelaw, Ralph T. 44, 46, 55, 66, 78, 81, 82, 105, 110, 153, 180, 183, 216, 219

Whittington, William 156, 167, 168, 178, 188, 280

Wignall, Alexander 133, 134, 136

Wilcocks, John 2, 15, 56, 58, 63, 68, 69, 71

Wilcox, John 228

Wilkins, Anne 253

Wilkins, Bridgett 252, 253

Wilkins, John 67, 72, 96, 105, 252, 253

William 270, 272

Williams (Willyams), John 226

Williams, Walter 117, 125, 168, 177, 178, 181

Williamson, Anne 253

Williamson, Roger 253

Wilson, Henry 93

Winbery (Winbrow, Wingbrough), Barberry 194, 210

Windley (Winley), David 240, 241

Windley, (Winley) Joane 238, 239, 265, 267

Winona 185

Winthrop, John (Governor) 112

Wise, Jennings Cropper 55, 60, 69, 129, 131, 141, 142, 180, 262, 263

Witchery 210

Wood, Thomas 266

Wryth, Richard 53

Wyatt, Sir Frances (Governor) 1, 2, 5, 7, 8, 10, 11, 13, 36, 56, 57, 106, 261

Wyatt, Goodman 31

Wyatt, Hautt 56

Y

Yardley, Argoll xx, 21, 29–31, 79, 101, 102, 104, 105, 107–113, 116–118, 130, 132, 137, 138, 140–142, 146–148, 150, 159, 163, 164, 166–168, 172, 177, 179, 182, 186, 209, 233, 263, 280–284

Yeardley, Sir George (Governor) *xii, xvi, xvii, xviii,* 1–5, 8, 11–18, 20, 25, 27, 28, 33–35, 38, 39, 56–58, 63, 68, 72, 82, 101, 104, 111, 265, 273, 276, 277

Yeo, Colonel 198, 202, 210

Yeo, Hugh 260

York County 261

York River *xxv,* 102, 109

Young, Pharoah 241

Young, Richard 240

About the Author

Jenean spent thirty years working as a school psychologist and special education director before retiring to devote her time to family research and other history projects. She lives most of the time on Virginia's Eastern Shore and part time at her home in south central Virginia. Her first book was *Victoria Stories: Glimpses of a Virginian Railway Town* (2011). Her second book was *An "Uncertain Rumor of Land: New Thoughts on the English Founding of Virginia's Eastern Shore* (2022).

www.ingramcontent.com/pod-product-compliance
Lightning Source LLC
Chambersburg PA
CBHW051934290426
44110CB00015B/1975